CONTENTIOUS
JOURNALISM
AND THE INTERNET

CONTENTIOUS JOURNALISM AND THE INTERNET

Towards Democratic Discourse in Malaysia and Singapore

Cherian George

SINGAPORE UNIVERSITY PRESS

in association with

UNIVERSITY OF WASHINGTON PRESS
Seattle

Published with the support of the Institute of Policy Studies, Singapore.

Published simultaneously in Singapore and the United States of America.

Singapore University Press, NUS Publishing
AS3-01-02. 3, Arts Link
Singapore 117569
www.nus.edu.sg/npu

ISBN 9971-69-325-9 (Paper)

University of Washington Press
PO Box 50096
Seattle, WA 98145-5096, U.S.A.
www.washington.edu/uwpress

Library of Congress Cataloging-in-Publication Data

George, Cherian.
  Contentious journalism and the Internet : towards democratic discourse in
  Malaysia and Singapore / Cherian George.
    p. cm.
  Includes bibliographical references and index.
  ISBN 0-295-98578-X (pbk.)
  1. Online journalism—Malaysia. 2. Online journalism—Singapore.
  3. Journalism—Political aspects—Malaysia. 4. Journalism—Political aspects—
  Singapore. I. Title.
  PN5449.M35G46 2005
  079'.595—dc22   2005024392

To

Zuraidah

CONTENTS

ACKNOWLEDGMENTS

This book would not have been possible but for the cooperation of the journalists and activists quoted in this work, and others who are not named. I benefited from Malaysians' and Singaporeans' deep love and concern for their respective societies, which made them generous with time and information when I was conducting my research between 2000 and 2003.

The manuscript began as my doctoral dissertation at Stanford University. My doctoral research and writing was funded by Stanford's Department of Communication; the Rebele Fellowship; the O'bie Shultz Fellowship, administered by Stanford's Institute for International Studies; the Stanford Center for Conflict and Negotiation; and Singapore's Institute of Policy Studies, where Tommy Koh and Arun Mahizhnan made me feel at home. The National University of Singapore's Asia Research Institute, under Anthony Reid, then gave me the luxury of a post-doctoral fellowship, helping me turn my dissertation into this book.

My intellectual debts are harder to enumerate than my sources of funding, but my creditors certainly include a dream team of a dissertation reading committee. Larry Diamond, François Bar and Purnima Mankekar provided a thoughtful blend of encouragement, stimulation and critical prodding from their diverse academic fields. François and Christian Sandvig provided guidance on a paper that evolved into Chapter 3. Thomas Hughes' seminar on the history of technology management, and Doug McAdam's on social movements, were critical launching pads for key discussions in this work. Fred Turner read my draft and contributed a timely adrenaline boost. My greatest scholarly debt is owed to Ted Glasser, who opened my eyes to new ways of looking at a profession that I'd thought I already knew. Ted was the complete adviser and mentor, exacting in his standards, inspiring as an intellectual, generous with his humanity.

A key theme in this book has to do with the importance of real-world social networks, even for projects described as "virtual." It is with pleasure, therefore, that I acknowledge the informal networks outside of Singapore that I relied on in ways big and small. Brendan Pereira eased my entry into that so-close-yet-so-far world of Malaysian politics and journalism. At Stanford, I could always count on the camaraderie of my fellow graduate students, especially Christian, Francis, Isabel, Karin, Marcus and Purcell. Other friends helped to make the Bay Area home: Cheong Soon and Jen, Euan and Gillian, Sajit and Lathika, and Teng Lang and Wee Chong.

Zuraidah, my wife, came with me in the Bay Area. She tolerated my hours lost in concentration, made the times in between the happiest I've known, and gave me the one thing no dissertation writer can do without: the incentive to finish.

Cherian George
Singapore, 2006

CHAPTER 1

BRINGING CYBERSPACE DOWN TO EARTH

In late 2001, the governments of Malaysia and Singapore began arresting dozens of individuals whom they claimed were members of terrorist cells linked to the notorious Al Qaeda network. The men were allegedly planning to bomb American targets, destabilize governments, and lay the ground for the creation of Islamic theocracies across Southeast Asia. For citizens of the two neighboring countries — among the most stable, peaceful, and economically vibrant outside of the advanced industrial west — the revelations were stunning, bringing home a storm that just months earlier had seemed confined to cities far away. The drama continued to play out over the coming months, in the pages of the nations' newspapers, and on radio and television news bulletins. These media reports focused on the terrorist threat to national security, the continuing hunt for more militants, and the implications of radical Islam for inter-ethnic relations. In Malaysia, the first *New Straits Times* editorial on the subject called for "zero tolerance" for "religious extremism as an instrument of politics," under the headline "Weed out the roots." Across the border in Singapore, *The Straits Times*, beneath the headline "Cohesion at all costs," said that the battle against terrorism had to be fought "using whatever means necessary, including force."[1]

There was, however, another angle to this running story — one that struggled to enter the agendas of the mainstream media. In dealing with the alleged militants, each state's instrument of choice was the Internal Security Act (ISA), a sweeping statute that permits arrest without warrant and detention without trial. A common legacy of British colonial rule, the ISA has been retained in both Malaysia and Singapore on the grounds that it is needed to preserve order. Many citizens seem to agree. However, opposition parties and human rights groups have long protested against the ISA, calling for its repeal or reform. Both governments have been known to use the ISA against political opponents who pose no credible, imminent threat to national security — except perhaps in the eyes of officials who equate the security of the ruling party with that of the nation as a whole.

Coming in the wake of the terrorist attacks of September 11, 2001, the governments' revelations of an Islamic militant plot were certainly more credible than some of their past justifications for using the ISA. However, the issue of civil liberties continued to hang over the affair. Whether the alleged militants should be tried in court, and whether they were being treated humanely in detention, were questions that were virtually absent from the mainstream media, which are closely supervised by the government. However, these topics were not entirely excluded from the public sphere. The two countries' alternative media, operating mainly through the internet, kept these issues alive from the moment the news of the arrests broke. Although not oblivious to the terrorist threat, these media incorporated the perspectives of human rights groups and opposition politicians, or wrote their own editorials to argue that liberty and justice should not be abandoned in the struggle to maintain order.[2] Thus, in Malaysia, the independent news site Malaysiakini accompanied its first news report on the arrests with a story titled, "Gov't rapped for latest ISA arrests, urged to show evidence."[3] It quoted a statement from the country's main human rights NGO, which was not carried in *New Straits Times*. In Singapore, the editor of Think Centre's website launched its coverage of the affair with an appeal that the detainees be treated well, and that they be charged in open court.[4]

Contentious Journalism

On this and other occasions, the internet-based alternative media engaged in what can be called *contentious journalism*, challenging the consensus that powerful interests try to shape and sustain through the mainstream media. This book tries to explain the emergence and development of contentious journalism on the internet in Malaysia and Singapore, two countries where government controls have severely constrained the opportunities of dissent. Malaysia and Singapore were early and aggressive adopters of internet technology, making them apt locations for studying the impact of the internet outside of the advanced-industrial, liberal-democratic west. Like most countries, they lie in the under-studied zone between the two extreme poles of liberal democracy and closed authoritarian regimes. Dissenting journalists here have enough political space to practice their craft openly on the internet (unlike in, say, China), but not the constitutional protection from political censorship or politically motivated reprisal that their American counterparts enjoy.

By conventional measures, the protagonists in this tale will seem decidedly unimpressive. It would be an understatement to say that they lack the economic muscle of the corporations that dominate the media industry everywhere. Most run on voluntary spirit, grants and subsidies, rather than the promise of profits. In most cases, their market shares — in terms of the readers and viewers they reach or the advertising dollars they attract — is not something about which the chiefs of mainstream media companies lie awake at night worrying. Even the issues they champion are not always populist causes that would sway the majority of voters. Their coverage of anti-terrorism operations is a good example: trying to persuade the public to care about the civil liberties of alleged terrorists is an uphill struggle, in Malaysia and Singapore as anywhere else. To those who value order, stability and the routines of institutionalized politics, these websites can appear annoying, unruly and irresponsible. The efforts of these intrepid journalists are, nevertheless, worth more than a cursory glance. Their struggles on the margins of the polity tell us something about the nature of mainstream journalism and politics. In addition, their experience with the internet helps to clarify how technology can be used to democratize public discourse.

The websites studied are examples of "alternative" media. It is not their online mode that classifies them as such; after all, mainstream newspapers and broadcasters also use the internet. Nor is the "alternative" label meant to imply that these media are interchangeable with mainstream print or broadcast news products — against which they do not have the capacity to compete directly. Rather, they are alternative in that they serve a distinct purpose, adding to the diversity of the media system. They democratize access to the media, inviting voices and viewpoints that are underrepresented in the mainstream for want of status, skill, or capital. Within this broad category of alternative media, those engaging in what I call "contentious journalism" form a subset. They are journalistic in the sense that they report and comment on current events in order to serve a public purpose (in addition to other private purposes they may have).[5] They are contentious in that they directly and explicitly challenge the authority of elites in setting the national agenda and in forging consensus. This is not to say that mainstream media are solely and always propaganda vehicles for the state, even in tightly controlled societies such as Malaysia and Singapore. However, whereas contentious journalism is the rare exception in the mainstream, it is the rule, and the *raison d'etre*, for the media dealt with in this book.

These websites are engaged in more than just a struggle against government domination. They also embody competing normative notions of journalism and its role in democracy. All the projects examined here subscribe to a more morally-engaged and less disinterested mode of journalism than their mainstream counterparts. At the same time, each is unique, illustrating different dimensions of alternativeness. Sintercom <www.newsintercom.org> is an experiment in doing journalism through open, informal and organic networks, distinguishing it from the institutionalized and hierarchical mainstream media. Think Centre <www.thinkcentre.org> blends advocacy into its journalism, breaching the mainstream's firewall between observation and participation. Both are run by amateurs and volunteers, and come out with new editions irregularly. Harakah Daily <www.harakahdaily.net> is the official organ of a political party, challenging the conventional wisdom that views partisan journalism as an oxymoron. Organizationally, Malaysiakini <www. malaysiakini.com> is the most similar to mainstream media, but it includes editors and reporters with activist backgrounds that, they readily admit, influence its agenda. Such features make many a professional journalist balk at the very suggestion that these alternative websites can be considered journalism at all. There is thus a double meaning in the label I have given them — the very claim that they are practicing a form of *journalism* is itself *contentious*. However, Chapter 4 will highlight the traditions of journalism that give them a greater pedigree than is usually acknowledged, and Chapter 10 will argue that contentious journalism, whatever its faults, is an essential ingredient in any democratic media system.

In academic terms, this book is oriented mainly towards theory building, rather than the testing of specific hypotheses generated from existing theory. Research on the internet and its democratizing potential has tended to assume, perhaps based on its global reach, that its effects will be uniform and homogenizing. Hence, the misplaced confidence with which scholars have ventured into this field of enquiry with quantitative studies. Equally misguided is the widespread intellectual exercise of pitting technology and law in hypothetical wrestling matches, as if these macro-structural factors can predict outcomes. They cannot, because no matter how well we think we understand the internet's technological characteristics and a regime's legal and political structure, our understanding is incomplete if we do not take into account human agency.

Therefore, the following pages attempt to build the case for a different way of looking at the internet. This book is, at one level, an argument for paying attention to social and political context when analyzing the impact of new communication technologies. Comparing Malaysia with Singapore helps to make this point. The two states introduced the internet to their populations at about the same time, and within broadly similar regulatory regimes: both claimed jurisdiction over online activities, but promoted the technology aggressively, and generally refrained from prior censorship or blocking of journalistic sites (Chapter 3). Malaysia, being the larger and less wealthy of the two countries, has unsurprisingly achieved significantly lower levels of internet penetration than Singapore. About 17 per cent of Malaysians were internet users in 2000, compared with 32 per cent of Singaporeans.[6] Given these starting conditions, one might expect contentious internet journalism to be more vibrant in Singapore than in Malaysia. Indeed, you might be accused of verging on tautology if you were to hypothesize that the prevalence of online media correlates positively with the level of the internet access.

In fact, the outcome has been exactly the opposite. Technologically-inferior Malaysia is home to the significantly superior contentious online media. This inverse relationship between technological availability and technological application is a paradox — but only if we start out with fundamentally misconceived notions about the relationship between media and society. The Malaysia-Singapore comparison becomes less surprising when we disabuse ourselves of the notion that communication technologies are "independent variables" appearing from out of the blue, and appreciate instead that their forms and functions are shaped by the societies that absorb them, even as they influence those societies. As we shall see, Malaysia's more fertile social and ideological ground allowed media activists to make limited technological capital go a longer way than their counterparts in Singapore.

Aside from comparing the two countries, this book will compare the four prominent contentious media projects selected for in-depth case studies. When comparing these groups, the overall picture is one of diverse outcomes that, once again, cannot be predicted entirely from either technology or regulation. Presented with the same internet opportunity, in technological and regulatory terms, media activists made unique choices. Some chose to work through informal and open networks facilitated by internet technologies, others through traditional, formally structured organizations. Some took full advantage of the medium's low economic barriers to entry and invested negligible funds into their enterprises, while others opted for a high-investment strategy that required a more business-minded orientation. Some exploited the internet's disintermediating potential by celebrating a deliberate amateurism, while others were committed to bringing the values of professional journalism to their projects. Indeed, although the four case studies were picked purely on the basis of their prominence, no two are alike. This was serendipitous: their differences open up fertile ground for further theory building. Comparing the four projects, it appears that the key mediating factors between opportunities and outcomes are social actors embedded in communities with different histories, resources, values and interests. It will also be argued that the internal diversity of the contentious online journalism movement reflects unresolved contradictions and dilemmas that plague the journalistic vocation. Simply put, there is no one media model that is self-evidently superior to all others, even if there is agreement on a common normative touchstone, such as "democracy."

Much of the discussion about the internet assumes that it is one fixed thing, with a particular "nature" or "essence". In fact, media activists — like other users — deploy the technology selectively and strategically, such that the internet opportunity takes on quite different meanings from context to context. Take, for example, the popular metaphor of cyber "space." This has spawned the theory that the internet is a geography-defying site where "netizens" can remain out of the authorities' reach, and, if they wish, engage in a kind of guerrilla insurgency. This conceptualization captures an important meaning of the internet in the eyes of media activists — but it is not the only one. Indeed, most of the activity studied in this book does not leverage on the place-transcending capability of the technology. On the contrary, the media activists featured here are firmly rooted in their real-world communities. Defying the popular notion that the internet may diminish "social capital,"⁷ they use the internet not to escape, but to intensify their interactions with society and the polity, often in parallel with traditional media and face-to-face communication.

The Internet and Democratization

Few contemporary phenomena demand scholarly analysis as much as the internet "revolution." This study has no trouble acknowledging the novelty and transformative power of the technology, although it views with skepticism many of the claims that have been made about it. We need to clear some of the clutter and moderate the hyperbole. By specifying the causal processes and mechanisms at work, instead of indulging in sweeping statements, we should be able to pinpoint the genuine difference that the internet has made in democratizing media systems, while at the same time making clear that the technology alone cannot fully explain many of the dynamics of that democratization.

   The prosaic guts of the internet comprise thousands of computer networks, linked by common protocols that allow dissimilar computers to communicate with each other. Internet communication breaks each message into small "packets," each encapsulated in the digital equivalent of an envelope, bearing the intended address. Computers in the network read the envelope and pass it on. If one route is blocked, another is tried. The different packets making up a single message can take different routes to their destination, where they are reassembled. Through the internet, millions of computers are linked through many millions of possible paths. This decentralized design was developed partly as a robust communication network for the military, able to withstand even nuclear attack. It would later become the bane of censors.

The impact of new media on politics has come under close scrutiny in recent years. Scholars have followed a number of different lines of inquiry, such as whether online space can revive the public sphere.[8] Some have content-analyzed online deliberation, showing that it shares some but not all characteristics of socially-cohesive communities.[9] Others have assessed information and communication technologies' value in bringing government closer to the people, pointing to various promising experiments but also significant gaps.[10] Studies on the relationship between journalism and the internet have focused mainly on what the new media mean for mainstream news organizations. Some have focused on how the internet medium changes the way journalists gather material and tell stories, making it easier for them to provide readers with access to primary source materials, to solicit feedback and discussion, and to integrate text, audio and video.[11] Others have argued that the internet's compression of time can weaken the role of sound editorial judgment — as when internet journalist Matt Drudge set the pace for the coverage of the Monica Lewinsky scandal.[12] (The concern that new communication technologies may compromise quality by bypassing responsible editors is not new, having been expressed before in the context of live television news.[13])Another line of inquiry compares online media with traditional media on such dimensions as credibility and impact.[14] Some writers worry that the internet threatens to undermine the newspapers' business model without itself offering to play the civic role that newspapers have. For example, Colin Sparks argues that the commercial newspaper press, whatever its faults, is one of the main sites of the public sphere, providing readers with a unique bundle of advertiser-supported material that includes detailed reporting and commentary on politics, economics, society, international affairs and so on.[15]

Unlike these other studies, this book focuses on the relatively unknown world of media insurgents — and not on the well-studied incumbents. There has been some scholarly interest in how the internet has been used as a vehicle for organized forms of resistance, social movement mobilization, lobbying, and dissent. Within this literature, Mexico's Zapatista movement has achieved celebrity status as a case study of early — and by most accounts stunningly successful — radical internet use.[16] The Zapatistas, led by the enigmatic Subcommander Marcos, used the internet to distribute communiqués about the uprising in Chiapas to officials and journalists in the capital and around the world. With public attention focused on the conflict, the government restrained its use of military force and agreed to peace talks in 1996. One writer, contrasting the outcome with the loss of one million lives in the Mexican Revolution earlier that century, muses: "Did the Internet, with instantaneous communication and 'the whole world watching', short-circuit similar slaughter in Chiapas?"[17]

The Zapatistas were not the only group that understood how to use the internet to communicate rapidly across long distances, and thus achieve a mobilizational power out of proportion to its physical resources and institutional strength. The Tamil "Tigers" of Sri Lanka have been equally adept at harnessing the internet to reach out to the Tamil diaspora around the world.[18] Democratic movements in various authoritarian societies have also taken advantage of the medium. In Indonesia, for example, pro-democracy activists in the last days of President Suharto used the internet to circulate news about the regime's abuses and to publicize demonstrations.[19] In Serbia under Slobodan Milosevic, the independent radio station B92 made use of the internet when its transmitters were cut off by the authorities. The station sent its content over the net to sympathetic stations overseas, which then transmitted the reports back into Serbia over the airwaves.[20]

Transnational civil society networks have used similar tactics. The successful protest against the developed countries' Multilateral Agreement of Investment in 1997 started with a leaked draft document that was disseminated over the internet as well as by traditional means, quickly snowballing into a movement of 600 organizations in 70 countries. A coalition of similar size was brought together, initially by phone and fax but later by internet, to campaign successfully for an international treaty to ban landmines. Such internet-assisted mobilization is remarkable not only for its scope but also its speed, which can catch governments and inter-governmental organizations off-guard.[21] Women's organizations have used the internet to create networks within which alternative forms of self-understanding and community can be fostered.[22] Note that while many of these civil society groups can be thought of as enhancing democracy, there is no reason to assume that their tactics cannot be shared by less savory forces. Extremists of all stripes — ranging from Neo-Nazis to Islamic militants — can and do use information and communication technologies for propagating their views and for command and control.[23]

The case of China is deservedly attracting considerable interest. Although enthusiastic about the internet's economic potential, the Chinese Communist Party (CCP) has introduced a national firewall to block internet users' access to non-approved websites. Administrators of online chat-rooms censor anti-government messages, and dissidents using the internet have been arrested and made examples of. Still, faith in the medium's democratizing potential was high enough for one political scientist to predict in 1998: "Despite the intentions of regimes like the CCP, their sway over the ideational and organizational character of domestic affairs will be diminished as a result of the Internet."[24] Observers continue to believe that the government's controls are not watertight and may ultimately fail. However, the state's response so far has been undeniably formidable: an extensive 2002 study counted more than 19,000 websites being regularly blocked.[25] A more recent study concedes that "although its methods are increasingly tested, the state has for the most part managed to dampen the emerging sphere of independent communication by employing a mixture of regulation, policing, and threats."[26] If Chiapas helped inspire the old techno-optimism, China is the main source of a rebounding realism. Reflecting the new conventional wisdom, *The Economist* declared the triumph of geography over what now seems like a "glorious illusion": "The Internet is often perceived as being everywhere yet nowhere, as free-floating as a cloud — but in fact it is subject to geography after all, and therefore to law."[27]

The several years' worth of theoretical exploration and comparative analysis can be pieced together to form a more nuanced picture of the internet's political impact than was available before. Some of the details of that picture have guided the present study; these are described below in the form of four broad principles.

The internet is special

First, even after stripping away the hyperbole, it is clear that we are dealing with a unique communications technology with extraordinary capabilities. Digitized data are carried in small packets through a global network that automatically picks the best route between any two endpoints. The endpoints do not have to be custom-built, but can be general-purpose devices such as personal computers and telephone modems. This foundation and its superstructure have evolved steadily since the internet was invented in the 1960s. The key innovations in the 1990s, this study's main period of interest, were the commercialization of the network, which made the internet available beyond the research community, and the invention of graphical web browser software, especially Netscape, which enabled easy publication and retrieval of attractive pages.

Most of the internet's individual features are shared by other media. Broadcast technology is as instantaneous as the internet; the telephone is as interactive; fax machines enable a single person to reach a large number of known recipients almost as easily as e-mail does. However, the internet offers a unique bundle of capabilities that makes it especially attractive to insurgents of all types as a medium for communication and coordination. In this regard, perhaps its most significant feature has been its "end-to-end" architecture. Its key design principle, at least at birth, allowed those at the edges of the network to create new ways of using that network, regardless of the views of its owners or any power in the middle.[28] This has allowed an extraordinary amount of innovation, by individuals and groups outside of the centers of corporate and political power.

The internet's capacity to reach across space, linking farflung individuals and groups in virtual communities, is well known. Its potential for manipulating time is equally dramatic. Activists prize the speed with which the internet delivers messages. Its opposite capability — time shifting — is probably of equal value to alternative media. A difficult problem faced by communicators outside the mainstream is their inability to gather a large audience at any one given time and place — unlike major broadcasters who can count on people to congregate in front of their television sets at prime time, or newspaper publishers who depend on the morning ritual of picking up a newspaper from one's doorstep. Achieving such coordination between communicators and audiences is a marketing challenge for which small alternative publishers do not have the resources. The internet, however, does not require publishers and readers to fix the time and place of their meetings. Publishers send out material on the web or by e-mail, and readers can open it at times of their choosing. Past issues can remain available to visitors, since digital storage makes it easy to archive a large volume of material. Search engines such as Google, as well as hyperlinks, further reduce the necessity for coordination. These technologies allow readers who are searching for information on a particular topic to land on a website that they had never heard of before.

Not surprisingly, all the groups studied in this book believe that the internet is special. But, the features that are most valued vary from group to group, and over time. Most tended to overestimate the technology's special powers initially, and had to adjust their strategies when reality bit. Some capabilities emerged gradually, allowing the activists to use the medium in ways they had not foreseen. The case studies in this book will trace these shifting uses and meanings.

Power matters in cyberspace

While the case could be made that the medium was decisive in the overthrow of Indonesia's President Suharto by the country's Reformasi movement, other control-minded governments, such as China's, continue to retain more power over internet communication than thought possible just a few years earlier. The internet does not transcend space. As one writer observes, information "does not flow in a vacuum; rather, it moves through political space that is already occupied."[29] Another points out that the rhetoric about the virtual liberation of cyberspace should not obscure "its material foundations and the economic realities of the culture in which it exists."[30] This is not only to make the fairly intuitive point that we should not confuse actual uses and outcomes with what are thought of as a technology's inherent characteristics — what C.S. Fisher calls the "impact-imprint" fallacy, and François Fortier calls the perspective of "ahistorical inherence."[31] It is also to say that "the internet" itself does not have a "nature" or "essence" that is independent of power relations. Behavior in cyberspace is regulated by software protocols and architectures — "code" as Lawrence Lessig puts it: "*Code is law*. ... Code is never found; it is only ever made, and only ever made by us."[32]

Lessig and others point out that the "end-to-end" paradigm, which encouraged innovation, is under serious threat. Most of the hype surrounding the Net in the mid-1990s assumed this open, libertarian architecture, when there was nothing immutable about it. Indeed, the same forces that were contributing to the internet's rapid expansion were changing it. The end-to-end principle has been undermined by internet service providers that try to compete with others by providing enhanced services within their own virtual enclaves, by users who prefer a convenient, consumer-type experience on the Net, and by third parties such as governments and employers that want to control what they consider to be abuse of the system.[33] All these pressures are creating a higher premium on trust than on freedom, the addition of greater functionality at the nodes of the network, and reduced flexibility at the ends. The internet revolution, Lessig notes, is thus being tamed by changes introduced by powerful incumbents:

> Some of these changes are legal; some are technical; and some use
> the power of the market. But all are driven by the desire to assure
> that this revolution doesn't muck things up — for them.[34]

Scholars have observed parallels with the history of radio, which similarly went through a phase of democratic flowering in the early 20th century, before government and business interests moved in and exerted their influence.[35]

When trying to address the question of government power, Lessig's advice comes in useful. He argues that we need to distinguish between two claims. The first, which is true, is that "*given the architecture of the Net as it is,* it is difficult for government to regulate behavior on the Net." The second, which is not true, is that "given the architecture of the Net, it is difficult for the government to *regulate the architecture of the Net.*" He adds:

> Even if it is hard to regulate behavior given the Net as it is, it is
> not hard for the government to take steps to alter, or supplement,

the architecture of the Net. And it is those steps in turn that could make behavior on the Net more regulable.[36]

To believe otherwise is to slip into the "fallacy of 'is-ism' — to confuse how something is with how it must be," he says.[37]

This study therefore aims to identify the creative work done, not only by insurgents, but also by government authorities as they grappled with the internet. There was nothing "given" about the technology. The two governments had to decide whether to establish connections to the global internet, and what architecture to build within their sections of it. These decisions had no obvious answers, as they were subject to conflicting priorities and pressures. Chapter 3 will try to trace the political-economic processes and interests that account for the internet being introduced and developed in the way that it was in Malaysia and Singapore.

People are technologically promiscuous

We may label them as internet users, but in fact people profess no loyalty to the medium. Instead, internet use is woven into a web of multiple media and face-to-face interactions. This is the third principle that can be teased out of the literature. In Mexico, Marcos depended on mainstream newspapers to carry his internet statements, while Serbia's B92 relied on foreign radio stations. In Indonesia, activists distributed missives through e-mail and the web, which were downloaded at public internet kiosks in cities and near university campuses, printed out, and then photocopied for mass circulation in hardcopy form. This sort of two-step-flow — from the internet, through printouts, to the street — has also been observed in Tibet, where internet use is even less widespread.[38] Thus, even if the vast majority of people in a country have no computers or internet access, the technology can have a significant impact if it is in the right hands (or wrong ones, as the case may be). Knowing the medium's penetration rate in a society may give the quantitatively-minded the comfort of firm ground, but it tells us little about the internet's utility.

For this reason, cross-sectional studies that try to correlate macro indicators of internet use with some social variable — such as David Richards' inconclusive attempt to link internet connectivity with government respect for human rights — are theoretically flawed.[39] What matters is not the overall or average level of internet use in any quantifiable sense, but the qualitative success with which agents of change exploit specific aspects of the technology within a broader offline strategy. Seen in this light, the fact that Malaysia has the more vibrant internet journalism scene, despite enjoying lower levels of internet access than Singapore, appears less paradoxical.

Technological promiscuity also suggests that internet use will always be contingent, with people trying to use new media for objectives that cannot be met through old media. The less press and personal freedom people have, the more attractive the internet looks as a safe site for anti-government political expression. Accordingly, when researchers analyzed more than 2,300 messages in 41 newsgroups devoted to individual countries, they found that the newsgroups for less-democratic countries contained more messages expressing opposition to individual policies, politicians or the government as a whole. Among Asian countries, for example, the newsgroups for Burma and China each contained more than 20 per cent anti-government messages (many of them presumably from people outside those countries), compared with under 5 per cent for India and the Philippines, which enjoy much greater press freedom.[40]

The internet is an idea

Much of what was said about the internet was hype, but hype is not without real effect. In the mid-1990s, it moved billions of dollars and inflated the dot-com stock market bubble. Similarly, ideas about technology can influence the actions of political entrepreneurs and the policies of governments. Despite its roots in the military-industrial complex, the internet was strongly associated with libertarian and even anarchic values. This was partly due to the end-to-end paradigm described earlier. In addition, one writer speculates, the manner in which people experience the internet has a psychological impact. They sit alone in front of the computer, logging-in with their personal online names and secret passwords, and start within their private space of email boxes and customized browsers. Thus, they begin each journey into cyberspace as an individual.[41]

> Communities, social structures and collectives may all appear to the virtual self as built from virtual individuals, not because of a prior political commitment to theories that posit the self-interested individual as the basis of all social life, but as a simple conclusion drawn from a recurring experience in cyberspace. From this basis, it is no surprise that the political ideologies that most emphasize individual liberty and the right to self-government have been powerful on the Internet; libertarianism and anarchism.[42]

These values flew in the face of the two governments' centralized model of information control. For people sold on the internet as the medium of the future, government control of information looked increasingly dissonant and plainly wrong. In addition, these ideas about the internet boosted activists' sense of self-efficacy and their perceived chances of success. The internet symbolized revolutionary change. Its terminology — "cyberspace," "netizens," and so on — evoked the potential for reconfiguring space and power relations. It was also associated with an "information revolution."

It should be noted that this hypothesis about the internet's ideological value is at odds with the "dimensional" or "variable-based" approach to the study of media.[43] The dimensional approach unbundles a technology into various variables of interest — such as speed, interactivity and capacity — rather than studying it as a single "thing." It regards any individual technology as an instantiation of these different dimensions, rather than a unique object. Its main benefit is that it opens the door to scientific research and theory-building about the effects of technology. A dimensional perspective helps to refine theories about media effects. For example, it was noted above that cost is a key dimension affecting a medium's potential for radical use. Therefore, other low-cost media ranging from buttons to street theatre — and not just the internet — offer radical possibilities. Similarly, in discussing internal mobilizing structures, speed is a key dimension, making the fax machine and text messaging through mobile phones possibly as powerful a communication tool for this purpose as the internet.

However, technologies are sometimes greater than the sum of their dimensions. Throughout history, certain technologies have seized the imaginations of their times, strongly influencing how people view their world. The computer has been described as the latest of a series of "defining technologies" that have served as metaphors for people's understanding of themselves and their environments.[44] Particular dimensions of the technology may influence the interpretation of its role, but ultimately a widespread technology does not become a *defining* technology by any predictable process. Instead, the vision of particular philosophers, theologians and poets has proven critical. The internet is one such technology, whose cultural impact can be linked to, but not reduced to, its specific characteristics.

Thus, one writer notes that "virtual-place metaphors" surrounding the internet — electronic frontiers, cyberspace, information superhighway and so on — can be put to opposing uses.[45] "The metaphors encourage control, surveillance, and capitalist expansion through computer technologies — and also evasion and resistance through computer technologies."[46] Virtual-place metaphors "take for granted that people can act on things at a distance by manipulating symbols" but they do not determine who can act, or to what end.[47] "The power of metaphors lies not in metaphors themselves but in the hands of their users," he concludes.[48] This study will therefore have to consider the work done by actors in using ideas about the internet according to their own interests.

Not Just About the Internet

The networked computer has stimulated huge academic and journalistic interest; it is the interface that launched a thousand scripts. Indeed, so exciting and evocative is this new medium that it is sometimes assumed that what goes on in cyberspace constitutes a separate field of study, with few worthwhile connections to be made with the social science of the pre-internet era. However, the leitmotif of the four principles highlighted above is that the internet's role is always contingent, and that the quest for macro-level generalizations about the internet's political impact will continue to frustrate. Does the internet democratize communication? This is one of the big questions that has guided a decade of inquiry within media studies, political science, sociology and other disciplines. The above survey suggests that the relationship between new media and political actors is far too dynamic and interdependent to be reduced to simple causal statements. The less democratic the society, the more attractive the internet looks as an emancipatory medium — but the more likely radical internet use will be blocked or punished. Furthermore, the internet cannot be treated as an independent variable. The technology has been and will continue to be shaped by political and economic forces. The outcome is "not up to the technology itself," as one scholar puts it.[49]

If context matters at least as much as technology, then scholarship on "the internet" cannot provide the only, or even the most important, intellectual guideposts. Accordingly, this book will demonstrate that there is much to be gained by suspending our enthusiasm for the technology, and instead treating the contentious journalism of the web as belonging to certain families of phenomena that have been analyzed by scholars since well before the internet became vogue. Two such scholarly traditions are especially illuminating and will be explored in Chapter 4. The first is a disparate literature on "alternative media" — small and varied print publications and broadcast stations that embody visions distinct from those of the mainstream. The internet projects studied here can be seen as continuing a long and colorful tradition that includes workers' publications in industrialized countries in the 1920s and '30s, anti-war newspapers in the 1960s, and community micro-radio.

Second, we can draw on political sociology's research into social movements. Contentious journalism possesses movement-like qualities: it operates from the fringes of the political system, uses tactics that place it on the edge of legitimacy, challenges the status quo, and takes advantage of social solidarities within loose networks. Understanding contentious journalism this way will unlock analytical tools that have been productively used to study social phenomena as diverse as the civil rights movement, the Zapatista uprising, and the international campaign against the World Trade Organization.

Good social science strives to move from particular towards more general knowledge, to use the facts we know to learn about facts we do not know. However, we should abstract and infer only after we understand the history and culture around the facts, lest we make "simplifications that are simply wrong."[50] In recent years, reviewers have acknowledged that a lot of the scholarship about the internet and society has made this mistake, rushing prematurely to test broad, law-like hypotheses about the internet and democracy. Thus, an article in the *Annual Review of Sociology 2001* argues that the way forward requires "more nuanced and circumscribed understandings of how internet use adapts to existing patterns, permits certain innovations, and reinforces certain kinds of change."[51] A reviewer in the *Journal of Politics* has noted that we are "still at the stage where we can learn most from detailed ethnography and participant observation."[52] This study takes such advice to heart, responding to the increasingly apparent need for close-to-the-ground accounts of internet use. Contentious media's founders, supporters and detractors are interviewed in depth; their online discourse and offline actions analyzed; and their internal correspondence examined where available. Whereas variable-oriented research aims to show that a certain probabilistic relationship holds for a certain population — often building a simplified conception of cause into the statistical model so that it can digest a large number of cases — the case-oriented approach adopted here is geared towards comprehending diversity and causal complexity.[53] The goal is "to account for the differences among instances of a certain outcome" — namely, contentious online journalism — with exceptions, deviations and contrary evidence treated as raw material for historical explanation, and as a basis for refining theory.[54]

Although the internet, and globalization more generally, has prompted grand prophecies of the demise of nation-states, state power remains the single most irresistible and immovable political force in the lives of billions of people around the globe. Even in places where there is a discernible weakening of state capacity as a result of long-term structural trends, the reality on the ground and in the moment is one of struggle. Non-state actors do not slip smoothly or inevitably from the fringe to the mainstream. Challenging the state, especially in societies where civil liberties are not guaranteed, is an enterprise that is fraught with risk. Nowhere does the state simply roll over and play dead. Neither, however, do all oppositional groups. As the president of the United States' National Endowment for Democracy has noted: "The governing principle here is the power of human ingenuity — if a technology is available, people will find ways to use it, even in the most difficult circumstances."[55] Thus, although the technology has played a transformative role, the real stars of the piece are social actors contesting on an old fashioned terrain. There is room for human agency on both sides, resulting in a complex and dynamic contest to which the internet has added new dimensions. This book will focus squarely on the ingenuity of the actors in their attempts to twist technology and circumstance to their own advantage.

CHAPTER 2

STATE AND MEDIA IN MALAYSIA AND SINGAPORE

Contentious internet journalism in Malaysia and Singapore is practiced under the noses of the authorities. The most prominent and organized alternative websites are published by people who do not go to great lengths to conceal their identities or their whereabouts. This distinguishes contentious journalism here from most of the cases of radical internet use that have dominated the literature reviewed in the previous chapter. Whether we look at the legendary Zapatistas, or dissidents in China, or transborder terrorism, we find the internet being used to evade authority. The insurgents are outlaws, the internet their hideout. Something else is going on in Malaysia and Singapore. The two societies are open enough for the internet to be used publicly as a medium for dissenting communication, although not so open that their citizens can take their freedom to communicate for granted. These are neither liberal democracies with constitutionally guaranteed freedom of expression, nor closed dictatorships.

The next chapter will pick up the story of how the internet provided activists an opportunity that was not available with earlier media. This chapter sets the scene, describing the two countries' political regimes and media systems. One of the challenges besetting such a task is that Malaysia and Singapore do not fall into either of those polar categories that have dominated discourse for the better part of the past century. Perhaps, however, this is a blessing, as it compels us to consider more carefully certain constructs that are often used too loosely, including democracy, the state, and power. Certainly, the tendency to dichotomize democracy and dictatorship — an intellectual legacy of the west's epic battles against fascism and communism — tends to achieve ideological clarity at the expense of descriptive fidelity. Within the field of communication studies, the classic work in this tradition is *Four Theories of the Press*.[1] It describes Authoritarian, Libertarian, Social Responsibility and Soviet Communist models. One critique perceptively recognizes *Four Theories* as really a single theory with four examples: it views the political systems through the prism of classical liberalism, promoting "a white/black, good/bad understanding" of the world.[2] Although the limitations of *Four Theories* are by now widely recognized, the impulse to dichotomize liberal democracy and its antithesis continues to influence communication scholarship.

Scholars working within the comparativist tradition of political science suggest that the binary perspective no longer works, if it ever did. They have faced a paradox in recent decades. On the one hand, democracy's minimum standard of competitive elections has proliferated. Its main ideological competitors have crumbled, and it has attained a normative status that is unprecedented in world history. The most repressive, politically closed regimes — such as China, Burma and (until recently) Iraq — make up a dwindling proportion of all countries, from one-fifth in 1974 to one-tenth in 2001, according to one count.[3] On the other hand, it has become increasingly clear that the many political transitions that have taken place in that period have not followed a clear and consistent path towards a single model of democracy. While plain-old dictatorship is becoming rarer, democracy appears to be getting more diverse. Philippe Schmitter muses:

> It is as if, having swept all of their 'systemic' opponents from the field, the proponents of democracy have at long last been freed to squabble among themselves over the meaning and application of their preferred political order.[4]

Larry Diamond notes that liberal democracy and politically closed authoritarian regimes account for fewer than half of all countries. In between, he suggests, are at least three other regime types: electoral democracy, competitive authoritarian, and hegemonic electoral authoritarian. The distinction between the first two of these three is so fuzzy that he also includes a category for "ambiguous regimes."[5] All these "hybrid" regimes conduct elections. However, in competitive authoritarian regimes — such as Russia and Malaysia, in Diamond's categorization — competitive elections produce outcomes that deviate markedly from popular preferences, partly because civil and political liberties are so constrained that significant interests are unable to organize and express themselves. In hegemonic party systems — such as Egypt and Singapore — a "relatively institutionalized ruling party monopolizes the political arena, using coercion, patronage, media control, and other means to deny formally legal opposition parties any real chance of competing for power."[6]

Categorizing regimes in ways that are sensitive to their diversity is only part of the challenge. Another difficult task is to explicate the relationship between the media and the state. Again, *Four Theories* provides a cautionary example of how not to do it. The book conceptualizes media praxis as a straightforward extrapolation of state ideology:

> To see the differences between press systems in full perspective, then, one must look at the social systems in which the press functions. To see the social systems in their true relationship to the press, one has to look at certain basic beliefs and assumptions

which the society holds: the nature of man, the nature of society and the state, the relation of man to the state, and the nature of knowledge and truth. Thus, in the last analysis the difference between press systems is one of philosophy....[7]

Hence, the authors assume that Lenin's vision for the communist press represents Soviet journalism. In fact, the archetypal totalitarian press under the Soviet bloc or Chinese communism was more diverse over time and space than could be predicted from official ideology.[8] Furthermore, the press in the liberal West has been subject to authoritarian practices — if authoritarianism in communication is defined in terms of concentrations of power, including economic power, that restrict people's freedom of expression.[9] A comparative study by Daniel Hallin and Paolo Mancini of two liberal democracies, the US and Italy, provides a more nuanced view of the relationship between political systems and the news media.[10] It argues that while the media's forms of representation are shaped by the political and social processes they try to reflect, media practices in turn affect politics and social interaction. Thus, the relationship of US journalism to political authority is "intensely ambivalent and very unstable."[11] The US media sometimes identify themselves with the authority of the state, thus virtually collapsing into the latter; and at other times force the state to spend most of its time trying to tame the processes through which they form public opinion. Hallin and Mancini have also pointed out that media systems vary in "political parallelism" — the degree to which they reflect their respective political systems.[12]

Old habits die hard. One recent work, *Twilight of Press Freedom*, implicitly takes the same fallacious tack as *Four Theories*.[13] Its authors cite Singapore as representing a neoauthoritarian "Order Paradigm" that espouses "social stability and harmony that really can come about with orderly and predictable media control."[14] Although this is a reasonably accurate representation of official ideology in Singapore, the authors fail to recognize that Singapore leaders' views about journalism do not necessarily represent Singaporean journalism as it actually operates. *Four Theories* and *Twilight* thus fail to consider the diversity of media practices, in particular those that are at odds with official ideology or national culture. Such blinkers may have been assets when providing intellectual support for Cold War rhetoric or for neoliberal arguments, but they would be fatal for the present project. By definition, contentious journalism goes against the grain, often at great personal risk to its practitioners. That being the case, to define a country's media according to official statements of what the press should do — or for that matter in any essentialist terms — is to deny the existence of the alternative possibilities that contentious journalism represents, thus adding academic insult to political injury.

Another problem with many comparative accounts of the press and politics is that they hinge on assigning democracy ratings to the regimes in question. Measuring a country's level of democracy may be worth the trouble, and the oversimplification, when conducting large-scale correlational studies — relating economic growth and democratic development for dozens of countries, for example.[15] However, the impulse to categorize can be more harmful than beneficial when we are trying to account for complex developments within a small number of cases. The danger lies in exaggerating the explanatory power of coarse categories. For that reason, this study does not dwell on Malaysia's or Singapore's democratic standing. Among the labels that others have assigned to the two regimes are: semi-democracy, Asian democracy, illiberal democracy, soft authoritarian, authoritarian, and dictatorship. This book is indifferent to such nomenclature. This is certainly not to say that there is no meaningful normative distinction between democracy and authoritarianism. One of the premises and guiding motivations of the present project is this writer's belief that the more democracy, the better — and that Malaysians and Singaporeans do not have enough of it. However, the analysis in the following pages is not premised on any judgment about the two countries' aggregate scores on any democracy index. Instead, the approach taken in this chapter is to try to understand the nature of state power in more universal terms, and how it relates to the media.

State Power and the Media

The purpose of this section is modest: to find appropriate lenses through which to look at the two countries that are the setting for this study. The chosen perspective can be summed up in three points. First, states are in the business of force and control. Second, states obtain cooperation through a range of non-coercive as well as coercive means. Third, cooperation is never total; resistance and contention are always present.

Coercion as the guarantor of control

This first principle draws from Max Weber, who laid the groundwork for studying the modern state, pointing out its autonomous organizational features and its control over territory.[16] The state, in Weber's view, is "a compulsory organization with a territorial basis." It claims binding authority not only over its citizens "but also to a very large extent over all action taking place in the area of its jurisdiction."[17] The state's insatiable appetite for control has been commented on by various scholars. James Scott argues that the modern state handles its classic functions — taxation, conscription and prevention of rebellion — by simplifying, standardizing and organizing society in order to make it more "legible" and thus more manipulable.[18] Michel Foucault has likened the art of government to running a household. The rationality of government, then, is jealous and possessive as well as protective:

> To govern a state will therefore mean to apply economy, to set up an economy at the level of the entire state, which means exercising towards its inhabitants, and the wealth and behaviour

of each and all, a form of surveillance and control as atten-
tive as that of the head of a family over his household and
his goods.[19]

To Weber is also owed the shrewd observation that what
distinguishes the modern state from a criminal gang with guns is that
the former is entitled to use violence while the latter is not. "Today
legal coercion by violence is the monopoly of the state," he writes.[20]
This monopoly may be latent, but it is omnipresent and definitive
of the modern state, Weber reminds us. The articulation of this
rather unflattering perspective was choked by the pluralist tradition
in political science. Pure forms of pluralist theory conceptualized
American democracy as comprising private interest groups that
compete for resources, and governments as "figurative cash registers
or as literal referees" as one reviewer has put it.[21] American political
science has since come round to acknowledging that democratically-
elected governments need not be so benign. Even game theory has
been used to demonstrate that a democratically-elected sovereign
can get away with transgressing fundamental rights, by exploiting
the fact that divided publics find it difficult to coordinate their
political actions. By displeasing sections of the public selectively or
non-simultaneously, he can still maintain support among a sufficient
subset of the citizens to retain power democratically.[22] Therefore,
while much of the present study is devoted to investigating how the
state in Malaysia and Singapore exercises its coercive powers, this is
based not on any presumption that they are non-democracies, but
merely on their status as modern states.

Obtaining compliance by consent

A more complex theme to deal with than coercion is how states
secure the willing cooperation of its citizens. The state's coercive
power may seem the obvious guarantor of cooperation. However,
states do not rule through force alone. Ronald Wintrobe argues
that even a dictator — at least, a rational one — would not rely

on repression.[23] Indeed, repression increases the likelihood that his subjects and his officials hide important information from him. Better to cultivate loyalty, by distributing rents, for example, in a way that "overpays" supporters. Mancur Olson arrives at similar conclusions from a different angle.[24] Observing the behavior of mafia families in city neighborhoods and bandits in China in 1920s, he finds both limiting their predations despite their virtually limitless power over their subject populations. It is in a dictator's rational, long-term self-interest to practice self-restraint rather than slaughtering the goose that lays the golden egg, he concludes. Therefore, even if we are inclined to believe that Malaysia and Singapore are dictatorships, political theory advises us to look for non-violent methods of rule. The two regimes' stability in the absence of extreme repression should further alert us to the possibility that these are not political systems that are solely dependent on force.

David Held has provided a useful scale that marks various kinds of compliance on a continuum ranging from coercion to pure consent.[25] Held's complete scale is as follows:

1. Coercion: People have no choice but to accept it.
2. Tradition: Alternatives have never occurred to people.
3. Apathy: People don't care one way or another.
4. Pragmatic acquiescence: People know it's not ideal, but it seems like fate.
5. Instrumental acceptance: It's not satisfactory, but it gives people some long-term benefit.
6. Normative agreement: People believe it is the right thing to do in the circumstances.
7. Ideal normative agreement: People believe it is the ideal outcome.

The examples given by Wintrobe and Olson would fall in the category of securing cooperation in the form of "instrumental acceptance." Note that their theories are based on the behaviorist assumption that people will support whatever furthers their self-interest. Respect for property rights emerges as being of central importance: dictators need to allow their subjects their livelihoods. However, it is not self-evident that civil liberties, such as press freedom, need to be included in the bargain. Indeed, many relatively stable, autocratic regimes seem to be counting on precisely their ability to parse out rights, respecting those directly required for the market economy, and denying those that may one day be used to mobilize opposition against them. Wintrobe notes that such regimes — including China with its free-market communism and as well as soft-authoritarian Singapore — perpetuate democrats' "recurring nightmare" of economic power without democratic politics.

As a means of securing moral legitimacy or normative agreement, there is today no more powerful instrument than free and fair elections. However, Diamond points out that many hybrid regimes are merely adopting the outward appearance of electoral democracy, and that, indeed, they are "quite deliberately *pseudodemocratic*," fashioned for "the contemporary era, in which democracy is the only broadly legitimate form, and regimes have felt unprecedented pressure (international and domestic) to adopt — or at least to mimic — the democratic form."[26] The idea of democracy as a performance staged for an audience is an important one. Even more important to keep in mind is the fact that the show is interactive, and that skilled performers modify the script based on the audience's response. Thus, cunning regimes will comply with the formal requirements demanded by the opposition and election monitors, while looking for less obvious means of subverting the process. "Their dream is to reap the fruits of electoral legitimacy without running the risks of democratic uncertainty," says Andreas Schedler.[27] He reminds us that "the modern history of representative elections is a tale of authoritarian manipulations as much as it is a saga of democratic triumphs."[28] If regular elections are to serve their democratic function as mechanisms of social choice, a series of conditions must be met, he says. For example, if there is to be genuine *range* of choice, citizens should be free to form, join and support parties, candidates and policies. Citizens should also have access to alternative sources of information, to *know* their choices and form preferences. Decision-making authority should be delegated to elective officials, and elections must have effects, and not be reversed by preventing elected officials from serving their terms. There are thus a number of links in the democratic chain that governments can manipulate to subvert social choice, even in country with regular elections.

A state is of course most powerful when citizens are at levels 6 and 7 of Held's scale: when they do not even feel that they are "obeying," because they are doing what they ideally wanted to anyway. Note, however, that in practice it would be difficult for one to distinguish between "ideal normative agreement" (a perfect "7" on the scale) and "tradition" (a mere "2"), since one's imagination of an ideal world is constrained by tradition. Indeed, the construction of a consensus around the status quo that seems to be based on common sense — because alternative worlds are unthinkable — represents ideological domination at its most complete. This is the realm of hegemony, a term is most closely associated with Antonio Gramsci, who used it to denote (among other things) the bourgeoisie's ideological subordination of the working class, enabling a consensual form of rule in Western Europe that makes the routine application of force less necessary.[29] Gramsci's powerful intervention in Marxist thought is his recognition that domination and subordination are, in the words of Raymond Williams,

> a saturation of the whole process of living... to such a depth that the pressures and limits of what can ultimately be seen as a specific economic, political, and cultural system seem to most of us the pressures and limits of simple experience and common sense.[30]

One of the chief goals of critical and cultural studies has been to expose the ideological nature of that common sense. Thus, Stuart

Hall argues that social order and consensus must be problematized, by asking who produces the consensus, in what interests it functions, and on what conditions it depends.[31] The media are implicated in any such discussion. Ralph Miliband has observed:

> The mass media cannot ensure complete conservative attunement; nothing can. But they can and do contribute to the fostering of a climate of conformity, not by the total suppression of dissent, but by the presentation of views which fall outside the consensus as curious heresies, or, even more effectively, by treating them as irrelevant eccentricities, which serious and reasonable people may dismiss as of no consequence.[32]

Miliband, like Hall, argues that ideological control is never total; indeed, the media are more effective hegemonic instruments when they are not merely tools of the ruling class. This aspect of hegemony makes the concept a subtler and more sophisticated one than Marx's false consciousness. In the view of these critical theorists, people retain a modicum of genuinely independent judgment and capacity for action. Foucault's concept of power includes a similar dimension. By his definition, power — as opposed to sheer physical force — presupposes that the people who are acted upon are agents with some freedom of action themselves. This has important implications for the rationality of government, which he describes as "a way or system of thinking about the nature of the practice of government (who can govern; what governing is; what or who is to governed), capable of making some form of that activity thinkable and practicable both to its practitioners and to those upon whom it is practiced."[33] In other words, the very possibility of a way of governing has, in order to work, "to be credible to the governed as well as the governing."[34]

The inevitability of contention

In Foucault's view, therefore, although power is everywhere in human relations, it is never absolute. Even as governments try to conduct and demand, people generate dissenting counter-conducts and counter-demands. "At the very heart of the power relationship, and constantly provoking it, are the recalcitrance of the will and the intransigence of freedom," he says.[35] This recalcitrance is the third key point that should be drawn from theories of the state. Regardless of the level of political stability or social consensus, resistance and contention against the state is part of politics. There is no room for such recalcitrance in theories that deny the state any autonomy to begin with. However, once it is understood that states are, in Theda Skocpol's words, "not simply reflective of the demands or interests of social groups, classes, or society," it becomes clear that some things that states do will always generate dissent.[36] Thus, James Scott, studying peasant life in Malaysia, tells us not to be fooled by public displays of acquiescence to the hegemony of dominant values.[37] Such "public transcripts" are deliberately shaped to appeal to the expectations of the powerful, he says. Behind the scenes are locations where "the unspoken riposte, stifled anger, and bitten tongues created by relations of domination find a vehement, full-throated expression."[38] It is there that mass defiance gathers energy, before suddenly erupting and taking by surprise ruling elites as well as social scientists who have been paying attention only to the public transcript.

Confrontations between ordinary people and elites have always been a feature of human society, but contentious politics took on a new form from the 18th century, associated with the rise of the modern state. Sidney Tarrow notes:

> [T]he framework for their actions was increasingly the opportunities for collective action provided by the national state. In making war, provisioning cities, and raising taxes, as well as by building roads and regulating associations, the state became both a target for claims and a place in which to fight out disputes with competing groups. Even when access was denied, the standardizing and unifying ambitions of expanding

states created opportunities for less well endowed people to mimic and adapt the stratagems of elites.[39]

The contours of contention are shaped by the fact that the state is not a single thing, but stands for a number of separate but interrelated institutions. Miliband notes: "It is these institutions in which 'state power' lies, and it is through them that this power is wielded in its different manifestations by... the state elite."[40] Sometimes, focusing on the reified state may overestimate the level of democracy on the ground, as when citizens face corrupt petty bureaucrats and functionaries in a formally democratic country.[41] At other times, deficiencies in the state's capacity for repression, or the presence of allies within the elite, may give people more autonomy than would be predicted from a country's non-democratic status. In either case, what is clearly needed are close-to-the-ground accounts of interactions with state power — a principle that the present study tries to adhere to.

While it is no longer heretical in social and political theory to speak of consensus as ideological domination and contention as a natural response, practicing politicians and their supporters, including in the media, are bound to view things differently. Thus, as we shall see in Chapter 4, there is a strong tendency in even the most democratic of societies for the press to frame collective action that takes place outside institutional channels as socially deviant. Similarly, in Singapore, a 1991 Government White Paper on "Shared Values" proposed that the nation adopt "Consensus, Not Contention" as one of five core principles to live by.[42]

Politics in Malaysia and Singapore

Malaysia and Singapore are neighboring countries that in recent decades have experienced sustained periods of rapid economic growth and political stability. However, the post-war British colonial period was marked by fierce communist insurgency that was forcibly put down through various emergency measures. The non-communist nationalists who led their countries to independence were thus endowed with both the tools for controlling insurgency and hypersensitivity towards organized dissent.[43] The two new states were also shaped by ethnic politics. Malays, Chinese and Indians make up the main ethnic groups in both territories. However, their proportions differ. In Malaysia, Malays and other indigenous peoples form the majority, while Chinese are dominant economically. The Malaysian social compact has included affirmative action for the economically-backward indigenous or *bumiputera* population. Singapore is three-quarters ethnic Chinese. Its multi-ethnic ruling party has governed on a platform of largely non-racial policies. Between 1963 and 1965, Singapore was a state within the Malaysian federation but the merger broke down, resulting in full independence for Singapore, because of irreconcilable differences over how to manage their ethnically plural societies.

Singapore's expulsion from the Malaysian federation in August 1965, together with its tiny size, has given its leaders an acute sense of national vulnerability, which they believe can be compensated for only through a strong state. Malaysia's own historical consciousness includes the trauma of race riots in 1969. These have similarly fostered a premium on order and strong government.[44] At independence, both countries adopted parliamentary systems based on the Westminster model. Members of Parliament are popularly elected, and the prime minister is drawn from the party that controls the legislature. While both governments have subjected themselves to elections at the constitutionally-mandated intervals, neither has seen the need to limit its power substantially between those elections. Malaysia and Singapore are not constituted as liberal democracies with deep civil liberties and failsafe checks against the abuse of government power. The executive dominates the legislative and judicial branches of the state. Dissent is forcibly dampened, and opposition parties and interest groups are routinely hampered in their efforts to organize and mobilize. Much of this control is effected through laws and regulations inherited from the colonial authorities. These include a licensing system for the press, and the requirement of permits for public gatherings. Thus, although the two countries have regular multiparty elections, they lack some key democratic features.

Underlining the exceptional stability of their hybrid political systems, Diamond notes that of the seven "electoral autocracies" that existed around the world in the 1960s and 1970s — states that had "elections without democracy" — Malaysia and Singapore are the only two that have survived as such. (They have since been joined in this category by scores of others.[45]) That stability is evident not only in the political system as a whole, but also at the level of parties and premiers. Both Malaysia and Singapore have been described as dominant party states, with the ruling parties never having lost power since gaining independence. Malaysia is governed by the Barisan Nasional or National Front, a coalition dominated by the United Malays National Organisation (UMNO). Its main coalition allies are the Malaysian Chinese Association (MCA) and the Malaysian Indian Congress (MIC). In the main period covered by this book, Malaysia's prime minister was Mahathir Mohamad. He had been in office since 1982, making him Asia's longest serving leader. He stepped down in 2003. In Singapore, the country's first prime minister, Lee Kuan Yew, stepped aside in 1990 after 31 years in the office, but remained highly influential in cabinet as "senior minister" and later "minister mentor". His People's Action Party has enjoyed a virtual monopoly of parliamentary seats since independence.

In trying to account for the longevity and stability of the two regimes, the concepts introduced in the previous section come in useful. Although the two governments have impressive instruments of coercion at their fingertips, it is not the case that force and the threat of force are the main means of maintaining order. Instead, the two states appear to be backed by a significant degree of consent on the part of the ruled. Part of this is accounted for by the people's "instrumental acquiescence," to use Held's term, based on their not-unfounded faith that the governments will continue to deliver rising standards of living. As we shall see in the next section, the promise of financial reward has also been an important means of securing the loyalty of the mainstream news media industry. In addition, there is also evidence of a normative consensus at work, maintained through the state's ideological domination. Part of the thesis of this study is that this consensus is less complete than the state makes it out to be, and that the appearance of consensus should not be allowed to foreclose debate. At the same time, it is important to understand that the consensus is not all an illusion. It is not based on lies, such that, to borrow Adam Przeworski's line, "once the king is announced to be naked, the equilibrium is destroyed instantaneously."[46]

Instead, the sources of hegemony are formidable, presenting a genuine challenge to insurgents.[47] First, the governments have drawn upon the legitimating power of elections. Of course, there is little doubt that both Malaysia and Singapore would fail Schedler's test for elections discussed above. More than one link in the democratic chain is completely sundered. However, elections have at least been free and fair enough to attract the continued participation of all major opposition parties. Even Malaysia's Islamic Party, the organization with the best chance of success if it embarked on an extra-parliamentary struggle — an idea that it flirted with in the 1960s — has committed itself to the ballot box. For all their weaknesses, elections have been recognized by the vast majority of Malaysians and Singaporeans since the 1960s as "the only game in town."[48] The winners of that game are broadly accepted as legitimate representatives of the people. Of course, the two states' illiberal features constantly pressure their legitimacy. While they do not deny that civil and political rights matter, they usually frame such claims as Western in origin, excessively contentious, and opposed to Asian values that are said to emphasize consensus and harmony. "Asian" democracy, for which Mahathir and Lee were key spokesmen, stressed economic and social rights instead. Both governments add that they are in favor of moving towards greater political openness, but insist that such reform must be incremental and carefully managed. In Malaysia, reforms have included the setting up of the Malaysian Human Rights Commission. Singapore has intensified the use of official feedback channels for greater citizen consultation.

William Case suggests that such "semi-democracies," may in fact enjoy "more intrinsic stability than 'purer,' ideal-type regime forms."[49] By offering electoral opportunities to opponents, ruling elites are able to claim greater political legitimacy than allowed under authoritarianism. At the same time, by retaining strong powers, they are able to contain ethnic tensions and pursue developmentalism, thus avoiding the strains that have precipitated breakdowns of full democracies. This brings us to the second big idea around which hegemony is constructed: that of nation-building. The idea evokes a sense of collective purpose, to fight common threats and work towards common goals. The main threat is that of social discord in their multi-ethnic societies. A history of occasional race riots, and examples of internecine bloodbaths in places as far away as Yugoslavia and as close as Indonesia, are mustered in defense of strong government, the only guarantor of order. The positive goal of nation-building is rapid socio-economic development. Note that the idea of economic growth in these societies does not carry merely private and instrumental meaning. Growth is linked to nationalism, and thus possesses normative social significance. In Malaysia, for example, the government's "Vision 2020" target and its rallying cry of *"Malaysia Boleh"* (Malaysia Can) are not merely about individual wealth-creation, but also about arriving collectively as a developed country. In Singapore, the equation of nation and economy is stated more prosaically but no less powerfully: for many years, the first sentence out of the prime minister's mouth in his annual message marking the country's independence day was the announcement of the second quarter economic growth figure.

The two regimes have not been immune to political strains of either a long-term or short-term nature. Two will be highlighted here because of their prominent roles in motivating the contentious journalism that surfaced on the internet. One challenge can be described as liberal-democratic in orientation, questioning the lack of civil liberties, press freedom and government accountability, in terms that would sound quite familiar to western ears. A second line of criticism has been directed against a style of modernization that is seen as culturally and spiritually impoverishing, elite-oriented, and — in Malaysia's case — corrupted by money politics and cronyism. This is in particular the line of PAS, Malaysia's opposition Islamic party, but it is also the nub of the discontent that Singapore's Chinese-language lobby has with the establishment.

These simmering antagonisms did not amount to a serious electoral threat for either government, as long as it was able to deliver rapid economic growth with sufficiently effective redistributive policies to prevent extreme disparities of wealth. In the late 1990s, however, the Asian financial crisis flattened the economic growth that for years had lent legitimacy and leverage to less-than-democratic governments. It sparked what activists called a Reformasi movement for political reform in Indonesia, Malaysia and, to a lesser extent, Singapore. In Malaysia, the financial shock sharpened the differences between Mahathir and his deputy, Anwar Ibrahim. In a stunning turn of events, Mahathir sacked Anwar, accusing him of sexual misconduct. The charismatic Anwar refused to go quietly. Giving press conferences at home and speeches at mosques, he said that his dismissal was politically motivated, accused the government of corruption, and incited street demonstrations. He was subsequently arrested and convicted, spending the next six years in jail.

Mahathir won the 1999 general election, but with significant loss of domestic prestige and international stature. For the first time, his UMNO party accounted for fewer than half of the ruling alliance's seats, as Malays shifted loyalties to PAS. PAS is thought to be able to continue growing in strength, and perhaps even unseat the government if it can forge a stable alternative alliance with smaller opposition parties. In the near term, however, Barisan Nasional is firmly in charge, especially as the worst of the country's economic problems appears to be over. Under Mahathir's successor, Abdullah Badawi, the ruling party strengthened its position in the 2004 elections.

Singapore, the perennial socio-economic outlier at the geographical heart of Southeast Asia, was relatively quiet throughout the Asian financial crisis and the Reformasi movements of its neighbors. The economy suffered only two quarters of recession during the Asian crisis, and the ruling People's Action Party emerged with its international reputation for economic management enhanced. However, the tumbling of economies and governments nearby showed that stability could not be taken for granted. To the extent that the PAP drew prestige from being part of the wider East Asian "miracle," the end of that miracle robbed it of some of its gloss. When Singapore, following the US economy, slipped back into recession in 2001, it became even harder for the PAP to claim the performance-based legitimacy that it could once take for granted. The opposition was too weak and disorganized to take advantage of Singaporeans' unhappiness with the stumbling economy. Indeed, in the general election of late 2001, the PAP secured a popular vote of 75 per cent — higher than the previous few elections — and hemmed-in opposition parties to the mere two seats (out of 84) that they already held. Observers concluded that voters, sobered by the recession, decided in favor of stability rather than political experimentation.

Although Singapore's opposition was no better off in 2001 than in 1991, civil society made some advances over the same decade. The government under Lee's successor, prime minister Goh Chok Tong, had invited citizens to participate more actively in public affairs. It had also called for a reactivation of civil society as a way to increase people's attachment to the nation, and so that civic groups could take over some of the state's fiscal burden in such areas as welfare and education. The government's intention was to facilitate a kind of apolitical activism; there was no hint that it was changing its stand towards contentious politics. Nevertheless, more politically-oriented groups chose to extend the government's argument for a more active "people sector" into the realm of politics. Thus, even Singapore has witnessed a moderate intensification of activism. Explicitly-political groups protested against government restrictions on free speech and association, while an assortment of civic groups and non-governmental organizations stepped up their efforts to stake out an autonomous space for civil society.

The media's role in all of this is as multifaceted as the concept of power. What is certain is that they have not been mere bystanders in the politics of the two countries. At one level, the press is at the receiving end of the state's coercive force, in fairly direct and obvious ways. At another, the mainstream media are themselves functionaries of the government and part of what Miliband called the state system, helping to create and maintain hegemony.[50] The cooperation of media workers and owners, like that of the public, is based on instrumental considerations and ideological conviction as well as fear.

Media Control

Government regulation of the media in Malaysia and Singapore can be seen as operating at two levels. The first is the level of media content: the stories that comprise the news, and the information on which those stories are based. Various laws allow the government to impose prior restraints on publication, post-publication punishments, and penalties for the acquisition of official information. The second level is that of media access: who owns and operates the means of media production. Licensing laws and accompanying regulations are used to keep media within the control of the establishment.[51] These two levels of control have effects that are not always easy to distinguish, and they are certainly not mutually independent. For example, when editors engage in self-censorship, it can be difficult to tell whether they are afraid of legal repercussions under content regulations, or the career consequences of displeasing publishers who fear losing their licenses to publish. Even if the violation is at the level of media content, the punishment may be at the level of media access. Unhappy with a series of stories, the government can revoke one's publishing license and thus close down a newspaper.

The distinction between these two levels may seem trivial when we examine the controls on print and broadcast media in Malaysia and Singapore, but its significance will emerge when we turn our attention to internet regulation. As we shall see in the next chapter, many of the traditional content rules apply online as well as offline, but access rules have been radically liberalized for the internet. Under Malaysian and Singaporean law, cyberjournalists are no less accountable for what they write than print journalists. However, the internet is the first and only mass medium for which one does not need a production license. It is this loophole that contentious journalism exploits.

Controls at the level of media content

As a result of their common history, Malaysia and Singapore have many similar laws affecting the work of journalists. Most of these are broad and open-ended, making it extremely difficult for anyone to defend oneself against a charge, once the state has decided on its course of action. The most feared piece of legislation is probably each country's Internal Security Act (ISA), which empowers the authorities to arrest individuals without a warrant and detain them without trial. Originally introduced to deal with communist insurgency and used more lately against Islamic militancy, the ISA is regarded by even some of its critics as a justifiable instrument for preserving order. However, there have been a number of occasions when the governments appear to have abused the ISA to crush political dissidence without convincing evidence of any clear and present danger to national security. Recourse to the ISA was rampant in Malaysia during the Anwar crisis, although it has not been used against journalists.[52] Since the late 1980s, the Singapore government has been relatively restrained, using the ISA to combat espionage and terrorism, but not political opposition.[53] Nevertheless, since the government has not expressed second thoughts — let alone remorse — over the way it used the ISA in the past, its existence continues to have a chilling effect on political expression.

Each country also has a Sedition Act, which outlaws any tendency to bring the government into hatred or contempt, or otherwise excite disaffection against it. Malaysia's, amended after the race riots of 1969, includes in its definition of sedition the promotion of ill-will and hostility between races or classes. The act also declares out-of-bounds any questioning of the Malays' Constitutional privileges. Zulkifli Sulong, the editor of Harakah (one of the case studies to come), was found guilty of sedition, but got off with a fine. Malaysia's main press law, the Printing, Presses and Publications Act (PPPA) of 1984, also prohibits "maliciously publishing false news," with the executive given wide leeway to interpret the law.

Key state institutions receive special protection from journalistic assault. Commenting on the role of the judiciary has proved especially tricky. In both countries, the courts have regularly ruled against critics of the government in defamation and other cases, but anyone who suggests that judges are politically motivated or lack independence risks prosecution for contempt. In Malaysia, a Canadian journalist spent four weeks in jail in 1999 over an article about the judicial process, published in the Hong Kong-based *Far Eastern Economic Review*. The Singapore regime's readiness to use this instrument was clearly demonstrated in 1994, when an op-ed article in the

International Herald Tribune earned it and the writer fines — despite the fact that Singapore was never named in the offending article. Journalists must also beware being cited for contempt of Parliament, under the acts that define the privileges and powers of the two countries' legislatures.[54] The House is the ultimate judge of what constitutes contempt, for which offenders can be jailed or fined. In Singapore, this writer was threatened with a contempt of parliament complaint for allegedly implying that the Speaker of Parliament was stifling debate. In Malaysia, a journalist who criticized MPs' perks was held to be in contempt in 1957.

Both countries also have an Official Secrets Act, making it a crime to receive or publish government information without proper authorization. It covers not just documents stamped "secret," but also virtually any classified material. Malaysia's *New Straits Times* fell foul of the OSA in 1995, over an article about military aircraft contracts. Singapore's *Business Times* got in trouble over a seemingly innocuous economic growth figure. In pursuing the case, the government did not claim that the data were highly sensitive, arguing instead that it wished to demonstrate that leaks would not be tolerated. The newspaper's editor and a correspondent were fined, together with a civil servant and two private-sector economists.

The two countries' defamation laws do not follow the American tradition, in which plaintiffs who are public officials must show "actual malice" on the defendant's part. Unconcerned about the chilling effects that libel suits have on political debate, courts in Malaysia and Singapore have ruled for the plaintiffs in almost every action brought by a politician of the ruling party. Opposition politicians have felt the brunt of such action. In 1998, for example, Singapore courts awarded plaintiffs S$265,000 for a libelous article published in *The Hammer*, the newsletter of the Workers' Party. In 2004, *The Economist* agreed to pay S$390,000 in damages to Lee Kuan Yew and his son, the new prime minister, for suggesting that nepotism was at work in their family.

Malaysia has used these various instruments against the foreign press as well as the domestic media. In Singapore, the regulation of choice when dealing with foreign media is an amendment to the press act that bans "offshore newspapers" — foreign publications with significant sales in Singapore — from "engaging in the domestic politics of Singapore."[55] In practice, the government deems periodicals to be playing politics when they refuse to give it the right to an unedited reply to an offending article. A quota is then imposed on their Singapore sales. They are not banned outright because, the government says, its objective is not to curtail free speech but to hold publications financially accountable for their editorial judgments. The list of publications that have been gazetted in this manner since the law was introduced in the mid-1980s includes *Asiaweek, Asian Wall Street Journal, The Economist, Far Eastern Economic Review* and *Time*. A similar provision was introduced to the Broadcasting Act in 2000. Although offshore publications campaigned furiously against the law at first, both the officials and their critics believe that it has met its objective of giving the foreign press cause for pause before criticizing the Singapore government.[56]

Neither government has used its powers against journalists as frequently or as brutally as many other states have. Laws against contempt and protecting official secrets have rarely been invoked. The more draconian ISA and costly defamation suits have tended to be targeted at opposition members and political dissidents, rather than against professional journalists. Indeed, the generally calm relationship between press and state raises the question of whether it is actually ideological and material comfort with the status quo, rather than fear, that keeps journalists in line. On the other hand, one does not need to be burnt more than once to realize that one should not play with fire. The senior-most gatekeepers within media organizations measure their experience in decades; they have witnessed and learnt from the uglier episodes of government repression. As neither state has repealed any of its security or press laws, it is not unreasonable for editors to assume that officials can, at any time, dust off a rarely used instrument to deal decisively with media that go out of line. Thus, a former *Straits Times* chief editor has said:

> The press laws and political culture are such that the Government, with a vast array of powers at its disposal, will not countenance the press taking any determined stand against it on any issues that it considers fundamental.[57]

Controls on media access

Content regulations leave journalists in no doubt about the one-sided balance of power between press and state in Malaysia and Singapore. However, it does not represent the routine, on-going mode of political control, which is instead more cooperative in character. This is effected mainly through licensing systems that control access to the media industries. Newspaper laws require publishers to apply for annual permits, which can be revoked at any time. It may seem odd to characterize licensing as an instrument to secure voluntary cooperation. Certainly, the many publishers and journalists who have suffered the suspension or cancellation of their publications' licenses would be inclined to regard such action as a flagrantly coercive use of state force. The casualties include, in Malaysia, *The Star* and *Sin Chew Jit Poh* (suspended in 1987); and *The Singapore Herald* (license revoked in 1971).

The key point to note about media permits is this: while deprivation is coercive, possession is a powerful reward. Indeed, their scarcity enhances their economic value. As long as a media organization holds one — and especially when would-be competitors are denied them — a license is a ticket to monopoly profits, and induces cooperation with the licensing authority. Even in a free market, media industries show a strong tendency towards monopoly.[58] A licensing system heightens the already formidable economic barriers to entry, to the benefit of existing players. It is in this sense that access regulation has been used to obtain the media's instrumental acquiescence in Malaysia and Singapore.

This effect of licensing is further assured by the choice of licensees. While neither government has felt the need to nationalize the press, both have intervened in the market to create media companies that are closely allied to the ruling elite. In Malaysia, an UMNO holding company took over the country's main newspaper company in 1972, partly to wrest control of a strategic asset that was then in the hands of Singaporean and British interests, and also to give UMNO a cash cow that would reduce its financial dependence on its ethnic Chinese allies.[59] The publishing company, New Straits Times Press (NSTP), has since been transferred to UMNO cronies. NSTP publishes the broadsheet English-language daily *New Straits Times*, and the second-largest Malay-language daily, *Berita Harian*. Utusan Melayu, which publishes the largest-circulation Malay daily, is similarly linked to UMNO. The leading English daily, *The Star*, is controlled by Huaren Holdings, the investment arm of the Malaysian Chinese Assocation, UMNO's main ally in the national alliance. Huaren also owns two of the three largest Chinese-language papers, *Nanyang Siang Pau* and *China Press*. *The Sun*, the third-largest English paper, is owned by the Berjaya Group, whose owner is close to UMNO elites. The small Tamil-language press is largely under the control of the president of the Malaysian Indian Congress (the third major partner of the ruling alliance).

The structure of Singapore's newspaper industry is simpler, but the means of control subtler. Virtually all daily titles — three English, three Chinese, one Malay and one Tamil — are published by Singapore Press Holdings (SPH), a public-listed behemoth. The Singapore government, generally more respectful of the market than is Malaysia, found a way in the 1970s to make the boards of newspaper companies accountable to the state while leaving equity in private hands. The new press act of 1974 required newspaper companies to institute management shares, which have 200 times the voting rights of ordinary shares. Under the Act, the government decides who holds management shares. In effect, this allows the government to control the composition of the board of directors of newspaper companies, and through them, senior editorial positions. Top editors have always come from within the profession, rather than parachuted in from government. However, since the 1980s, the board and management team has been headed by former senior officials from government. The only daily newspaper outside the SPH stables is *Today*, published by MediaCorp, the privatized, but still 100-per cent government-owned, national broadcaster.

In both Malaysia and Singapore, the behind-the-scenes strings that tie the press to the government mean that the latter does not need to micromanage journalists by, for example, requiring articles to be submitted for vetting. The political leadership can instead count on editors to act in the interests of the nation, the state, the government, and the party (all of which in the politics of the two countries tend to be conflated). Editors do not always get it right, which is why the newspapers occasionally get in trouble with the government. Hegemonic control, after all, is not failsafe. The price of giving the dominated some choice in their domination is the risk that a few of these democratic decisions go astray. By and large, however, the mainstream press is ideologically aligned with the state, readily embracing their nation-building role, and recognizing the government of the day as the legitimate interpreter and trustee of the national interest.

The Case of Television Policy

The governments of Malaysia and Singapore have been successful at controlling the press because, as suggested above, they know the importance of carrots as well as sticks. Publishers have been given something that they value more highly than editorial freedom: the license to print money. Despite their instinctive suspicion of the press, government leaders understood that rich media need not be politically threatening. Indeed, financially successful media were likely to align their interests with a state that promoted economic growth and political stability. Therefore, political censorship could be achieved without destroying newspapers as a business.

This aspect of the media regime in Malaysia and Singapore is seen even more clearly in the case of television policy. In the 1980s and 1990s, both governments decided to liberalize their broadcasting regimes partially. The changes of the 1990s are particularly illuminating because this was also the period when the governments were formulating their internet policies. Internet regulations contained novel loopholes. One question that arises is whether this was a symptom of wider political liberalization. Examination of TV policies, devised around the same time, shows that this was not the case.

Privatization of television in Malaysia

For 20 years after its introduction in December 1963, television in Malaysia was the monopoly of a government department under the Ministry of Information. Radio Television Malaysia (RTM) was charged with the mission "to explain in depth and with the widest possible coverage, policies and programs of the government in order to ensure maximum understanding by the people."[60] By the 1980s, however, the Mahathir government was convinced that state-owned enterprises could not be as profitable or efficient — or as lucrative for the taxman — as private companies. Privatization was also seen as a way to develop a new class of Malay businessmen.[61] As part of this new national policy, a television license was awarded in 1983 for a commercial station, TV3. Service began the following year.

TV3 quickly made an impact by being more entertainment-driven and risqué. Its earliest coup over RTM was to purchase the rights to broadcast the 1984 Los Angeles Olympics. Its aggressively commercial thrust was not uncontroversial. It was attacked for importing sex and violence — via *Miami Vice, Dynasty* and the like — into conservative Malaysia. However, the station did produce the policy-makers' desired effect. Its focus on ratings-driven entertainment succeeded in increasing the size of the broadcasting industry as a whole.

Zaharom Nain writes that TV3's increasing commercialization created at best "an illusion of freedom," since the imports comprised mainly genres that would not challenge the political status quo.[62] TV3's programming priorities were clear from the fact that it did not even wait to set up a news department before launching its service. Until it launched its own newscasts in 1985, TV3 simply acceded to the government's request to carry RTM's main news bulletin.

The lack of diversity in broadcast news, even as entertainment options proliferated, was no accident, but the direct result of government policy. The station's political impotence was assured by the government's choice of licensee. TV3 was owned by a joint venture controlled by the Fleet Group, the holding company of Mahathir's political party. Other major shareholders included the holding companies of Daim Zainuddin, a close associate of Mahathir who would become finance minister soon after.[63] Zaharom Nain notes of Malaysian TV:

> [T]he selective privatization exercise continues to extend the tentacles of the ruling coalition and its allies even wider across the Malaysian economy, adding economic and cultural domination to what is already virtual political domination.[64]

To formalize its control of private broadcasters, the government pushed through the Broadcasting Act of 1988, giving the information minister authority to intervene in the stations' operations. The TV3 model of privatization was subsequently extended to new entrants into the industry. Two additional commercial free-to-air stations and a subscription TV service were launched in the 1990s, all with equity control in the hands of establishment institutions and cronies of the ruling elite.

From a democratic perspective, the true test of privatized television came in the 1997 economic crisis and the political crisis that followed. Broadcast news was uniformly uncritical of government, and instead purveyed "feel-good news and blame-it-on-others news," notes Zaharom.[65] Shortly before the shock ouster of deputy prime minister Anwar Ibrahim, a senior executive of TV3 and two newspaper editors were forced out, as Mahathir cleared the decks of Anwar loyalists, demonstrating the political realities within which private media companies operate. Thus, the Malaysian model of TV privatization retained the ruling elite's leverage over political content and editorial direction, while increasing its economic resources by exploiting television's commercial potential. Zaharom argues:

> Despite there having been greater expansion of the Malaysian media over the past decade, legal, economic, and political controls on Malaysian television particularly, and the media generally, have not been relaxed but, instead, have been tightened considerably.[66]

Introduction of satellite television in Singapore

Singapore's government, like Malaysia's, engaged in partial liberalization of television, harnessing the benefits of economic competition while continuing to protect itself from political pluralization. The dominant broadcaster, MediaCorp, is descended from state television and remains 100 per cent government-owned. The sole cable operator is Starhub Cablevision, owned by Singapore Technologies, a government-linked conglomerate with roots in the defense industries and which used to be run by Lee Kuan Yew's daughter-in-law. Competition in the free-to-air market began in 2000, when a license to operate two channels was awarded to Singapore Press Holdings, the government-friendly publishing giant.

The government's policies on satellite television are particularly illustrative. Until the early 1990s, ownership of dishes for receiving satellite TV signals was completely banned. The finance sector's need for timely information prompted a rethink. At the outbreak of the Gulf War of 1990–1, the government was persuaded that its closed, CNN-less TV regime handicapped the country's financial industry in the global marketplace. A member of parliament wrote that the outcome of last-ditch talks between US Secretary of State James Baker and his Iraqi counterpart Tariq Aziz was evident on their faces as they emerged from their meeting. Traders elsewhere could see their expressions on live TV and knew what to do. "They sold US dollars. Our bankers and businessmen here, without such immediate access, bought. Who were left holding the baby?"[67]

·A month later, the government announced that it was allowing banks and financial institutions to operate satellite dishes with immediate effect, because "timely access to information is essential especially for forex and futures trading."[68] The new policy was formalized shortly after, allowing businesses to apply for annual licenses to operate satellite dishes. Applications would have to be supported by the Economic Development Board or the Monetary Authority of Singapore. Licensees were required to ensure that there was no unauthorized tapping of signals from their dishes. Other than these special cases, the ban on private ownership remained — anyone found guilty of installing or operating any broadcasting equipment without a license could be fined up to S$2,000 or jailed up to a year.

The Singapore case, as Garry Rodan suggests, shows that it may be "possible for sophisticated authoritarian regimes to reconcile commercial transparency with significant political and media control."[69] The approach works because businesses have a narrow concept of transparency — one that is "indifferent to "media liberalization."[70] Similarly, the government has succeeded in attracting even media corporations to Singapore, creating simultaneously "a regional media centre and a site of media repression."[71]

Determined to develop Singapore into a regional hub for international satellite broadcasters that were showing growing interest in Asian markets, the government liberalized regulations on satellite "up-linking," making it easier for satellite broadcasters to beam their programs out of the island state and into the region. Although the ban on dishes for receiving those same signals domestically remained, the benefits of operating out of Singapore were sufficiently attractive for HBO, MTV and other giants to locate their Asian operations on the island. They eventually tapped the Singapore market through cable.

In an assessment that echoes Zaharom's on Malaysia, Rodan says that in Singapore, "rapid and increasingly sophisticated market development has actually coincided with more effective control of the media."[72] In that sense, the governments of both Malaysia and Singapore were able to have their cake and eat it too. This has confounded the critics who — convinced of the conventional wisdom that economic and political liberalization must go together — expect the Malaysian and Singaporean media systems to collapse under their own ostensible contradictions. The critics have waited in vain for decades. The print and broadcast sectors continue to grow, enjoying commercial vitality while serving the hegemonic interests of the state. It is only with the internet that cracks have finally appeared in this edifice. Suddenly, the governments found themselves having to choose which they wanted more: economic growth or political control. The choice they made radically transformed the landscape for contentious journalism.

CHAPTER 3

"NARROW TAILORING" AND THE INTERNET DILEMMA

In the mid-1990s, the governments of Malaysia and Singapore gave their public access to the global internet. It became the first medium that citizens of either country were allowed to use for mass communication without first having to secure a government license. This qualitative shift in the media regime, which enabled the flowering of contentious journalism on an unprecedented scale, cannot be accounted for by any fundamental change in either government's political philosophy as described in the previous chapter. At the time when authorities were introducing the internet, their treatment of print and broadcast still bore all the hallmarks of their authoritarian styles. Indeed, neither government disavowed post-publication punishment as a legitimate response to online journalism. On the contrary, both governments made clear that writers and publishers in cyberspace would enjoy no immunity from prosecution if they broke the laws of the land. Still, the lack of prior restraints on internet communication made the medium considerably more hospitable to contentious journalism.

In trying to explain internet exceptionalism, it is easy to slip into the fallacy discussed in Chapter 1: that the internet has certain inherent powers — "ahistorical inherence" as François Fortier calls it — that determine a particular outcome irrespective of context.[1] Indeed, policymakers themselves engaged in such rhetoric, depicting the internet as a global force that they could do little to resist. In fact, however, they always had options other than the ones they chose. They could have gone the way of Myanmar or North Korea and simply not provided general access to the internet. Later, China would demonstrate the feasibility of censorship, blocking access to thousands of websites. The failure to adopt such controls in Malaysia and Singapore cannot be explained away as an oversight or by a lack of authoritarian imagination. Initially, perhaps, the authorities may have been taken by surprise by the internet's applications as a medium for dissent. Before long, however, they were fully aware of the need for explicit policy on political websites. At that point, Malaysia adopted and flaunted a no-censorship policy. Singapore blocked access to exactly 100 pornographic sites as a symbolic gesture but declared that it would not ban any political site.

This chapter offers an explanation for the authorities' uncharacteristic behavior. The argument, in brief, is that the internet's perceived economic value dominated the authorities' policy formulation, subordinating the goal of political control that historically shaped media policy. It was not the first time that the governments had to balance economic and political objectives in media policymaking. However, when dealing with print and broadcast media, the authorities had been able to tailor their political interventions narrowly, such that these actions did not smother their largely pro-market economic priorities. In contrast, the internet was not as amenable to narrow tailoring. Rather than abandon their economic dreams for the internet, the two governments decided to tolerate a lesser degree of political control than they were accustomed to, and that continued to prevail in their treatment of other media.

Narrow Tailoring and the Internet Discontinuity

The rhetoric of "Asian democracy" professes no contradiction in principle between market-driven economic growth and authoritarian government. Nevertheless, in practice, both governments were sensitive to a particular policy tension in their economic and political goals for mass media. On the one hand they wanted media organizations to serve and obey the market. After all, markets require efficient circulation of information. Furthermore, the media are industries in their own right, creating jobs, producing goods and services, and contributing to (or draining from) tax revenue. On the other hand, political and ideological imperatives nudged the governments to intervene in the industry, and to treat media as tools for maintaining hegemony and extending their control over their societies.

Much of the policy work in the media sphere had been directed at trying to resolve this tension. The basic strategy involved treating political expression as a separate category requiring special management, while other activities were given more freedom. Indeed, all states give political expression special treatment, distinguishing it from other forms of communication. However, the nature of that treatment varies. In liberal democracies, political expression earns special protection from government censorship — protection that may not be accorded to, say, commercial speech. In more authoritarian societies, political content in the media is usually singled out for extra control and manipulation, either through explicit legislation or through selective exercise of sweeping state powers. In either case, effective state action depends partly on the authorities' ability to discriminate between political and non-political uses of the media, and to tailor their interventions narrowly to fit the intended goal. The term "narrow tailoring" is borrowed from American First Amendment discourse. The United States Supreme Court requires the government to show that any restriction it wants to impose on protected speech is necessary for achieving a compelling state interest — and that such a restriction is narrowly tailored to achieve that goal. Thus, two parts of the Communications Decency Act of 1996 — an attempt to regulate indecency on the internet — were struck down by the court in part because the government failed to make the case that the legislation was narrowly tailored. The court ruled that in trying to regulate indecency, the law would also threaten internet users' valid First Amendment rights; this "overbreadth" problem would be tantamount to "burning the house to roast the pig."[2]

Authoritarian governments face their own narrow tailoring problem, but in a way that turns the US example on its head: They try to tailor intervention to fit the goal of political censorship without smothering other types of activity that are seen to require more latitude. In Malaysia and Singapore, the specific challenge for media policy-makers has been to couple illiberal political interventions with market-oriented strategies for economic growth. The previous chapter explained how Malaysia and Singapore employed narrowly-tailored political controls in their management of print and broadcast media. They were able to encourage rapid development of their terrestrial broadcasting, cable and satellite television industries while maintaining a tight rein on news and current affairs programming.

Narrowly-tailored political control can take a number of forms. First, communication *technologies* can be subject to discriminatory policies. For example, technologies serving mainly private, business functions can be treated more liberally than those serving mass media purposes. Thus, Malaysia's press law requires owners of printing presses to obtain a government license, but machines that are not capable of reproducing at least 1,000 impressions per hour — such as most photocopiers — are not defined as presses and therefore exempt from licensing.[3]

Second, media *organizations* can be selectively licensed — based on ownership, national origin, mission, or track record — to block those with suspect political agendas. The two countries' opening up of their airwaves only to companies with close ties to the government is a case in point.[4] Third, *audiences* can be differentiated according to their perceived levels of vulnerability or trustworthiness, with different groups granted different degrees of access to media. One example is Singapore's policy of allowing approved financial institutions,

but not the general public, to own satellite dishes.⁵ Fourth, media
content can be selectively policed, with special restrictions placed
on political expression. In Singapore, this includes the provision in
the press laws prohibiting foreign periodicals from "engaging in the
domestic politics of Singapore."⁶

The internet poses a problem for narrow tailoring, because it
defies the kind of categorization to which older media technologies
are subject. E-mail, for example, can be used as a one-to-one
medium like a telephone, or as a means of distributing material to a
subscriber list the size of a newspaper's circulation base, or anything
in between. The kind of statutory distinctions drawn between
unregulated photocopiers and regulated printing presses — based on
the number of reproductions that the machine is technically capable
of making within a given time — are rendered meaningless by the
internet, through which material can be reproduced five or 5,000
times with equal ease.

The more functionally-dedicated a communication system is,
the more amenable it is to narrowly targeted policies. Characteristic
of older media, dishes for receiving satellite TV signals are good for
little else. Thus, banning them has no spillover impact. The internet,
on the other hand, is accessed through computers and modems that
cannot be banned without affecting all sorts of other activities such
as electronic commerce and corporate communication. The internet is
also harder to regulate because it is a two-way medium. Malaysia and
Singapore regulate newspaper publishing differently from newspaper
purchasing, and radio broadcasting differently from radio reception.
In general, production and distribution is more tightly controlled
than consumption. With the internet, however, it is difficult to
prevent an individual consumer from becoming a producer, as the
same technology can be used by either.

Since the internet is hard to categorize as a technology,
authorities could instead try to impose narrowly-tailored controls by
discriminating among consumers, among producers, or according to

content. Myanmar, for example, limited internet access to selected government officials and foreigners. Malaysia and Singapore, in contrast, decided in the mid-1990s to make the internet accessible to the general public. There was nothing inherent in the technology that determined this outcome. The explanation lies in political-economic factors that will be explored in this chapter. Once the internet was made generally available, the legendary volume and speed of its traffic would have made it harder to control producers or content. However, it was not impossible to impose some restrictions on producers or content, as Singapore itself showed when it required internet service providers to block access to proscribed pornographic sites. Again, the explanation for the governments' difficulties in imposing narrowly tailored controls of these sorts does not lie in the technology itself, but in the historical context of their policy options.

Not Just Another Medium

As much as by any of its special technical features, the internet is distinguished from earlier media technologies by the meaning that has been invested in it. It was seen as embedded within, as well as a bearer of, an information technology revolution that would usher in an entire new mode of economic development. A series of developments in the early 1990s proliferated the technology and enabled it to seize the popular imagination. The internet's design was conceptualized as far back as the 1960s, and has roots in the Pentagon-funded ARPANET network, which connected a handful of US research centers in 1969. By the 1970s, electronic mail had appeared, as well as the use of the "@" symbol for addresses, remote accessing of computers, and message groups. However, what has been called the internet's "Big Bang" occurred in the 1990s as a result of a number of parallel developments. First, it became possible to use the internet for commercial purposes. Until then, the National Science Foundation, which maintained the main long-distance backbone of the internet in the US, had prohibited commercial information and transactions. The acceptable-use policy was abandoned when the US government withdrew the NSF subsidy and commercialized the backbone in 1994. Second, computers were getting cheaper, allowing people to have them in their homes and offices. Third, the World Wide Web was born in 1990. Websites could include pictures, buttons, and hypertext linking to different pages. Users did not have to type complicated commands. They could navigate by typing web addresses and clicking on links. Navigation became even more intuitive and pleasurable when web browsers were launched in 1993, starting with Mosaic, the forerunner to Netscape. Fourth, hypertext markup language or HTML was accessible in 1991, providing users with a tool for creating documents for publication on the Web.[7]

Before the Big Bang, people were already talking about an ongoing information technology revolution, including the power of connecting computers within closed networks. However, the internet — a network of networks — was never part of these conversations. After the Big Bang, the internet was treated as virtually synonymous with the IT revolution, and was its most evocative symbol. Thus, the internet became tied structurally and symbolically to what Manuel Castells has called the new "informational mode of development," in which productivity arises out of information and communication technologies.[8] For policy-makers, the IT revolution contained not only promise but also a threat. Network externalities mean that while the benefits of being in the network grow exponentially, so do the penalties of self-exclusion. A node that disconnects itself will find resources bypassing it. "Thus, within the value system of production/consumerism, there is no individual alternative for countries, firms, or people," Castells writes.[9] Whether or not this assessment is accurate is not particularly important for our present purposes. What is significant is that this perception was shared by policy-makers. As one set of authors note, the communications revolution attracted considerable attention in Europe, Asia, and the

Americas as "both a central cause of globalized economics and the central playing field on which economic competition among nations takes place": "Analysts in each region alternatively fantasize about the prospect of their own success in seizing dominance, and fret over the dire possibility that others will."[10]

These meanings distinguished the internet from earlier media technologies. When newspapers emerged in Malaysia and Singapore in the 19th century, they carried intelligence important for commerce, but the technologies of mass printing and distribution were themselves peripheral to the main economic activities of the time, such as agriculture and trade. When broadcasting was introduced, the countries were industrializing. Radio and television became important advertising media, but broadcast technologies was not central to, say, ship-building in Singapore or the processing of rubber and palm oil in Malaysia. Thus, the strict licencing of presses or broadcast equipment had limited bearing on the wider economy. Centralization of traditional media industries in state-controlled monopolies mattered little one way or another to other sectors. In contrast, it was clear that regulation of the internet would have wide implications for the new information economy. Earlier media technologies were regarded first — both chronologically and in importance — as transmitters of political and cultural messages, and only then as modes of production. Those wanting to extract economic benefits from a particular medium had to appeal for concessions from regulators with entrenched policies of political control. Liberalization would then be managed in a manner that did not threaten political interests. In contrast, the development of the internet in Singapore and Malaysia was framed initially within the discourse of science, technology and the development of a new information economy. It was treated first as a productivity-enhancing extension of computer technology, rather than as a medium that would grow to challenge state hegemony over print and broadcasting.

The internet in Malaysia's Vision 2020

The previous chapter showed how broadcasting was born within information ministries, with the main policy objective being a desire to tap the technology's potential as a propaganda tool. In contrast, the internet's Malaysian seeds were planted within a technological and research environment, and later hothoused in an all-encompassing modernization vision in which private enterprise would take the lead. The Malaysian Institute of Microelectronic Systems, MIMOS, set up a university computer network in 1988 with four dial-up lines overseas and offering e-mail and newsgroups. MIMOS, which grew into a full-fledged government department within the Ministry of Science, Technology and the Environment, established the country's first internet service provider, Joint Advanced Integrated Networking (JARING, which is also Malay for "net"). In 1992, JARING obtained a permanent connection to the internet backbone via a satellite link to the US. In 1996, Telekom Malaysia, supervised by the Ministry of Energy, Telecommunications and Post, launched TMNet to compete with Jaring. TMNet is now the country's dominant ISP.[11]

Significantly, therefore, the Information Ministry — the custodian of the government's propaganda and censorship interests — was not a lead agency in the internet's development in Malaysia. The internet's arrival in Malaysia had the same unheralded and under-the-radar quality that characterized its early development in the United States and elsewhere. However, even after its social and political significance was appreciated, policy continued to be framed in primarily economic terms. It is difficult to overestimate the enthusiasm with which Mahathir Mohamad, Malaysia's prime minister, embraced information technology and later the internet. IT was to play a central role in achieving Vision 2020 — the goal of becoming a developed country within 30 years of 1990. Vision 2020 itself, announced in 1991, was more than an economic target in the narrow sense. John Hilley observes that it was "a millennial symbol of growth, wealth-creation and nation-building on an unprecedented scale."[12] The new informational mode of development was seen as a golden opportunity to wrest Malaysia free of its Third World past and thrust it among the advanced countries of the world. Structurally and symbolically, the heart of this strategy was the construction of a Multimedia Super Corridor (MSC), announced in 1995. About 15 km wide by 50 km long, it would stretch from the Petronas twin towers (the world's tallest buildings, appropriately enough) in downtown Kuala Lumpur to the new international airport (the region's largest airport) being built to the south. The MSC was to have the very best infrastructure and supporting incentives and regulations to attract IT and multimedia companies.

Mahathir cast the MSC in an epic role. It would be Malaysia's bridge "from the Industrial Age to the Information Age," he said.[13] Although Malaysia was a small country, the new technology offered an opportunity that he likened to America's in the 19th century:

> At that time, England launched the Industrial Revolution but America won it. Why? Because the technology could be moved to an environment much more conducive to realising its full potential. Malaysia has come late to industrialisation, and this has given us the will and skill to make sweeping changes that others cannot because we have much less to lose. The MSC provides all the critical components required to create the perfect environment to achieve the promise of the Information Age.[14]

The flurry of institution-building and law-making that took place from the mid-1990s reflected the government's belief that IT development should be led by the private sector, with the state serving as facilitator and enabler. In 1996, a National Information Technology Council was established to advise the government on IT development. Once again, the information ministry was not given a major role. The chairmen of its five working groups, set up in 1998, included the ministers in charge of the telecommunications, education, and international trade and industry portfolios. The chair of the E-Sovereignty working group, responsible for "enhancing the identity and integrity of the nation in an increasingly borderless world" — the most ideologically-oriented function — was handed not to the information minister but to a think-tank chief.[15] Also in 1996, the government established the Multimedia Development Corporation as the agency to spearhead the development and implementation of the Multimedia Super Corridor. It is "a fully empowered one-stop shop" set up as a government-owned company to allow it "to operate independent of civil service rules and regulations" but with a direct line to the prime minister and deputy prime minister.[16] Its website (which has a dot-com rather than dot-gov address) promises that it will serve as "champion, facilitator and partner" of foreign investors:

> As a performance-oriented, client-focused agency, it endeavors to cut through the proverbial bureaucratic red-tape to provide timely information and good advice, expedite permit and license approvals, and introduce companies to potential local partners and financiers.[17]

Singapore's intelligent island vision

Singapore was an early and vigorous adopter of computerization and information technologies. Computerization was seen as an essential means of transcending the country's small manpower pool. Government strategy was articulated through a series of masterplans, beginning with a National Computerization Plan (1981–5). This saw the establishment of a National Computer Board, a key task of which was the computerization of major functions in all government departments. The National Information Technology Plan (1986–9) was directed mainly at developing an export-oriented IT industry and the raising of business productivity through IT. Specialized computer networks were developed for electronic data interchange, including to make customs procedures paperless at the world's third busiest port.[18] In 1992, the government launched its IT2000 masterplan, painting the vision of an "intelligent island" in which IT would permeate every aspect of the society, enhancing national economic competitiveness and improving the quality of life of its citizens.[19] IT2000 was succeeded by the Infocomm21 Masterplan, which aims to develop Singapore into one of the top five Information Societies in the world. The government's vision of a networked society was initially first centered on Teleview, the world's first national interactive videotext system. This centralized network quickly degenerated to dinosaur status when the internet's potential was recognized.

The internet's emergence in Singapore had the same backdoor quality as it did in Malaysia and elsewhere. Access was originally provided through Technet, set up in 1991 by the National University of Singapore and the National Science and Technology Board for the use of researchers and academics. The general public was able to gain access from July 1994, when the government-owned Singapore Telecom launched Singnet as the country's first commercial internet service provider.[20] With the internet having overtaken the white-elephant Teleview system, the government came to define the "digital divide" as "the gap between those who are Internet savvy and those who are not." Hence, the goal for personal computers and the internet was "ubiquitous adoption," rather than limiting it to a "small privileged group."[21] By the mid-1990s, Singapore officials, like the Malaysians, were talking about the internet as an irresistible historical force. George Yeo, then in charge of the Ministry of Information and the Arts (MITA), likened the internet to a big city with "wholesome, well-lit parts and ... dark alleys with dirt, sleaze and crime":

> But we cannot not visit a city just because there are parts of it we do not like. There will always be bits that we do not like in any city.... In any case, even if we want to avoid the city of Internet, we cannot because it will eventually envelop us, like an expanding urban conurbation absorbing small towns in its path.... When books are commonplace, it is important to be able to read. In the same way, those who are not adept in information

technology will be at a severe competitive disadvantage in the 21st century.[22]

Like Malaysia, therefore, Singapore framed the internet within an all-encompassing IT vision that had been conceived as part of a national strategy for survival in global economic competition. As in Malaysia, Singapore's institutional framework for IT policymaking reflected this priority. The National Computer Board was an agency under the Ministry of Finance. The National Science and Technology Board, which introduced the internet to Singapore by funding Technet, was an agency of the trade and industry ministry. When Singapore Telecom launched Singnet, it was overseen by the telecommunication regulator, under the communications ministry. The information ministry did not figure in the formal decision-making structure for internet development. Awareness of convergence in communication industries eventually brought broadcasting and IT regulation under the same institutional umbrella, with MITA becoming the Ministry of Information, Communications and the Arts in 2001. Only then, a decade after the internet was introduced, was the medium's development overseen by the same ministry that dealt with censorship, propaganda, and press and broadcast licensing. By then, in any case, the information ministry was not thought of as any less Net-savvy than the economic ministries. Under George Yeo, its first minister and the government's most eloquent prophet of information society, MITA had, for example, transformed its public library system into one of the most IT-intensive in the world, partly by handing its top management to officers inducted from the National Computer Board to remove any vestiges of pre-digital thinking. The Singapore Broadcasting Authority, the content regulator under MITA, had already reoriented itself into the role of industry promoter, having spent several years facilitating the development of Singapore as a regional broadcasting hub. Its name was changed to the Media Development Authority to reflect this role.

This is not to suggest that the government was not concerned about the internet's ideological threats. Nor is it to say that the information minister of either Malaysia or Singapore was blind to the medium's economic potential. Authoritarian impulses as well as economic priorities transcend particular ministerial portfolios. What the pattern of institutional evolution does show, however, is that both governments framed the internet first and foremost as an economic challenge and opportunity, and only secondarily as a political medium. Furthermore, the existence of government agencies tasked with a promotional role was not an unimportant factor in the emergence of contentious politics on the web. As later chapters will show, these agencies provided insurgents with elite allies who occasionally tempered the reactions of more control-minded officials.

Dealing with Net Politics

As much as the two governments wanted to treat the internet as economic infrastructure, there were citizens who had other ideas for the medium. Therefore, although the authorities introduced the internet without articulating any policy on political content, they could not ignore the fact that their citizens were using it for forms of expression that would not be tolerated in the mainstream media. The trend was noticeable enough to be reported in both domestic and regional newspapers even before the Net's Big Bang.[23] The governments' first response was to join the contest of ideas in cyberspace. As early as 1994, the government-linked Singapore International Foundation was e-mailing a twice-weekly bulletin to Singaporeans overseas.[24] In 1995, Singapore's information ministry launched Singapore Infomap, a portal for Singapore-related content.[25] One study of the national homepages of small states names Singapore's as the most attractive and appealing, beating 17 other countries, including 12 in Europe. "The page is cleverly designed for the international investor and tourist, and its features convey a state firmly linked to the world's high-tech networks," the study's authors write.[26] In addition, activists of the ruling parties of both countries began posting pro-government views on websites and bulletin boards to counter what they felt were unbalanced, ill-informed and irresponsible opinions circulating in cyberspace.[27]

Within two years of the commercial launch of internet service providers, Malaysia and Singapore announced their respective stands on internet content regulation. Previously, political websites' freedom from prior restraint had been the governments' position by default; it now became deliberate policy. Conventional wisdom in the mid-1990s stated that anyone who knew anything about the internet would know that it was impossible to censor. It followed logically that any government that tried to censor the internet must be ignorant about it. Conventional wisdom would shift by the end of the decade, but for a while it was enough to stay the hands of governments accustomed to authoritarian methods of dealing with media. Of course, this silver lining was accompanied by a forbidding gray cloud. Just because political sites would not be blocked did not mean that they were immune from criminal prosecution or civil action under existing laws ranging from sedition to defamation. Whether the governments would actually use such laws against internet journalism was another question altogether. Malaysians and Singaporeans would not have to wait long for the answer.

Malaysia's no-censorship assurance

Consumed by its IT vision, the Malaysian government began issuing assurances that its well-known proclivity for censorship would not leak into the internet or its beloved MSC. Speaking in California in January 1997, Mahathir promised investors that the MSC would have "the world's best soft infrastructure of supporting laws, policies, and practices" including a 10-point Multimedia Bill of Guarantees. One of its guarantees read: "Malaysia will ensure no censorship of the Internet."[28] The Bill of Guarantees in literal terms applied only to companies granted MSC status by the Multimedia Development

Corporation. However, the spirit of the law covered internet users throughout the country, since the MSC was touted as the first phase in a national plan. As Mahathir put it, the MSC was "a pilot project for harmonizing our entire country with the global forces shaping the Information Age."[29] If they wanted to create the image of an IT-friendly regime, the authorities would have to live up to that spirit, and not just the letter of the no-censorship guarantee. Officials clarified that the policy did not grant individuals blanket immunity from Malaysia's security laws. If someone presented seditious or libelous content to Malaysian audiences, action could be taken under existing laws that applied to television, for example. Such threats were usually issued by officials from the information ministry or the home ministry, in charge of security. These officials also raised the specter of reviewing the no-censorship policy. Invariably, officials from the multimedia ministry — the champion of IT and the MSC — would subsequently come out with reassurances that the government's policy of openness remained intact.[30]

Remarkably, the Malaysian government lived up to its no-censorship commitment through the Reformasi protests of 1998, when online dissent was scathing and vitriolic in its criticism of public figures. "Even when Mahathir went through the lowest of the low, and there were calls to block the worst websites, he resisted," says one official.[31] In an incident unrelated to the reform movement, four individuals were arrested in 1998 for spreading rumors on the internet about knife-wielding Indonesians rioting in a Kuala Lumpur neighborhood, which led to panic buying.[32] Yet, there were no reports of sites being closed down by the government — at least not directly. In 2001, more than a dozen anti-Mahathir websites were suddenly taken off the web, not by the government, but by Tripod, a free hosting service owned by Lycos Inc of the United States. The action was ostensibly taken because the sites breached Tripod's rules against material deemed hateful or defamatory, and it is not known whether it was initiated by a government complaint.[33]

The government's omnipresent threat to use existing laws against offending internet publications finally materialized in 2003, when the independent news site Malaysiakini was investigated by the police for publishing an allegedly seditious letter. The investigations entailed seizing Malaysiakini's computers, effectively shutting it down for half a day.[34] This story is taken up in the case study on Malaysiakini in Chapter 8.

Singapore's accountability laws

Singapore's government was one of the earliest in the world to devise internet content regulations.[35] Parliament enacted a new broadcasting law in 1994, formally extending the government's jurisdiction to electronic communication. At the time, however, no specific rules were set down for online media. The authorities finally introduced new regulations for the internet in July 1996. They required internet service providers to route traffic through proxy servers so that they could filter out sites that regulators found objectionable.

The other main feature of the regulations was a "class license" system. This introduced into new media the old principle of licensing. However, instead of having to apply for individual licenses, internet content providers were deemed automatically licensed as a class, and could therefore operate as before. Sites that sought public attention and dealt with what were deemed to be more sensitive areas, principally religion and politics, had to meet an additional requirement. They would have to register with the regulatory agency. Registration required the editorial team to sign a declaration saying that they would take "full responsibility for the contents on the website(s) and ... all reasonable steps to ensure that such contents comply with the laws of Singapore."

Singapore's stand was certainly less liberal than Malaysia's no-censorship guarantee, announced half a year later. This did not reflect a difference in political ideology: Malaysia was no more tolerant of dissent in print and broadcast media than Singapore. The difference in internet policy is instead best explained by the two countries' relative standing in the eyes of foreign investors. Malaysia, not yet regarded as a high-technology haven, may have felt a stronger need to make the dramatic gesture compared with Singapore, already a magnet for high-tech investments. It is quite possible that Malaysia's no-censorship stand was consciously designed to differentiate itself from its neighbor. Dr. Mohamed Arif Nun, chief operating officer of Malaysia's Multimedia Development Corporation, told an interviewer from a business publication that he recognized that US companies were "very emotional" about free speech. He added: "I've met many people who are very upset with Singapore's decision to censor materials on the Internet."[36]

Indeed, Singapore's mid-1996 announcement was greeted with vociferous protest from the internet's passionate early adopters — including the founders of Sintercom, the subject of the case study in Chapter 5. International news coverage was largely negative, associating the moves with Singapore's reputation for draconian rule. In response, the authorities said that the proxy server barrier was intended only for pornography and not for political sites — a distinction that has not been forthcoming in the regulation of other media. Even when regulating pornography, the government acknowledged repeatedly that it knew that imposing watertight censorship would be impossible. To emphasize the symbolic intent of its actions, it named exactly 100 "high-impact" pornographic sites to its proscribed list.[37] The government also appointed a National Internet Advisory Committee chaired by a scientist. As a result of the committee's recommendations, the regulator revised the Internet Code of Practice to explain the responsibilities of licensees in less alarming terms.[38]

The regulators also amended their content guidelines. Their original list of discouraged material included content that jeopardized public security or national defense; excited disaffection against the Government; or undermined public confidence in the administration of justice — terms borrowed from existing legislation. These items were expunged from the new code, placing the emphasis squarely on sexual content and material harmful to racial and religious harmony. The regulator, the Media Development Authority or MDA, describes its content regulation as taking a "light touch" approach. Its website goes to the extent of addressing so-called myths about its regulations. For example:

> Myth: MDA is stifling religious and political discussion on the Internet. Fact: MDA does not stop religious and political bodies from putting up web sites. We ask that they register with us as content providers to emphasize the need to be responsible in what they say. This is important, given the multi-racial and multi-religious nature of our society, and is consistent with existing regulations pertaining to print and other electronic material.[39]

Singapore's first prosecution of an individual engaged in political expression on the internet took place in November 2001, more than seven years after the medium's commercial launch. A man was arrested for allegedly posting an inflammatory article on the Singaporeans for Democracy website. Alleging that the prime minister had entered a polling place in violation of election laws in 1997, his article urged Singaporeans "to break the same law" in the forthcoming elections. The writer's act was classified as an attempt to incite disobedience to the law in a way likely to lead to a breach of peace, an offence punishable by up to three years imprisonment. The authorities later dropped the charges, saying that he was mentally ill.[40] The case confirmed fears that the regulators' "light-touch" policy did not mean that they were not watching online politics closely, or that they would refrain from removing the kid gloves from time to time.[41] A second case involved Fateha.com, a site purporting to be the genuine voice of Singapore's Muslim community. The authorities threatened to charge its editor with criminal defamation for articles critical of senior establishment figures, but he fled to Australia before investigations were complete.[42]

Counter tendencies in the internet revolution

It is probably no accident that government crackdowns on online dissent in Malaysia and Singapore occurred after the dot-com crash of 2000, and after the terrorist attacks of September 11, 2001. The authorities' earlier self-restraint had been based partly on the calculation that any authoritarian action would damage their international reputation and prove economically costly. As the international environment changed, so did their calculations. First, the stock market bubble burst, deflating the hyperbole surrounding the internet. In the mid-90s, governments had hung on every word of tech gurus and geeks promulgating their visions of a New Economy. After the crash, those same words seemed like so much irrational exuberance. As internet investors' net worth shrank, so did the perceived importance of respecting their libertarian sensibilities.

Second, the terrorist attacks on the US shifted the center of gravity of American values. The land of the free suddenly developed an appreciation for order. The export of democracy and human rights became a priority of the past; the US was now seeking allies to join its war against terrorism. Within a month of the attacks, Mahathir was gloating that his government's use of preventive detention all these years had been vindicated.[43] In this new international context, Malaysia and Singapore could start dealing with internet dissent with less fear of condemnation. Government regulation might no longer be totally aberrant or abhorrent, but merely a local instantiation of a global response to an increasingly untrustworthy world.

Even before September 11, the internet's libertarian ethos had started to shed. That ethos had its roots in the so-called "end-to-end" paradigm of network architecture, which invoked user empowerment, voluntary cooperation, and lack of controls within the network.[44] David Clark, who had touted end-to-end almost 20 years earlier, predicted a new premium on trustworthiness. Shortly before September 11, he wrote with uncanny prescience:

Today, there is less and less reason to believe that we can trust other end-points to behave as desired.... The situation is a predictable consequence of dramatic growth in the population of connected people and its diversification to include people with a wider range of motivations for using the Internet, leading to uses that some have deemed misuses or abuses.... If the communicating parties are described as 'dissidents', and the third party trying to wiretap or block conversation is a 'repressive' government, most people raised in the context of free speech will align their interests with the end parties. Replace the word 'dissident' with 'terrorist', and the situation becomes less clear to many.[45]

This chapter has tried to explain internet exceptionalism in Malaysia and Singapore: why the medium was spared the kind of prior restraints that continued to apply to print and broadcasting. We have also seen that the freedom of cyberspace is neither permanent nor absolute. There was nothing magical about the technology that gave its users immunity from the powerful. The internet was *less* regulable mainly in the sense that narrowly-tailored prior restraints on communication are harder to apply. It was not *totally* unregulable. Lawrence Lessig warns us against "is-ism," reminding us that whatever is true of the internet's architecture today need not be true tomorrow.[46] Governments can modify the architecture of the internet to make it more regulable. Singapore took such a step when it required service providers to install proxy servers, enabling them to block proscribed sites as well as monitor messages. That the government did not use this system to block access to any political website was a matter of choice, based on political calculations. It was not determined by the technology.

By now, states' power to regulate the internet is well recognized and indeed represents the new conventional wisdom. Back in 1996, John Barlow had issued a Declaration of the Independence of Cyberspace to world leaders at the annual Davos summit. "I declare the global social space we are building to be naturally independent of the tyrannies you see to impose on us," he said. "You have no moral right to rule us nor do you possess and methods of enforcement we have true reason to fear."[47] Five years later, that "glorious illusion" was certified dead by *The Economist*. The internet, the magazine said in a cover story, "is subject to geography after all, and therefore to law."[48] In keeping with the new mood, a multi-country study published by the Carnegie Endowment for International Peace in 2003 concluded that "the Internet is not inherently a threat to authoritarian rule."[49]

Such assessments serve as important correctives to the claims of the past. Now, unfortunately, we face the opposite risk, of overestimating the state's power to control the changes it has set in motion by adopting the internet. In the cases of Malaysia and Singapore, it is tempting to conclude based on the evidence of recent reprisals that the more things change, the more they stay the same. To understand why that conclusion would be erroneous, we need to remind ourselves of the nature of political domination in those two societies. Traditionally, the two regimes have maintained control partly through coercion, but mainly through hegemonic consensus. As noted in the previous chapter, their preferred mode is not routine repression of dissident opinion, but an ideological domination that makes compliance with the regime seems like common sense. Restricting the range of opinions publicly uttered — by prior restraint of media outlets through licensing — is a key part of this strategy. The governments' failure to apply this mode of control to the internet, and their resulting need to reach for more coercive methods, should be seen as representing strains on their hegemony.

To regard the post-2001 government crackdowns as representing a total negation of the internet advantage is also incongruent with the perspectives of the insurgents themselves. Most of the individuals engaged in contentious journalism — unlike some of the commentators who wrote about them — had been under no illusions about the liberating potential of the internet when they embarked on their projects, and even at the height of the hype. They did not seek guarantees of safe passage, let alone success. The glimmer of opportunity they perceived in cyberspace was compelling only when compared with print and broadcast routes that were completely closed to them. They knew the internet offered no certainties, only risky possibilities. For some, however, that was good enough.

CHAPTER 4

CONTENTIOUS MEDIA IN THEORY AND PRACTICE

Like their counterparts elsewhere in the world, the Malaysians and Singaporeans who use the internet as a medium of mass communication have created a bewildering spectrum of websites and mailing lists. They range from individuals drawing ego gratifications from personal homepages or blogs, to government departments and corporations pursuing publicity and profits. This book is concerned with a small subset of these users: individuals and groups who practice contentious journalism. Chapter 1 defined contentious journalism as the reporting and commenting on current events with at least some intention of serving a public purpose (the "journalism" half of the definition), and with the explicit objective of challenging the authority of elites in setting the agenda and forging a national consensus (the "contentious" half of the definition). Before delving into four in-depth case studies of contentious online journalism, it may help to capture a sweeping overview of the terrain. First, this chapter will provide a brief historical survey, to try to reflect the number and range of such projects in the two countries. Then, it will suggest ways to make sense of these projects: it will explicate key concepts from the literature on alternative media and social movements, which will guide our investigation of contentious online journalism.

Birth of a Movement

The first Malaysians and Singaporeans to use the internet for communication resembling contentious journalism were participants in the open online forums soc.culture.malaysia and soc.culture.singapore, and their Southeast Asian precursor, soc.culture.asean. Postings on these newsgroups, which predated the world wide web, occasionally ventured into free-for-alls on politics and current affairs. The birth of the web inspired the publication of amateur online magazines, probably starting with Singapore's Sintercom in 1994, which is discussed in the next chapter. In early 1996, opposition parties began entering the web. The first were the National Solidarity Party in Singapore and the Democratic Action Party in Malaysia.[1] The DAP — whose leader Lim Kit Siang championed information technology with an enthusiasm matching that of his nemesis Mahathir Mohamad — beat even the ruling parties in the race to cyberspace. In Malaysia, one of the first professional journalists to exploit the disintermediating power of the internet — bypassing media organizations to reach readers directly — was M.G.G. Pillai, who launched his Sang Kancil mailing list for political news and commentary in 1997.[2] For Pillai, who earns his living writing for various print publications, his online venture is not a commercially-driven exercise. A senior government leader once expressed surprise at his choice to carry on despite the lack of any financial return. He says he replied to the minister: "If I have to explain, you wouldn't understand, so I won't bother."[3] Similarly, the overwhelming majority of contentious journalism projects march to the beat of non-commercial drums.

The Anwar Ibrahim affair and the Reformasi movement in Malaysia was the catalyst for an explosion of activity on the internet. It sparked the launch of dozens of sympathetic sites in 1998. A year later, an anti-defamation committee of the ruling UMNO party identified more than 40 websites that it said were being used to slander the government and its leaders.[4] Most of these sites became dormant after 2000, when Anwar lost his court appeals and started his prison term. Much of the content on some of these sites was indeed crass and outlandish.[5] The government was not the only target. Chandra Muzaffar, a respected public intellectual who helped establish a pro-Anwar opposition party, Keadilan, found himself under anonymous online attack when he criticized Keadilan's leadership after he left the party. Several of these comments were "vulgar, obscene and crude," even insulting his ethnic origin and his physical disability.[6]

However, there were also instances of independent journalists who tried to provide more responsible and professional contributions in the heat of the protests. They included Sabri Zain's eyewitness accounts in his online Reformasi Diary, and Saksi, which carried the work of some of the country's best-known independent writers.[7] Sites established a year or more after the Anwar sacking took this more professional tack. These included Malaysiakini and Harakah Daily (Chapters 7 and 8) in late 1999, and Agenda Daily in 2000.[8] The social reform movement, Aliran, launched a website with daily updates to supplement its monthly print magazine.[9] Radiq Radio, the country's first alternative radio network, experimented with the web as well as broadcast transmitters in nearby Indonesian islands to deliver its independent news programs.[10]

In Singapore, a search by a team of sociologists over four months in 2000 found 82 Singapore-based or Singapore-related political websites providing alternatives to dominant discourses.[11] The researchers grouped the sites into five categories. First, there are the sites of registered opposition parties, such as the Workers' Party, the Singapore Democratic Party, and the National Solidarity Party. Second, some sites promote freedom of speech, including that of Think Centre and the personal sites of opposition politicians. Third, several civil society groups maintain sites promoting legal and regulatory reform in their specific areas of concern. These include the Nature Society of Singapore, the Association of Women for Action and Research, Action for Aids, and People Like Us, a gay rights advocacy group. Fourth, there are religious and linguistic groups claiming fairer treatment, including the banned Unification Church (the "Moonies"), and a Speak Dialect Campaign resisting the government's promotion of Mandarin among Chinese Singaporeans. Fifth, some sites are internationally oriented but use Singapore as a base to escape persecution at home. These include the official website of the Bahais of Iran, and the Falun Gong of China.

Among these sites, two older ones that fit our definition of contentious journalism are Singaporeans For Democracy and Singapore Window.[12] Both are anonymously edited, but are believed to be run by Singapore dissidents who are in exile in Australia. As they carry very little original content, instead republishing articles from other sources, they have not captured the public imagination the way Singapore-based sites have done. Think Centre (discussed in Chapter 6) has a relatively higher profile.[13] Another prominent site was Fateha, which challenged the elite's claim to represent Singapore's Muslim community.[14] Fateha has championed causes such as the right of Muslim girls to wear headscarves with their school uniforms. The government in turn has labeled it a "fringe" group. Contentious journalism has also surfaced in some non-traditional venues. A rock music magazine, BigO, operates a website and mailing list that include stinging observations on local politics.[15] It does not deign to mention *The Straits Times* by name, referring to it instead as "the nation-builder press." As part of its house style, it also replaces the S in the country's name with a dollar sign, $ingapore, to protest the over-commercialization of music and culture. Even more irreverent is Sammyboy, which mixes political commentary with reviews of brothels and links to pornography.[16]

The researchers in the Singapore study quoted above note that not all of the 82 political sites they found reach out to the broader public; many cater to the internal communication needs of their respective communities. Therefore, while they can all be termed sites of "resistance" because they try to insulate their discourse from state domination, not all meet the definition of "contention" used in this book, which hinges on making claims on the state in a public and sustained manner. In addition, while all are obviously engaged in information dissemination, not all look like journalism as we have defined it. Such distinctions are of course debatable. However, although it is possible to quibble endlessly about where to draw the lines, there is a surprising degree of consensus among the practitioners interviewed. "Alternative" media recognize themselves in that label, and "mainstream" journalists similarly have no difficulty with that self-identification.

As for the term "contentious journalism," this is a construct of this study and is unlikely to ring a bell among practitioners. Nevertheless, even if they do not use the term, practitioners seem to have no trouble recognizing the existence of such a family of projects within the wider community of alternative media. They show this by their networking patterns. For example, the members of the Malaysian independent media activist group KAMI all fall squarely within the category of contentious journalism as defined here. They include the editors of Harakah, Malaysiakini and the banned print magazine *Detik*, for example — but not non-journalistic, informational party websites. One of the clearest manifestations of this tacit acknowledgment of family resemblance and solidarity is the choice of hotlinks within each website. Thus, Think Centre, under the heading "Political news and NGOs," provides links to Sintercom, Singapore Window, Singaporeans For Democracy and Fateha, as well as to the sites of four single-issue lobby groups. Think Centre also provides links to four Malaysian sites, all of which were mentioned above as belonging to the contentious journalism movement: Malaysiakini, Saksi, M.G.G. Pillai, and Aliran. Singapore Window in turn has front page links to Think Centre, Sintercom, Singaporeans For Democracy and Malaysiakini.

Even within this narrower category of contentious journalism, the variety of form and function is striking. Some of the websites employ full-time staff, while others are amateur-run. Some are backed by political organizations, while others are independent projects. There are those with formal business plans, while others seem to fly on the seat of their pants. Making sense of this diversity is a challenge that will require intellectual tools that the literature on the internet alone does not provide. In the rest of this chapter, we turn to two other sets of scholarly research for guidance.

Contentious Internet Journalism as Radical Alternative Media

Scholarly as well as popular accounts have long recognized a distinct category of "alternative" newspapers, magazines, broadcast stations, and other media. They are alternative *not* in the sense that they employ unique modalities or technologies, but in the ways they organize themselves, and the uses to which they put their resources. The label usually refers to media that are small, independent, and self-consciously oppositional, in the sense that they embody visions that challenge the status quo. Ultimately, however, these media are defined not in any absolute terms, but in relation to the mainstream. Indeed, large-scale and long-term studies of newspaper markets suggest that there is a kind of ecological link between mainstream and marginal media, such that the evolution of the former shapes the development of the latter. Typically, large daily newspapers defeat competitors and dominate the market by exploiting economies of scale, a strategy that entails taking a general-interest, middle-of-the-road editorial approach. In doing so, however, the specialized interests of certain niche audiences are neglected, presenting an opportunity for smaller publications.[17]

This ecological relationship makes the concept of alternative media difficult to pin down with precision. They may be easily identifiable within any one context, but definitions get slippery as we move from place to place and over time. One society's alternative media may be another's mainstream. These important caveats aside, there have been some noteworthy attempts to provide a systematic analysis of alternative media. In their recent books, John Downing and Chris Atton both view such media as vital for a genuinely democratic communication structure (a theme to be explored in the final chapter of this study).[18] According to these authors, alternative media's democratizing potential rests on two limbs: their emancipatory missions, and their structural positions. The former is the more obvious of the two, referring to a commitment to alternative editorial content, going against the grain of the status quo. The latter refers to alternative organizational features that make them more independent of dominant social forces, and more accessible to excluded groups.

Alternative content

Downing describes "radical alternative media" as expressing "an alternative vision to hegemonic policies, priorities, and perspectives."[19] They are "relatively free from the agenda of the powers that be and sometimes in opposition to one or more elements in that agenda."[20] Many have emerged in association with social movements. An early genre was the labor newspaper. Germany's *Arbeiter Illustrierte Zeitung*, for example, was founded by a workers organization and claimed a circulation of 450,000 at its height in 1931. The first illustrated workers' magazine in the world, it reported on workers' difficult lives and featured their interests and hobbies.[21] In the US, the weekly *Appeal to Reason* had a subscription list exceeding 500,000 and employed more than 100 staff at the peak of its success around 1900–10.[22] Another type of class-based media is run by rural communities underserved by metropolitan media. Usually referred to as "community media," they serve both democratic and developmental goals. Such media have been championed in poor countries by Unesco, the United Nations Educational, Scientific and Cultural Organization.[23]

The large readership of some early workers papers notwithstanding, alternative media are usually niche products with small audiences. Colin Sparks suggests that it would be a mistake for them to try to achieve a mass circulation, as such a target would dilute the medium's editorial mission.[24] The history of *Appeal to Reason* bears this out: its high subscription was achieved partly by reporting sensational news stories.[25] Conversely, editors of mass-circulation newspapers and of wire agencies have known since the 19th century that partisanship is incompatible with mass readership, and that the way to reach everyone in general is to serve (or offend) nobody in particular.[26]

In the US, the wave of activism in the late 1960s and early 1970s was a high point for alternative media. David Armstrong's history reveals the sheer variety of concerns and causes that alternative media represented. They included anti-war pamphlets, rock and roll magazines, newspapers on sexual politics, weeklies on city living, and investigative journalism.[27] Hundreds of offset-printed underground papers emerged, together with more prominent political weeklies such as *The Guardian* and monthlies like *Ramparts*. Likewise, the protest against the World Trade Organization's 1999 summit in Seattle was the catalyst for the "Indymedia" movement, a network of Independent Media Centers around the world.

Radical alternative media, says Downing, are usually the first to articulate and disseminate the concerns and perspectives of social movements. In contrast, mainstream media are notoriously unsympathetic to such activism, tending instead to sensationalize protesters' tactics and under-report their underlying support and beliefs. Thus, one recent study of media coverage of anarchist protests in Minneapolis found that the most powerful predictor of content differences between stories was whether the source was a mainstream or a radical one.[28] (This, the researchers admit, was not part of their initial research concerns — a symptom of the neglect of alternative media in much of communication research.) In his classic study of the 1960s anti-war movement, Todd Gitlin observed similar dynamics in the coverage of *The New York Times* and the largest news station, CBS News.[29] What Gitlin called "the movement-media dance" is fundamentally one-sided, as movements need the publicity more than mainstream media need their news or views.[30] While journalists may claim to report things as they really are, they have considerable discretion in the way they frame the groups they cover. The words reporters use can portray a group as serious-minded or irrational, representative or fringe, trustworthy or dangerous. "When Nazis assemble, they're a platoon; when members of the Sierra Club get together, they're a group," Pamela Shoemaker notes.[31] Her study of American newspapers found that the more deviant a group in the eyes of editors, the less favorably its activities are framed.

Herbert Gans' analysis of "enduring values in the news," similarly suggests that mainstream news upholds "moderatism."[32]

> Thus groups which exhibit what is seen as extreme behavior are criticized in the news through pejorative adjectives or a satirical tone; in many spheres of human activity, polar opposites are questioned and moderate solutions are upheld.[33]

Noting that one group's "order" could be another's "disorder," Gans argues that it is the perspective of the powerful that counts. "In short, when all other things are equal, the news pays most attention to and upholds the actions of elite individuals and elite institutions."[34] It is hardly surprising, therefore, that alternative media emerge to make up for such perceived biases of the mainstream press. While mainstream media may disingenuously claim to serve the neutral, value-free function of informing, educating and entertaining the mass audience, alternative media serve specific missions, more openly ideological and cause-driven. From this perspective, setting a distinct editorial mission is a necessary condition for launching alternative media.

However, an editorial commitment to alternative content may not be sufficient. It settles the "what" question, but not the "how." How an alternative medium is to achieve its goals and sustain itself are key decisions for any media activist. Again, much depends on what one considers the root of the mainstream media's deficiencies. There are two broad sets of theories explaining mainstream journalism's conservative attitude towards contentious politics. One focuses on the professional culture and operational routines of news production. Scholars note that institutions with power are by definition more "newsworthy" than those without, and that reporters' work habits and their touchstone of "objectivity" give authorized newsmakers, with their official spokesmen and clear lines of authority, a systemic advantage over often-anarchic movements and their ideas.[35] The second set of explanations highlights the political economy of the news business: commercial and political pressures on news organization dictate a bias for the status quo.[36] Either perspective turns the spotlight towards more structural, rather than purely content-based, aspects of alternative media.

Alternative structure

Raymond Williams has argued that to democratize the media, the public must have access to the "mode of communication." He notes that there are at least three kinds of barrier limiting such access in modern capitalist societies: capitalization, controls, and skills. First, the technologies for producing and distributing journalism require capital that is beyond the means of most people. Second, institutional hierarchies within a media organization means that even its own journalists have limited control over the newspaper or program they work for. Finally, craft and technical skills preserve a divide between consumers and producers of media.[37] Drawing on Williams, Chris Atton says that alternative media's definitive attribute is that they overcome one or more of these barriers by adopting a radical position within the relations of media production. Radical decapitalization, deinstitutionalization and deprofessionalization create room for a more authentic democratic discourse, he argues.[38] Most other studies of alternative media have arrived at similar conclusions.

The decapitalization principle addresses the problem that the mainstream media industry limits entry to those who can afford the capital outlay. Commercial news organizations cope with this challenge by targeting audiences with the ability and willingness to pay, and by selling audiences to advertisers. These strategies bias the media towards serving the mass audience, and niches with high socio-economic status. Although a capital-intensive approach provides resources for large-scale, regular and often high-quality production, some argue that a low-investment, not-for-profit approach can admit a greater diversity of form and content. Thus, Downing stresses the importance of cheap and accessible modalities — including graffiti, buttons, t-shirts, songs, street theatre and performance art. "If the public is not to be priced out of communicating via media, then low-cost formats become all the more crucial for democratic culture and process," he says.[39] Unesco's community media projects are similarly focused on small-scale, low-cost formats that can be sustained with limited resources.[40]

Within capitalist societies, the principle of decapitalization presents media activists with a dilemma. As adopting the business practices of the mainstream media may be the only way to grow, a policy of total abstinence can relegate alternative media projects to irrelevance. At the other extreme, market success can threaten their "alternative" identity. The latter category of poor little rich media includes the rock-and-roll magazine *Rolling Stone*, which was criticized by some of its competitors for selling out on the values of the 1960s.[41] In a similar vein, it has been argued that independent muckrakers such as *Mother Jones* operate not very differently from — and indeed have a symbiotic relationship with — the mainstream press.[42] This dilemma has probably been toughest on the socialist and communist newspapers operating within a capitalist system they aim to replace. In his study of radical newspapers set up in the US in the 1890s, Elliott Shore notes that *Appeal to Reason* experimented with various funding models, but only took off when it adopted some of the methods of profit-oriented newspapers, such as accepting commercial advertisements. To increase its output, it bought a linotype machine that made a number of typesetters redundant, to the horror of its socialist supporters.[43]

Deinstitutionalization is a response to the lack of internal democracy within most media organizations. Mainstream media institutions operate through internal hierarchies and bureaucracies over which even the individuals within them have little control. Alternative media have found various means to democratize their internal relations. *Arbeiter Illustrierte Zeitung*, for example, was run as a collective (which apparently annoyed some contributors who felt too many liberties were being taken with their submissions). It even used a system of voluntary distributors, making up a network of more than 45,000 people.[44] Contemporary "fanzines" — magazines produced by fans of music-based subcultures — and "open source" sites such as Wikipedia promote reader participation to the point of breaking down the very boundaries between reader and editor.[45]

The argument for deprofessionalization hinges on how skill requirements exclude wider participation in journalism. Certain technologies, such as equipment for television recording and broadcast, obviously demand more training than possessed by the average media consumer. Even writing a letter to a newspaper requires a certain level of sophistication if it is to be taken seriously by editors.[46] In addition to craft skills are professional codes that set industry insiders apart from lay people, and become conditions for public participation. The most powerful of these codes is probably that of "objectivity." The belief that it is desirable — even if not entirely possible — to report news from an objective, detached viewpoint has been a cornerstone of the professionalization of journalism.[47] However, critics have argued that objectivity has compromised journalism's public role. Gaye Tuchman finds it being used as a "strategic ritual" through which newsworkers protect themselves against criticism. For example, it is easier for a journalist to defend the exercise of "objectively" reporting the conflicting opinions of two newsmakers than it is to justify making an independent judgment about which one of them is more truthful — even though such truth-seeking might serve the public better.[48] Others have observed that the norm of objectivity restricts who can be quoted as an authorized source of news, and whose views can be treated as credible. Journalists' own autonomy is sacrificed, in favor of the bureaucratic sources around whom beats are organized. Officials become the "authorized knowers," to use Mark Fishman's term, and news media become vehicles for the transmission of expert opinion to the public. Thus, when a journalist tries to remove his or her conscious biases in the hope of laying bare the real facts of a story, the actual result is often to privilege certain interpretations of reality.[49]

Prevailing notions of professionalism are deeply entrenched. Although independent journalists who abandon them cannot be disciplined — in the way that true professions such as doctors and lawyers enforce their codes — they can certainly be treated with scorn and suspicion for breaking sacred norms. Critics point out that these norms have been reified, and that they are products of particular historical forces rather than clear moral principles. Journalism was once typified by partisan periodicals unfettered by pretentions of neutrality, they note. Indeed, the revered First Amendment — from which the mainstream press in the US draws prestige and power — was not framed with objective, professional journalism in mind, since this did not yet exist, but to protect polemical pamphlets and partisan newspapers. Thus, today's alternative journalism, although relegated to the fringe, possesses a pedigree that is seldom acknowledged.

While a policy of deprofessionalization might seem foolhardy and self-destructive to a mainstream newspaper, it can make good sense for a small, alternative periodical. Glenn Carroll suggests that small manufacturers in certain industries benefit from their identity as craft-like producers. Although often lacking in consistent quality, they appeal to loyal, tight-knit communities of customers who value the sense of being insiders in a small social network. Carroll has shown this to be the case in the microbrewery movement in the beer industry, and suggests that this sort of identity appeal may also apply to independent producers in the music recording, book publishing, and newspaper businesses.[50] For these alternative media, cultivating an emotional link with consumers could be of paramount importance. James Hertog and Douglas McLeod make a related point when they explain the alternative media's rejection of objectivity as a means of bringing together the author and the audience: "For the alternative press, remaining emotionally distant from the audience seems to be as much a violation of journalistic norms as is becoming attached for the mainstream author."[51]

Contentious Internet Journalism as a Social Movement

Alternative media have many of the attributes of social movements. In lay discourse, social movements are generally equated with such "causes" as feminism and environmentalism. Within political sociology, however, social movements are defined in terms of their actions and social location, rather than their goals or ideology.[52] They are networks of more-or-less organized groups marked by social solidarities. They have self-consciously shared interests, which their members do not believe are fully realizable through institutionalized political routines. These groups are on the margins or fully outside of the political mainstream and use non-routine methods to engage in sustained contention with power-holders. David Meyer notes: "The important point here about movements is that challengers pick tactics that place them at the edges of political legitimacy. They are defined by their dynamic interaction with mainstream politics."[53]

Not all alternative media, nor all internet media, fit this description. Some alternative media are mainly inward-looking, making no

claims on power-holders — at least for the time being. As for large
media corporations' online news sites, they are no more movement-like than their print and broadcast siblings. However, the
developments recounted in the first part of this chapter have all
the markings of a social movement. Many of the groups mentioned
were certainly engaged in political contention from the margins of
the polity, in this case by using the internet to disrupt the state's
control over information and ideas. There were also signs of a sense
of common purpose. Although representing diverse origins, the
groups had a shared interest in democratizing political communication and access to the public sphere. Social solidarities were evident,
both within and between the groups. Within each project, activists
took advantage of social networks to mobilize resources and enlarge
their constituencies. Solidarities between groups were expressed most
clearly in the hyperlinks through which they promoted each other.
While the websites of commercial news media strive for "stickiness"
— keeping eyeballs within their virtual walls and away from other
online news sources — alternative sites liberally direct visitors to
likeminded sites within the movement.

It is worth examining what political sociology has to say about
social movements because this tradition of scholarship — more
than most within the social sciences — has tried to treat marginal,
non-institutional forms of political contention as worth studying on
their own terms. Notwithstanding the literature on alternative media,
communication studies has been predisposed towards large-scale
organizations. Mainstream political science, similarly, has shown a
preference for formal institutions and their routines. It is this bias
that is challenged by scholars of social movements. Doug McAdam,
Sydney Tarrow and Charles Tilly argue that "the study of politics
has too long reified the boundary between official, prescribed politics
and politics by other means" — a disciplinary distinction that at
one time left unconventional politics to psychologists specializing in
abnormal behavior.[54] Although the non-institutionalized and often
unruly tactics of social movements may be unpalatable to those

who believe that democratic politics should be conducted in an orderly fashion, political sociologists tell us there is a rationale for movements' unconventional repertoire of action. It is within the so-called "proper channels" that elite members are most powerful, relative to insurgents. The use of non-institutionalized tactics, says McAdam, challenges elite groups in two ways:

> At a symbolic level, it communicates a fundamental rejection of the established institutional mechanisms for seeking redress of group grievances; substantively, it deprives elite groups of their recourse to institutional power.[55]

Decades of theorizing within political sociology have in recent years coalesced into a useful framework for the study of social movements. This is the so-called "political process" perspective, which sees the emergence and evolution of social movements as shaped by three sets of forces: political opportunities, mobilizing structures, and cultural framings.[56] This framework will be used in the present study and is elaborated on in the following pages.

Political opportunities

The "political opportunity structure" represents the movements' external environment, which ordinarily favors the political status quo. There are various dimensions along which political opportunity may shift in favor of insurgent groups. The institutionalized political system can become more open, or the state's capacity and propensity for repression may decline. Alternatively, the elite alignments that undergird the status quo may be destabilized, or allies for the insurgents may emerge within the elite.[57] In general, writes McAdam, "[A]ny event or broad social process that serves to undermine the calculations and assumptions on which the political establishment is structured occasions a shift in political opportunities."[58] Wars, industrialization, geopolitical realignments, economic depressions, and major demographic changes are typical events and processes that have been found to disrupt the political status quo, improving the prospects for social movements.

Mobilizing structures

An environment that is ripe with opportunity for contention cannot by itself explain movement activity. Actors also need mobilizing structures, or "collective vehicles, informal as well as informal, through which people mobilize and engage in collective action."[59] These include networks that provide a movement with key resources such as its leaders, activists and financial support, especially in its early days. Thus, for example, churches were critical to the emergence and sustenance of the US civil rights movement and democratic movements elsewhere. The movement groups must choose among various possible organizational forms and tactical repertoires, each of which has implications for their future development. Communication networks are another dimension of mobilizing structures, allowing groups to coordinate their actions and reach out to the public.

Cultural framings

Mediating between the political opportunities and actual insurgent action are meanings that people attach to their situations, says McAdam.[60] The third lens of the political process perspective focuses on social movements as interpretive accomplishments. If people are to engage in contentious politics, a number of changes need to occur at the symbolic level. These include: a loss of system legitimacy, increased belief in the potential for change, more awareness of one's rights, and greater perception of personal efficacy. Movements draw on what Anne Swidler calls "cultural tool kits" — the stock of widely-shared assumptions that people use in making sense of the world, and which can be deployed to cast a movement's aims and tactics in favorable light.[61] These stocks are not static, and their shifts can afford a movement with new cultural opportunities. There has been growing recognition in the literature that framing processes are not typically left to chance, but are part and parcel of the strategic work to be done by leaders of insurgency.[62] Nor are such projects straightforward in their application. A movement group's framing efforts are invariably contested by other actors, including the state and the mass media.

Merits of the political process approach

Proponents of the political process perspective readily acknowledge that it does not amount to a "theory" of social movements.[63] However, by being sensitive to both internal and external factors, as well as both objective structure and subjective perceptions, it has strong heuristic value, inviting rich, historically- and contextually-sensitive analysis. For the present study, a key merit of the approach is that it is based on fairly broad assumptions about the nature of power, making it suitable for export beyond the context of American democracy to which it was originally applied. First, it assumes that power is distributed unevenly between elites and excluded groups, with elites trying to maintain their advantage while the excluded strive to advance their interests as best they can. If this assumption holds in an established liberal democracy, it applies all the more to less-democratic societies such as Malaysia and Singapore. Second, the perspective assumes that the power structure is not rigid, but that excluded groups can exercise varying amounts of leverage to further their causes. This assumption appears equally sound, given the occasional success of social movements in even the most repressive of regimes.

The political process approach can illuminate some of the blind spots in previous research on the internet and democratization. While much has been written at the macro-social level on the internet's challenge to state policies, a political process framework gives due regard to the relatively neglected meso level of analysis, at which organizations and institutions interact in real-world settings. None of the three dimensions — political opportunity, mobilizing structures and cultural framings — is thought of deterministically. Each points to contests that are played out dynamically by social actors within, and in response to, movements.

Towards a comparative analysis

The literature on alternative media and social movements together provide the conceptual guideposts for the present study. Contentious journalism stands at the confluence of alternative media and social movements. It is a subset of alternative media: like other alternative media, contentious journalism democratizes media access by lowering financial or institutional or skill barriers. It is also a kind of social movement: it employs social networks to help compensate for a lack of material resources. It shares with other movements a marginal position in the political structure, from which it engages in public and sustained contention with power-holders, making novel claims and choosing methods that are not routine. Governments are not the only institutions targeted by this particular movement's claims. It is also in contention with the institutional news media and the norms of professional journalism. The transgressive methods used by contentious journalism include some — such as its advocacy or partisanship — that are opposed by the mainstream press. Thus, the claim that it counts as "journalism" is itself contentious.

The case studies

The case studies were limited to four, two each in Malaysia and Singapore, to keep the project manageable. There were roughly six to nine active sites that fit tighter or looser definitions of contentious journalism during the mid-2001 period when this study was begun. From these, those that published negligible original content and instead posted mainly articles from other sources were dropped. Of the remainder, four were chosen for in-depth study based on an impressionistic sense of their prominence — the degree to which they were cited in public discourse.[64]

As we explore the difference made by the internet in contentious journalism, the political process perspective provides a highly suggestive checklist of questions. The previous chapter has already shown how the introduction of the internet in the 1990s helped to shift the political opportunity structure for alternative journalism within Malaysia and Singapore. It made repression less attractive an option for the authorities. In addition, champions of technology within the elite may have served as allies to the activists — a hypothesis that will be explored in the case studies. The concept of mobilizing structures is similarly useful. It is clear from many other studies of internet use that the medium is a powerful mobilizing and organizing resource. In addition, groups engaged in contentious journalism may rely on pre-existing social networks, either virtual or real. As for cultural framing processes, the literature on the internet suggests that the technology is not only a value-neutral conduit for messages, but may itself be a symbol and template for robust resistance against central control and censorship, for individual empowerment, and for social change. The case studies in the following chapters will therefore examine how the media activists engaged in cultural framing work, to what extent they took advantage of the internet's symbolic power, and how their frames were received or contested by other groups, in particular the state.

Thinking of contentious online journalism as alternative media helps us to discern additional features of interest. We know that historically, such media have varied in their dimensions of alternativeness. Some have chosen radical ownership and control structures. Others have rejected prevailing professional norms. The four case studies in the following chapters demonstrate similar diversity. Sintercom is resolutely informal, non-hierarchical and voluntaristic, consciously modeled on what its founders understood to be the architecture and philosophy of the internet itself. Think Centre is formally constituted as a registered society, but like Sintercom has no full-time staff. Malaysiakini and Harakah are both run by full-time journalists working in newsrooms structured like those of mainstream news organizations. Malaysiakini is a profit-seeking company that brands itself as an independent news source, while Harakah is the official organ of a political party.

The case studies are an opportunity to explore these different structures and strategies, investigating how they arose, how they shaped the groups' responses to various challenges, and to what extent they succeeded in democratizing journalism. Systematically comparing these groups could help to generate theories about the dynamics of contentious online journalism. However, these are early days in the study of the internet and politics. It would be a mistake to rush towards law-like statements in answer to overly broad causal questions. To borrow the words of Clifford Geertz, theory-building at this stage should try to contribute through "the delicacy of its distinction, not the sweep of its abstractions."[65] The proper response is to engage in thick description close to the ground, and to be historically accurate and sensitive to context before making generalizations about the internet's role. The following case studies are therefore not enslaved to the framework suggested by the preceding discussion. While Chapter 9 will be devoted to more systematic comparison and tentative generalization, the following four chapters are driven by narrative. They represent an attempt to stay true to the particular, highlighting the idiosyncratic as much as the generalizable.

CHAPTER 5

SINTERCOM: HARNESSING
OF VIRTUAL COMMUNITY

It was not your typical Silicon Valley start-up. It neither bled red ink with spectacular abandon, nor promised obscene profits. The "com" at the end of its name did not stand for "commerce," but for "community." No stock options were dangled before the noses of its staff; they were all volunteers motivated by a sense of social mission that would seem almost quaint by the standards of the techno-entrepreneurs and corporations who eventually colonized cyberspace. This was Sintercom, the Singapore Internet Community, born 1994 at Stanford University.[1] It was a time when the internet seemed tailor-made for the nonprofit and civic sector, before corporate dominance and commercialization became "the undebated, undebatable, and thoroughly internalized truths of our cyber-times," as Robert McChesney has put it.[2]

Sintercom is worth a closer look partly because it is a relic from that more innocent age. In addition, it is the only one of the four cases in this study that predates the internet's take-off and rapid diffusion, and that straddles the pre- and post-regulation periods in either Malaysia or Singapore. As such, its history lets us analyze dynamics that are harder to discern in shorter-lived cases. Sintercom has seen the political opportunity for contentious journalism wax and wane, compelling it to reassess its mission and its methods, and ultimately forcing it out of Singapore. Although the least formally organized of the four cases — or perhaps because of that — Sintercom has proven surprisingly resilient against pressures from government. The social networks that it grew out of and cultivated were mobilized at critical junctures, allowing it to survive external shocks.

From Newsgroup to Website

The site was the brainchild of Tan Chong Kee, then a 33-year-old PhD student in Stanford's Asian languages department. He had been tossing about the idea of starting an independent forum for Singaporeans like him who did not find the country's newspapers and broadcasters sufficiently reflective of the full range of public opinion. He explored the possibility of starting a print magazine, but ran into the barriers described in Chapter 2. Formal regulations were only part of the problem. He also found potential backers reluctant to fund a project that might incur the government's wrath. Tan wrote to the Minister for Information and the Arts, hoping to obtain some form of written in-principle approval that he could then use to allay the fears of potential investors. The ministry, however, told him to submit a formal application — which would have had to include details of funding sources. Caught in this Catch-22 situation, and under increasing pressure from his own parents ("They demanded that I stop such nonsense."), Tan gave up the idea.[3]

This dead end turned Tan's attention to the small but hopeful alleyway that was the internet *circa* 1993. The arrival of Mosaic, a graphical browser software that enabled users to navigate easily through the world wide web, was an eye-opener. "When Mosaic hit the market and I saw what web sites could do, the idea that I could publish the forum on the Net very soon suggested itself," Tan said.[4] He was already participating in "soc.culture.singapore" (s.c.s.), a pre-web listserv that had spun off from "soc.culture.asean" in 1992. In one user's words, s.c.s ranged "from a place of lively intellectual debate, to a forum for name-calling and swearing, and nearly all shades in-between."[5] It was s.c.s. that brought together Tan and his future Sintercom collaborators, and that suggested the form Sintercom should take. Through s.c.s., Tan broached the idea of a website that would organize and archive his interlocutors' chaotic and evanescent musings. He called it the Singapore Electronic Forum (SEF). The idea dovetailed perfectly with his ambition to start an independent forum on Singaporean issues. "There are lots of very good ideas and discussions in there (overshadowed, unfortunately, by a lot of noise). I just thought it was a pity that these thoughts would disappear into the ether," he said. He also saw it as a step towards a more people-centered historiography.

> I thought of it as a project to write the history of the common man. Mass media like The Straits Times chronicle official history with official announcements and speeches and policy explanations. I wanted SEF to be the voice of the ordinary citizens, who respond to the current affairs of their time from a different perspective no less valid and worthy of attention.[6]

Tapping the technology was perhaps Tan's easiest task. He bought a book on HTML, the Hypertext Markup Language used to write web pages, and retired to his apartment in Stanford's verdant graduate community of Escondido Village. On his Apple Macintosh computer, connected to the university network, he read an online tutorial courtesy of Stanford's computing center. "Within a day, I was writing HTML," he recalled. Singapore Electronic Forum was established in October 1994 at the address, <www.leland-stanford.edu/~chongkee/singapore.html>.[7] The site grew organically into the Singapore Internet Community (a name suggested by a Singaporean piano student at the Oberlin College Conservatory of Music) as Tan's cyber-collaborators added more features.[8] Not all were political in nature. After SEF, the first new section was Cafe Vanda, a space for jokes, recipes and other Singaporeans, edited by a Yale undergraduate. Sintercom adopted a broad mission, "to build and maintain an Internet home where all Singaporeans, whatever their concerns are, can meet and feel at home."[9] The breadth of content reflected the varied interests of the editors, who at the peak numbered more than twenty.

As Sintercom evolved, there were "lots of false starts and dead ends," Tan said, including a travel section, two arts sections, and one for pop culture gossip.[10] One reason for their lack of success could be the entry of mainstream players into the web. In June 1995, eight months after the launch of the Singapore Electronic Forum, the country's media giant Singapore Press Holdings put its *Business Times* newspaper on the Net, followed by its mammoth flagship, *The Straits Times*, in December. Print magazines specializing in food and wine, arts, music and other lifestyle interests added electronic versions in subsequent years. These sites could draw upon full-time, professional staff and the voluminous content produced for their print or broadcast parents. As the web became more crowded, Sintercom found its niche as a space for open, public discussion of current affairs and national issues. This, after all, was precisely the role that the mainstream mass media found hardest to live up to, whether in print, on the airwaves, or online.

In addition to producing moderated and archived versions of soc.culture.singapore, Sintercom launched SGDaily, an e-mail service that disseminated articles on Singapore. These included news reports and opinion columns from the foreign press, as well as research papers by analysts and academics that the editors felt provided perspectives not emphasized in the local mainstream press. On rare occasions, SGDaily circulated *Straits Times* columns deemed noteworthy. The mailing list grew to some 1,200 subscribers by January 2000.[11] The feature that most clearly signaled Sintercom's status as a "contentious" medium challenging the status quo was its "NOT the Straits Times Forum" section. It published contributions that had been rejected, or carried in edited form, by the letters page of *The Straits Times*. It allowed

Sintercom visitors to see for themselves the extent of censorship of letters by the national newspaper. The site also launched a "NOT the Straits Times" section, to highlight cases of questionable journalism. One example was a short *Straits Times* article about the controversial Chinese group, Falun Gong. The contributor, "khang," noted that the story — attributed to the wire agencies Associated Press and Agence France-Presse — described the group as a "sect." However, the newspaper used the term "cult" in its headline: "US may give cult members asylum." He said that the newspaper's choice of noun caught his attention because he had read on a website dedicated to cultism that the Associated Press had decided two years earlier to use the word "sect" instead of the more pejorative "cult."

"Khang" typified the Sintercom participant: tapping information on the internet to develop independent views that were then circulated through the internet again. As for Sintercom's editors, practically all of Tan Chong Kee's collaborators were either studying in universities or working in information technology firms — a reflection of the state of diffusion of the internet at that time. More than half were studying or working abroad, in the US, Canada, Britain, Australia and Malaysia. However, contrary to some press reports at the time, Sintercom was not a site for and by Singaporeans overseas. "We never thought we were targeting overseas Singaporeans at all," Tan says. "However, I think it was true that at that time, many Singaporeans at home were rather afraid that joining and working on Sintercom might get them in trouble."[12] Nevertheless, some of the most active and influential editors were Singapore-based. They included Wynthia Goh, who was behind Sintercom's SGDaily. There was also Harish Pillay, an IT professional who would be at the forefront of the public opposition to the government's eventual Internet regulations.

Virtual, civic and flat

Three interrelated features of Sintercom are worth highlighting because they help explain its behavior at critical junctures when major decisions had to be made about its form and future direction. First, Sintercom was self-consciously a virtual community of the kind that so many writers have found deeply fascinating.[13] Its editors marveled at how the new technology enabled a new kind of social network. At the National Taiwan University, where he did his masters in Chinese literature after completing his bachelor's degree in computer science at Cambridge University, Tan had plunged into e-mail and bulletin boards. The world wide web had not yet arrived, but even minus the joys of WWW, the experience was an epiphany. "I loved the Net the moment I tried it. Made tons of new friends and found lots of long lost friends from Cambridge on it too. The sense of connectedness and its power still amazes me now," he says.[14] Terence Chua, another editor, waxed lyrical about communicating with Tan entirely online since 1992, before finally meeting face-to-face in 1995. "Like a lot of people I've gotten to know the insides of their heads before I've seen the outside. Isn't that just the beauty of it all? We're down to essences," he said.[15] Remarkably, the editors coordinated their activities across six countries on three continents. An introduction to the site read:

> You won't believe it, but many of the editors of this site collaborated for a year without ever meeting each other face to face. You often hear about Internet romances of two people meeting and falling in love through this most impersonal of medium [*sic*]. Similarly, the editors met solely through the Net, and fell in love with the idea of building a Web site where Singaporeans all over the world can meet and discuss things which concern them — A Web home away from home.[16]

Second, many of the editors felt strongly that they were creating a civic space, free from the state, but also from the market. Like others who came together to form Sintercom, Chua was struck by the Internet's implications for free expression:

> Cyperspace can be a liberating experience, and people are capable of abusing whatever liberties are thrust upon them, especially

when they have no experience in dealing with that kind of liberty to begin with. But I'm of the crazy notion that the liberty of cyberspace, the liberty to freely exchange viewpoints and information, the liberty to find out more about each other, and the way we think, can only be a good thing in the long run.[17]

Tan had originally wanted the site to be able to generate some income. "But most of the other editors were against it. They wanted it to be strictly non-profit. We discussed this once and I decided to bow to the majority."[18] Alvin Jiang, who had joined as a high school student, was within that majority. The youngest Sintercom editor, he was the archetypal teenage-"techie". At a time when most Singaporeans had not even heard of the internet, he had his own home page. He volunteered his technical services to Sintercom when he was around 16, and was responsible for writing some of the more complex programs behind the site, for surveys, search functions, automatic archiving, and so on. He saw his own work for Sintercom as a way to return to the Net community all the help he himself had received for free in cyberspace — "e-mails of advice, pages on how to program, and hours of entertainment." He believed the technology was becoming over-commercialized.

> I agree that one should be able to buy books over the Internet, but I'm not for intrusive or excessive ads, junk mail and all kinds of schemes to make money. In a perfect world, the primary objective of something like the internet should be interest or a desire to share, rather than to make money.[19]

Despite being a business school graduate, Wynthia Goh, similarly, believed that Sintercom should reside in the non-market space of the internet. Its value should not be assessed in terms of commercial success, she insisted.

> I think human beings are more than *homo economicus*. We have multiple and sometimes conflicting personalities. The preferences of a citizen can differ from the preferences of a consumer, but a human being is and wants to be both.[20]

Third, Sintercom adopted an open and non-hierarchical structure. With more than twenty editors taking responsibility for its various sections, Tan assumed the role of coordinating editor, but did not see the need to impose any authority. "We were growing so fast and in so many different directions that no top-down planning could do it justice, I think, especially when things were still so new," he says.[21] This informality also had much to do with the site's roots in the soc.culture.singapore newsgroup.

Coming Home

In September 1995, Sintercom's physical infrastructure migrated to Singapore, moving into the offices of a government-owned multimedia company, Sembawang Media, in the heart of the Orchard Road shopping district. Sembawang Media agreed to host the site and give it free bandwidth, and used its clout to obtain a donation of S$20,000 worth of hardware and software from Sun Microsystems.[22] The move, which put Sintercom on a more secure footing, demonstrated its ability to take advantage of establishment allies — allies who would soon come in even more useful when government regulators struck. It also tested Sintercom's resolve to remain non-commercial.

The idea appears to have originated with Jek Kian Jin, Sembawang Media's chief technology officer, who had met Tan on a visit to Stanford and was aware of the site's server problems. Free-of-charge campus computing resources had been an indispensable incubator for Sintercom, but they could not offer long-term or unlimited shelter for a growing site. Jek raised the idea with Philip Yeo, chairman of Sembawang Media's parent company, Sembawang Corporation. One of the country's most powerful mandarins and a champion of computerization and new technology, Yeo wrote to Tan and suggested they meet when he visited the Bay Area. Tan says: "After meeting Philip in San Francisco and talking about various things, I thought we spoke at the same wavelength. He suggested that I move Sintercom to Singapore and I agreed."[23]

Before meeting to formalize the arrangement, Sintercom editors fretted about whether the site's civic mission would be compromised by associating with big business. They decided that they were prepared to display the logos of their sponsors, but would not give up editorial control. As it turned out, they need not have worried. Sembawang Media and Sun did not want interfering rights in return for their sponsorship. Quite the opposite: The firms were anxious for indemnity, rather than itching for control. "Before we had the opportunity to talk about the importance of retaining control over our content, both Sembawang Media and Sun wanted an assurance from us that they would not be held in any way responsible for our content," says Wynthia Goh, one of the editors who represented Sintercom at its first formal meeting with the two sponsors. "After the meeting, we discussed among ourselves and decided to go ahead and ask them for their logo to put up on our website anyway, because it was the least we could do in return."[24]

On the face of things, Sintercom's relationship with Sembawang Media was a curious one. The former was a small cottage-industry network, the latter, an offshoot of one of the country's largest conglomerates. Both sides explained that, as dissimilar as they appeared to be, there was a cultural affinity between them. Despite its government links, Sembawang Media was itself something of the new kid on the block, with a maverick, underdog mentality. It was vying to take over Technet, Singapore's academic internet network, and enter the internet service provider business. Its competitors were Singapore Telecom, the monopoly telephone company, and Singapore Press Holdings, the newspaper monopolist. Of the three, only Sembawang Media had no traditional media or communication roots; everything was riding on the Net. The staff of Sembawang Media shared Sintercom's messianic zeal for the internet, at a time when they were surrounded by skeptics and naysayers. "The original

Sembawang Media team and the Sintercom group had a lot in common," recalls Wong Seng Hon, at that time the former's chief executive officer. "We were very impressed by the dedication, spunk and idealism of Chong Kee and his group. It wasn't PR or charity, but more of a shared vision."[25]

The timing was critical. "The people involved in the industry at this stage were very evangelical and passionate in trying to grow the Net," says Goh. "No Net trends were clear at that early time so anything was worth a try. I think the timing was significant. In my opinion, if Sintercom had sought the same sponsorship a year later, it would have been too late." At that time, even those working in commercial internet firms had a strong civic orientation, she adds. "I think we sort of reinforced one another then. 'Spreading the Net *karma*,' we used to call it." she notes. This was before the "get-rich-quick, IPO-before-creating-anything mentality" became the business culture of the internet and Silicon Valley.[26] Jek bears this out when he explains why he pushed for his company to give Sintercom shelter:

> I just thought it was a good thing to do, as Sintercom demonstrated the viability of grassroots, community-generated content and, dare I say it, activism, all in the cause of empowering users and giving them a voice through cyberspace. That was back in '95, when ideals and motives were purer. None of us, as far as I could remember, was in it for the money then. We just wanted to change the world a little.[27]

These declarations notwithstanding, Sembawang Media's behavior can also be understood in more self-serving terms. At the time, there was a dearth of online content, not just in Singapore, but all over the world. In early 1995, according to one estimate, it would have been possible to store the data of the entire global internet on fewer than 50 compact discs.[28] Sintercom, as one of the few existing providers of local online content, must have seemed an attractive partner to Singapore's new ISP — especially one that did not own print or broadcast media from which to draw content. From Sembawang's perspective, Sintercom must have represented what Tiziana Terranova calls free labor within the "social factory": taking place within society, "voluntarily given and unwaged, enjoyed and exploited."[29]

The partnership was announced a few months after the launch of Sembawang Media's ISP, Pacific Internet. Sembawang Corp's media-savvy chief Philip Yeo seized the opportunity for publicity mileage and to underline his belief in the wired world. "Sintercom captures the spontaneous and soulful side of Singaporeans on the Internet," he told the press.[30] The relationship did not last long. According to Thomas Hughes, technology firms in the 20th century have followed a typical evolutionary pattern: if the early growth is nursed by inventor-entrepreneurs with a love for the technology, maturity soon requires the entry of managers with a greater knack for counting the proverbial beans.[31] True enough, as Pacific Internet grew rapidly, Sembawang Media reorganized its management, and many members of its pioneering team moved on to other companies. The new management was less enthusiastic about non-revenue-generating obligations. Furthermore, the hosting deal had not been firmly institutionalized: it depended greatly on the convenient fact that Sintercom editors Wynthia Goh and Harish Pillay both joined Sembawang Media, and were working within feet of the hardware. When they too left the company, it became more difficult to maintain the arrangement.[32] Goh managed to find bandwidth sponsorship elsewhere: a company called Cybersoft. This did not last long either, as Cybersoft's system administrators felt that Sintercom's traffic constituted a hazard to network security. Their safety measures began to affect the editors' ability to operate the system, so the server returned to the site's founder. Tan Chong Kee, back in Singapore and working in his father's property development company, moved the server to his own office, paying for the bandwidth himself.[33]

The Regulators Strike

Sintercom first came to the broader public's attention in mid-1995, when its existence was reported in *The Straits Times*.[34] A year later, Singapore's newspaper of record noted Sintercom's role as a political forum, highlighting some of the controversial issues being discussed, such as the state of human rights.[35] This national attention made it all the more remarkable that the site continued to operate unregulated in Singapore. The internet free-for-all ended one and a half years after Sintercom's launch, when the Singapore Broadcasting Authority instituted new rules for the medium. The July 1996 announcement stated that websites that sought public attention and dealt with more sensitive areas, principally religion and politics, would have to register with the SBA. Sintercom was named as one of those affected.[36] Among other things, registration required the editors and publishers of a political or religious website to sign a declaration accepting "full responsibility for the contents of [the] website, including contents of discussion groups carried on it."[37] Holding those in charge of websites accountable for comments other people posted on it would make it impossible for sites such as Sintercom to carry on as before.

The reaction to the SBA announcement was revealing. It showed, first, the power of the internet as a mobilizing tool; and, second, the strong feeling among users at the time that the internet should remain free. Harish Pillay, a Sintercom editor, chronicled the episode on his own home page, starting with this entry:

> July 12th 1996: I am pissed off at the SBA and send an e-mail
> to the morning rag, Straits Times.
> July 13th 1996: I am very surprised that the morning rag did
> print my letter and verbatim at that — they did
> introduce a typo though.[38]

Pillay's letter to The Straits Times was less colorful, but no less clear:

As a Singaporean, I cannot understand why there has to be this
high level of distrust that the Government has of its people...
We do not need such draconian guidelines, even if the SBA
says that they will be interpreted gently.[39]

This was only the opening salvo in a long and vociferous
campaign against the regulations mounted by individuals associated
with Sintercom. Tan Chong Kee discussed the matter with his
fellow editors, but — not surprisingly for a committee of some 20
individuals — they could not agree about what should be done. "I
thought it was urgent, so instead of trying to forge any consensus
internally, I started campaigning in my personal capacity," Tan
says.[40] He wrote a detailed critique of the regulations and posted
it on the site. Tan's analysis quoted the SBA's reassurances that it
wanted to be "light-handed," and the generally positive responses
carried in *The Straits Times* and *Business Times*. He proceeded to
show how the regulations were not as innocuous as they had been
made to sound:

If the SBA thinks you should be banned, even if the public
disagree [sic], you will still be banned. They have not mentioned
any avenue of appeal. Does this set up sound 'light-handed'?
Would a disciplinarian who promises to be light-handed request
for an iron rod?[41]

Additionally, Tan wrote e-mail "to everyone I had ever talked
to on the net" — about 2,000 people — to raise awareness about the
situation. Wynthia Goh, meanwhile, launched a page for feedback,
which drew mainly adverse comments from day one. "Many people
signed with their real names, which was very encouraging," Tan
recalls.[42] Some were spooked by the regulations, seeing in them
the specter of government surveillance and censorship. Others were
confident that the internet's resilient architecture would render futile
any attempt to control it. A Gerard Lim wrote: "The vagueness
and carte-blanche nature of these criteria run counter to the clarity,

fairness and transparency that the rule of law is supposed to provide."
One Francis Chong called the regulations "just so much legalese to
cover what is essentially an exercise of unchecked power." Those
who spoke up even included a junior official from the Ministry
of Information and the Arts, the SBA's parent ministry. The civil
servant, Stephanie Sim, wrote:

> laws which cannot be enforced are not relevant or intelligent
> laws which are arbitrarily enforced are repressive laws which
> assume that people will never be mature and responsible will
> create societies which are selfish, childish and petty. yes, we
> want RESPECT, *NOT* REGULATION.[43]

Despite such protests, the government was never likely to
withdraw the regulations. After all, even at its height, the opposition
was largely confined to the small cyberspace community. There
was little danger of the unhappiness spilling over to either the
government's main electoral base of working class and middle class
citizens (most of whom at that time may have been suspicious of this
unregulated new medium and its possible threat to family values), or
to business interests (who were probably confident that the regulations
would not stand in the way of commercial exploitation of the Net).
The most the campaigners could hope for was to embarrass the
government, such that it would exercise self-restraint in interpreting
and applying its powers.

Sintercom's narrower mission — to evade the registration
requirement — was pursued primarily through private negotiations
with the authorities. Its ally in the public sector, Philip Yeo of
Sembawang Corp, again proved to be a friend in need. He brokered
meetings between Sintercom editors and the SBA chief, the chairman
of the National Internet Advisory Committee, and the Minister for
Information and the Arts. The editors told the officials that theirs
was not primarily a political site, since it carried everything from
jokes to recipes. Its political content was mainly the Singapore
Electronic Forum component, which was merely an edited version

of the bulletin board soc.culture.singapore. They pointed out that since bulletin boards were not covered by SBA regulations, it was inconsistent to demand that a website carrying one should register. However, what clinched the argument may have been Sintercom's preparedness to pack up and leave Singapore. "I said if SBA finds us too intolerable, we can move overseas again and host it on the servers of Stanford, Yale, Oxford, etc as before. They would look very silly if they blocked these sites," Tan says.[44] A week after the editors met SBA officials, the regulator wrote to Sintercom, saying:

> Based on our discussion and SBA's assessment of SInterCom's current webpage, and your assurance that your editorial group will exercise responsibility, intelligence and maturity in its selection of postings, we wish to confirm that SInterCom will not be required to register with SBA under the Class Licence Scheme.[45]

Tan suspects that the SBA was under instructions to try to persuade Sintercom to register, but not to insist: the government could live with the website being treated as a special case. Thus, Sintercom survived the new regulations unscathed. Of course, had the site gone beyond the limits of government tolerance, things may have turned out differently. It carried independent and critical commentary, but was not rabidly anti-government. This was an impression shared by *Business Times*, in a tongue-in-cheek snippet soon after the new regulations were announced:

> Soon after the SBA announcement, we checked out what material there might be on the site which might possibly be construed as 'exciting disaffection against the Government, or bringing it into harm or contempt'. Lo and behold, what caught our eye when we clicked onto it was a beaming Wee Cho Yaw, chairman of United Overseas Bank, who in a wide-ranging interview, talked about the potential of the Net for the bank, its arts sponsorship programme, and the promotion of Mandarin.[46]

Wee, a captain of Singapore's rock-solid banking industry, could hardly be mistaken for a poster-boy for political subversion.

Comfort with Sintercom grew. A hotlink to the site was even incorporated on the front page of "Singapore Infomap," a web window to Singapore maintained by the information ministry. In a speech on civil society in May 1998, the minister, George Yeo, named Sintercom as one of the civic organizations that "encourage us to be more socially conscious." "Singapore is a heterogeneous society and differences of opinion are natural," he acknowledged.[47] Sintercom carried more critical views than the mainstream media did, but it was not considered extreme. To Stephanie Sim, the young ministry official who had opposed the SBA regulations, Sintercom was little more than a "talk fest," and not a website that attempted to organize dissent. At the same time, it allowed the government to tell its critics abroad that Singapore respected alternative views. "I think it has become a very safe place which will never be shut down because it's great PR for the government," she says.[48]

The Regulators Strike, Again

Sim's prediction that the government would not threaten Sintercom's survival held for little more than a year. In 2001, the authorities revisited the issue of registration, resulting in the closure of the original site. This turn of events illustrates the fluid nature of political opportunities. Governments' calculations change with changing circumstances, in turn altering the environment for contention. In this case, the Singapore government appeared to be acting in advance of general elections due in late 2001. Although the ruling party does not flagrantly undermine the electoral process by, for example, stuffing ballots or buying votes, it is not above curtailing freedom of speech in order to limit citizens' access to alternative sources of information and their knowledge of the choices available to them. The mainstream news media are accustomed to feeling the leash get shorter in the run-up to elections. This time, Sintercom would feel it too.

Whether or not the coming elections were the motivating factor, the SBA wrote to Sintercom in July 2001 asking it to register.[49] Asked to explain its reasons, it reiterated its stand that registration "is used to emphasize the need for content providers to be responsible and transparent when engaging in the propagation, promotion or discussion of political issues relating to Singapore."[50] Sensing that the SBA did not wish to engage Sintercom in further dialogue, Tan filled out and submitted the registration forms, making him formally accountable for the site's content. In one small act of resistance, however, he modified the registration form, deleting a section that he believed violated his rights. Even with this amendment, however, registration placed Sintercom in a dilemma. "I do not want to be in a situation where I could be hauled into court anytime, depending on how someone in power has decided to interpret content in Sintercom," he wrote in an editorial. At the same time, he did not want to err on the side of caution. "To self-censor now defeats the purpose of our existence," he said.[51]

As a compromise, he decided to send all published material on the site to SBA for clearance. This, he felt, should satisfy the broadcasting law, which states that a licensee would be deemed to have used its best efforts to comply with the conditions of the license if it had taken "all reasonable steps in the circumstances."[52] "In this way, we will not self-censor, but we let SBA censor us whenever they like," Tan said.[53] Using the electronic feedback form on the SBA website, Tan submitted links to all of Sintercom's existing content, and requested an e-mail address to which he could continue to send published content for clearance. SBA replied two days later, saying that it did not pre-censor material. Internet content providers were required to exercise their own judgment and take responsibility for their content, it added. With the affair beginning to receive mainstream media attention, SBA also issued a general news release stating that "registration is a simple administrative procedure" and that there was "no cause for Sintercom to over react over such a simple request."⁵⁴ Tan e-mailed SBA again, asking whether its characterization of Sintercom's response as an overreaction meant that the site's contents were clearly well within SBA's limits. The authority again refused to be pinned down, reiterating that it was "unnecessary for Sintercom to seek advice from SBA on its posting."⁵⁵ Feeling that he had run out of options, Tan closed down the Sintercom site, seven years after its launch. One mark of the recognition it had gained in that time was that its demise was reported in *The Straits Times*, *Time* magazine's Asian website, CNET.com and other media.

New Sintercom

When Sintercom closed, a *Straits Times* columnist stated that Sintercom features such as Not The ST Forum would "fade into cyber-oblivion."⁵⁶ However, one week after Sintercom's disappearance from the World Wide Web, the site was reborn as New Sintercom, hosted on the Geocities service based in the US. By going back overseas, Sintercom's content moved beyond the reach of Singapore's regulators. As long as the government continued to refrain from blocking political sites, Singaporeans could still visit New Sintercom and most of the Sintercom archive. The reincarnation of Sintercom is a clear example of internet media's legendary resilience. In addition, it demonstrates the strength of Sintercom's weak ties: its open, informal structure and its communal ownership. Sintercom was set up as a community of acquaintances, rather than as a one-way or top-down medium. That community proved critically important when Tan decided to close down the original site.

Tan kept Sintercom's readers abreast of every move in his exchange with the SBA. He noted the option of moving the site overseas, but added that this would contradict "our belief that it is possible for openness to exist in Singapore." In the following days the SGDaily mailing list, primarily a vehicle for circulating articles about Singapore, was turned into an open forum for discussing the fate of Sintercom. From the start, support was expressed for the idea of placing Sintercom outside of Singapore's jurisdiction. Angela Oon wrote: "It is all very well to want to be a symbol of open discussion... in Singapore, but since that doesn't seem likely in the near future, it's better to have a Sintercom than none at all."[57] Another poster, Lok Yuin Chung, with a British academic e-mail address, said:

> I cannot understand why at this juncture are we still clinging on to the false belief that there can be true open and frank debate within the borders of Singapore... It's clear that they are not taking civil society, or indeed public opinion seriously. We have to demonstrate that they can't just push us around. By moving overseas, we not only escape the curtain of censorship that is now threatening to draw upon us, but also a rejection and protest against this violation of free discussion and debate.[58]

There was some disagreement over the timing of such a move. Some suggested that Sintercom should exit only if and when SBA tried to censor it. One argued for appealing to the minister and even the prime minister. Another idea was to run two parallel sites, one Singapore-based and regulated, the other overseas and unregulated. By comparing the content of the two sites, Singaporeans would be able to see for themselves the effects of censorship, said proponents of this idea. The sole writer who argued that Tan was overreacting and that the Sintercom should trust the government was swiftly told off by others, in a typical example of a virtual community's policing of its norms.

The community also offered concrete help. One asked if the real reason for the impending closure was financial, and said that, if so, he would be prepared to pay subscription fees. Another offered a one-gigabyte hard disk drive that was "collecting dust at home." Privately, away from the mailing list, Tan was also receiving offers from individuals who were prepared to take over the site. Some wanted to cannibalize the site, to exploit the parts that appeared to possess commercial potential. "I said no. It wasn't mine to give away," he says. For the same reason, he declined requests to "ordain" anyone as his successor. "I didn't want to make any public announcement of that sort."[59] Soon, however, assistance arrived from others who were more attuned to the spirit of the site. One week after Tan announced the closure of Sintercom, the SGDaily mailing list carried the message, "Just to keep you all in the loop… Sintercom lives," together with a link to the New Sintercom site.[60] The first to take over the keys was a Valeryj Andrzejewicz Szyszczenko, who transferred the Sintercom archive to a Geocities host in the US. A month later, Szyszczenko appealed on the site for someone else to take over. A non-Singaporean, Andreas Sabin, held on to website administrator's password until someone else could assume control. A Singaporean overseas eventually responded, and proceeded to run the site *incognito*.

Sintercom did not start out intending to exploit the internet's potential for evading authority. Instead, the internet advantage that had originally attracted Tan and his collaborators to the medium was the regulatory loophole that allowed them to publish legally without a licence. When the opportunity arose to relocate the site from overseas campuses to Singapore, its editors did not hesitate. The editors' presence in Singapore gave the site a more prominent and generally positive public profile. It secured allies within the administrative elite, even getting showcased on the official national homepage, Singapore Infomap. While in Singapore, the editors were also able to forge links with other groups in civil society, through an initiative called The Working Committee (TWC). TWC organized a civil society convention and fair, and spawned various inter-NGO projects. Sintercom served as the online vehicle for TWC publicity. However, as enthusiastic as Sintercom's founders were about their online community of the early 1990s, the TWC process moved mainly through face-to-face meetings, in which Tan was a key player.

New Sintercom's move overseas may seem to represent a fundamental break in the way it used the internet. For the first time, the site was accepting the internet's offer of refuge from the state's territorial jurisdiction. However, one should not make too much of this. It would be an exaggeration to say that New Sintercom was sent underground by government repression. Although its editor guarded his or her anonymity, other contributors were not so coy. One of its most active and outspoken new writers, a teenager by the name of Teng Qian Xi, was living in Singapore and used her real name. Furthermore, Sintercom's best-read feature, the SGDaily mailing list, was managed by two Singaporeans who did not bother to conceal their identities. One, Chang Li Lin, is a researcher at the Institute of Policy Studies, a government-linked think-tank; the other, Dharmendra Yadav, was a student in London who returned to Singapore to work as a lawyer. The online discussions about the future of the site suggests that the move overseas may have been mainly symbolic. As one of the participants in the debate put it, there was a need to show the authorities "that they can't just push us around."[61]

CHAPTER 6

THINK CENTRE: ACTIVISM THROUGH JOURNALISM

In the function hall of a budget hotel in Singapore, about forty people sit waiting for the start of a political forum. The main speaker is to be James Gomez, a colorful activist whose new book will be launched at the same event. A smiling Gomez eventually enters — in handcuffs. He welcomes the bemused audience and requests that everyone look under his or her seat for the key that will unlock the shackles. Drawn into the little performance, a wire-service reporter finds the key and frees the activist.

The forum proceeds. It is the first in the country to discuss the domestic political impact of the September 11 terrorist attacks in the United States and the subsequent arrest of a militant cell in Singapore. Nothing is reported in *The Straits Times* the next day, even though one of the newspaper's political reporters attended the event and dutifully took notes. However, the forum is covered in the organizers' own website, complete with pictures and the full text of speeches.

This is Think Centre in action. Since 1999, it has combined public meetings, performance, and internet journalism to push for a new kind of politics in Singapore. Anbarasu Balrasan, who served for a while as the website editor, says that the goal is to place issues such as justice and fairness on the agenda. "They may be abstract, but they are important," he says.[1] Think Centre describes itself as "an independent, multi-partisan political non-governmental organization." The group "aims to critically examine issues related to political development, democracy, rule of law, human rights and civil society." Its motto expresses a commitment "Towards a Vibrant Political Society."[2] Unlike Sintercom, which emerged from online communities, Think Centre's website developed as an adjunct to traditional offline political activities. Its founders were engaged in the printing of political tracts and the organization of public meetings — two ancient forms of democratic participation. They launched the website as a means of publicity and mobilization. Gradually, the site's role grew to include the more journalistic function of reporting and commenting on current events. More than the other three cases investigated in this book, ThinkCentre.org challenges conventional notions of journalism. It is "alternative" not only by virtue of its political stance and ownership structure, but also in practicing a model of activist journalism abhorred by believers in objective and disinterested reporting.

Activist Roots

In 1999, James Gomez, a writer and researcher, completed a self-published book that he titled *Self-Censorship: Singapore's Shame*. Unable to find a distributor, Gomez decided to use the internet to market the volume. He managed to get the Singaporeans for Democracy website to carry a short blurb and mail-order instructions. About 25 pre-publication orders arrived by post, including from two government ministries. The online marketing campaign was successful enough to capture the interest of Select, an independent distributor specializing in local and regional books. This in turn opened the doors of larger bookstores. *Shame* became a best-seller, and as it included Gomez's e-mail address, quickly put him in touch with several likeminded individuals.[3] Online and offline activities were thus mutually reinforcing; this multi-platform approach, combining old and new modes of political activism, would become the *modus operandi* of Think Centre.

Immediately after the book launch, Gomez and his newfound collaborators launched a political education program, Politics 21. The name was a twist on Singapore 21, a massive consultation process organized by the government to help form a public consensus on the country's direction in the 21st century. Gomez's main organizational partner was Socratic Circle, a political discussion society. Socratic Circle was not allowed to hold public events, under requirements imposed when it registered itself as a society. Gomez and friends decided to organize Politics 21 activities under the aegis of a new network that they called Think Centre. They set up a website in September 1999 to publicize the public forums and handle online registration. The site was revamped in January 2000 with more journalistic content, including reports on the Politics 21 forums, the full text of speeches, and longer features. It was officially launched in March 2000, during a reading of *Shame* at the Borders bookstore downtown. Over the next few months, new sections were added, including Human Rights Watch, Media Watch, Policy Watch and Election Watch. These carried some original content but mainly reports and commentary from other sources, such as international human rights groups, foreign publications and local press reports. Think Centre supplemented the website with a mailing list service, using the Yahoo! eGroups facility, which grew to more than 3,000 subscribers. A separate mailing list was added to send press releases and other announcements to the mainstream media.

Gomez had registered Think Centre as a sole proprietorship in July 1999. Since October 2001, it has been registered as a society. His job with the German foundation, Friedrich Naumann Stifftung, took him to Bangkok, Thailand, where he set up Think Centre Asia as the regional arm of Think Centre. The Singapore organization is run by an executive committee, one of whose members is designated as Editor of the website. All are volunteers. Its executive director, Sinapan Samydorai, was previously a program coordinator with the Hongkong-based Asian Human Rights Commission. The society has fewer than 30 members, with half a dozen actively involved with the website.[4]

As with Sintercom, pre-existing social networks were a key mobilizational resource in the setting up of Think Centre, although the latter drew from much more explicitly political groups. In addition to the Socratic Circle, the group forged links with Roundtable, a small non-partisan political discussion group that had achieved some measure of political acceptability. Gomez became a member of Roundtable and regularly drew on its members as speakers for Think Centre's public forums. Think Centre also had close relations with opposition parties and the Open Singapore Centre, a civic group established by two opposition leaders. The links were two-way. Opposition party members joined the executive committee and contributed regularly to the website. At the same time, Think Centre developed into an energetic and creative partner for the opposition. Gomez himself joined the Workers' Party and tried to run for election in 2001 (a bid disqualified by a characteristically inept administrative error by the party on nomination day).

The organization quickly appreciated the website's value as a vehicle for disseminating news about its own events. The first Politics 21 forum, "From Student Politics to Real Politics," was not reported in the mainstream press, leaving the newspaper-reading public clueless that an independent exercise in political deliberation had just been launched. The second was covered by *The New Paper*, *The Straits Times* group's afternoon tabloid, but not by the country's main daily. "It proved we were right to set up the website," says Melvin Tan, one of Think Centre's founders.[5] In December 2000, the group organized an Abolish ISA event together with the Open Singapore Centre, to mark International Human Rights Day. Once again, mainstream media reports revealed as much about their own bias as about the event they covered. *The Straits Times*, for example, reported that an opposition leader delivered a protest letter to the gates of the Istana, the government mansion housing the prime minister's office, but did not report what the letter said.[6] Television news referred to an "apparent" denial of human rights, and reported that the organizers "seized the opportunity" to sell their publications, implying that the event was a self-serving marketing ploy.[7] The mainstream coverage, ranging from blatant omissions to subtly pejorative framing of the event, was itself critiqued on the Think Centre website. Thus, the group introduced a media watch component to its activities. This achieved multiple goals. It not only justified the website's own existence, but also exposed a dimension of the very problem that Think Centre was protesting against — the lack of political freedom in a society where essential avenues for political expression, including the press, were controlled by the government.

Think Centre's activities regularly brought it into conflict with norms and regulations governing political life in Singapore. Its first Politics 21 talk earned Gomez and others a warning from the police for organizing an event without the required public entertainment license. The organizers had not applied for one because the talk was meant to be a closed-door, by-invitation-only activity. Invitations were sent out by e-mail to friends and contacts, and those who were interested were asked to register at the Politics 21 website. However, the authorities argued that since the website was accessible to anyone, and not just to invited guests, the event had to be categorized as a public one.[8] The case was one of many examples, in Singapore and elsewhere, of how the internet has fudged the distinction between "private" and "public." That the activists got off with a warning showed that the government was prepared to give them some leeway.

Think Centre continued operating at the edges of political acceptability, challenging the mental blocks and administrative obstacles in the way of political organizers in Singapore. Not all their plans materialized. Even so, the young activists succeeded in organizing more protest events and meetings than even established opposition parties. The government eventually used its legislative powers to create new rules of engagement. First, it introduced the Political Donations Act of 2001. This law banned political parties and political organizations from receiving any funds from overseas sources, and required them to declare local donations in excess of S$5,000. Think Centre and the Open Singapore Centre were the two groups gazetted as political organizations for the purpose of the new Act.[9] Think Centre had not yet received any foreign money, but its ability to attract international media attention suggests that it would have been only a matter of time before western benefactors came to its aid.

Next, the government amended the Parliamentary Elections Act's provisions on campaign advertising. Political parties were permitted to use their websites to publicize their candidates and manifestos, but political websites not belonging to a party were banned from campaigning. In response, Think Centre closed its online discussion board.[10] The group explained that it could not control what was said on the forum, and closing it was the only way to ensure that the site did not unwittingly fall foul of the new election advertising regulations. It labeled its move as a protest, although it is hard to see it as anything other than a victory for the authorities. It was around the same time that the regulators demanded that Sintercom register as a political site to bring it within the ambit of the election laws. As recounted in the previous chapter, this led to Sintercom closing shop entirely in Singapore, and resurfacing overseas. The difference in response between Sintercom and Think Centre was probably due to the fact that the open forum function was not central to Think Centre's mission and was a late addition to its website, whereas this was a core and indispensable part of Sintercom's identity. Think Centre's preparedness to live with registration certainly cannot be interpreted as a sign of acquiescence to government control in general. On the contrary, as we shall see in the next section, the group took political contention to a level of audacity not seen in Singapore for decades.

In addition to closing its Speakers' Corner Online forum, Think Centre decided not to update its Election Watch column during the campaign period. The group knew that the new legislation was written in catch-all fashion, with no clear definition of what constituted election advertising. The rules covered any material thought to promote candidates or parties even if it did not mention them by name. "We are a civil group of law-abiding citizens and will not knowingly break the law though we remain critical of this piece of legislation," it said in a letter to the head of the Elections Department. It also asked him to clarify what else might be construed as election advertising.[11] The authorities replied that publishing party manifestos and announcements of party events were examples of campaigning. The breadth of the regulations remained unclear.[12] However, if the activists were looking for a less ambiguous sign, they got one quickly enough. A terse two-paragraph letter informed Think Centre that it had contravened the election advertising regulations by publishing an article entitled "Young Singaporeans, Can the PAP Safeguard your Future?" It was directed to remove the article from the internet immediately, apparently because the author was a candidate of the opposition Singapore Democratic Party.[13] The group promptly complied.

Contention Through the Web

Although Think Centre activists were not interested in engaging in campaigns of civil disobedience against laws that they believed to be unjust, their style of protest politics was innovative in a number of respects. One tactic that must have annoyed the government to no end, but could hardly be deemed illegal, was to use the internet to publicize all their correspondence with officials, with the aim of increasing various agencies' levels of public accountability. Sintercom had pioneered this tactic in a more modest fashion: one of its contributors posted his lengthy exchanges with government departments on the site. The effect was to expose the dismissive manner in which bureaucrats often replied to members of the public. Think Centre escalated this tactic to new heights. When it organized public events, for example, it chronicled on its website the entire circumlocutory exercise of obtaining the necessary permits, demystifying the process and turning it into a spectacle. So novel and compelling were these little dramas that even *The Straits Times* occasionally reported them. One of these involved the organization of a rally to raise funds for an opposition leader, J.B. Jeyaretnam, who owed defamation damages that threatened to make him bankrupt and thus disqualify him from Parliament. Think Centre had to apply for a public entertainment license from the police to hold the rally, a permit from the Building and Construction Authority to hang banners, and even a license from the Public Health Commissioner to sell books, T-shirts and stickers under the Environmental Public Health Act — the law that regulates the country's popular street vendors of food.[14] Organizing the rally produced "a lot of learning on all sides about the license-issuing process," Gomez says.[15] (The rally was eventually held, but raised less than 5 per cent of its S$400,000 target.[16] Jeyaretnam declared bankruptcy and lost his seat in Parliament shortly after.)

Police investigations into Think Centre activities were also quickly reported in detail on the internet. The tone of these reports was sometimes morally indignant, but often humorously irreverent. The police probe into the Politics 21 forum, for example, was referred to as a "comedy-drama" and "festivities." The group even wrapped up the final interview with a photo session, the result of which was posted on the web, along with its written account:

> The group's request to take a picture of this 'warning' session, which took place in [the investigating officer's] room, was

predictably declined. Determined to have a group picture to commemorate this session at Tanglin [police station], the group thus enlisted the help of a gangster-type loitering at the station. He was very obliging and helped the group out with a few photographs. As the group turned to leave they thanked him for doing his part for the Singapore 21 process![17]

Think Centre also used the internet to turn the tables on government surveillance. "Watching the watchers," Gomez called it. Plainclothes agents are standard fixtures at any political event in Singapore. At large events such as election rallies, they make no attempt to conceal their presence, pointing video cameras at the crowd or opening briefcases full of tape recorders. The mainstream news media do not report their activities — perhaps because they are so taken-for-granted that they are not deemed newsworthy. The targets of surveillance also tend to shrug it off, "failing to acknowledge that they feel in some ways intimidated and violated," Gomez notes.[18] He launched his first "internet counter-surveillance offensive" in mid-1999, before Think Centre was formed. He posted on the web a detailed report of his observations outside the venue of a tea party organized by two opposition politicians. He counted eight to twelve individuals whom he believed to be agents, including women carrying boxy handbags that appeared to conceal cameras — "the camera lens was the size of a five-cent coin and was merged in the middle of an elaborate gold ornament in the front of the handbag."[19]

When Think Centre started organizing its own activities, "watching the watchers" became standard operating procedure. Members would approach suspected agents of the government, once even posting on their website a photograph of one such individual together with reports of the event. "The Internet has made surveillance interactive," Gomez says.[20] He says that the tactic appeared to have the desired effect: the exposed agents would leave and not be seen again. Of course, Gomez may be overstating the power of this approach. It is unlikely that the authorities would have aborted or scaled back their surveillance activities on account of Think Centre's confrontational response. At most, realizing that the group was not to be intimidated by overt surveillance, officials would have switched to covert methods. However, the activists' bold response certainly challenged the prevailing norm of helpless acquiescence to government intimidation. It was a way to enhance that sense of self-efficacy that any social movement needs.

Challenging the mainstream press

Think Centre also went on the offensive against the local press. Sintercom had already blazed a trail with its "Not the Straits Times Forum" section. Think Centre was considerably more confrontational. For example, it campaigned against the government-owned radio broadcaster, MediaCorp Radio, over an apparent instance of self-censorship. The three-month-long controversy began on the morning of December 11, when the news station 93.8FM broadcast a segment commemorating International Human Rights Day. It included an interview with a Think Centre director and an open letter to the prime minister from Jeyaretnam, the opposition politician. The presenter, Fauziah Ibrahim, announced that the segment would be aired again in the next hour. Later, however, she announced that management was unhappy with the original segment and that only a re-edited version would be aired. The new version dropped Jeyaretnam. The rare, if not unprecedented, public revelation by a journalist of politically-motivated gatekeeping by her superiors might have slipped by unnoticed if not for the Think Centre's direct interest in the program and its media-watchdog mission. The same day, the website and email list publicized the radio station's actions.[21] The station, obviously stung, responded on the air, saying that Think Centre got the facts wrong, although the company did not account for the presenter's own statements during the program.[22]

Over the next few months, the activists continued to track the case. They reported that Fauziah did not seem to be working at the station any longer, possibly because of the incident. In typical style, they shared with readers their futile attempts to get answers from the station.

> When Station Administrator, Ms. Florence Lim was contacted today ... about Ms. Ibrahim's disappearance, she informed that Ms. Ibrahim is on leave until January. Ms. Lim when asked about Ms Ibrahim's return was not able to provide any specific dates.[23]

Hearing new rumors two months later, Think Centre's public affairs manager, Jacob George, telephoned and visited MediaCorp to try to get to the bottom of the story. Broadcast journalists more accustomed to asking the questions found themselves portrayed as unwilling sources giving the amateur reporter the run-around:

> ... Jacob asked [Ms. Mun Fong] whether Ms Ibrahim had resigned and she said that she does not know about that since Ms Ibrahim works in another team. She went on to say that [Jacob] could talk to the co-ordinator in that team, Geraldine Chan, but she was away attending a course.[24]

Think Centre also applied for a permit to picket MediaCorp Radio on World Press Freedom Day. Predictably, the police turned down its application. Equally predictably, the unsuccessful attempt to organize a protest was sufficient to draw the attention of the international media.[25] Unable to picket, three Think Centre activists delivered a protest letter to the radio station's premises, demanding the resignation of MediaCorp Radio's chief executive officer for refusing "to come clean about this sordid affair."[26] The following week, the CEO replied, reiterating the station's right to edit its programs. The most noteworthy point in the reply — besides the fact that one was offered at all — was that it finally provided an official answer about the fate of Fauziah Ibrahim, albeit in classic management-speak: "Our presenter admitted that what she did was unprofessional on her part and a breach of her employment contract. She decided to resign."[27]

In its campaign against MediaCorp, Think Centre showed that its quarrel was with the political system and corporate media, and not with working journalists. This was, of course, a difficult line to maintain, given that most of its interactions with the establishment were with reporters from the mainstream press. On at least one other occasion, however, it stood by the principle that reporters should not be used as easy targets. Its report, headlined "Good forum marred by unnecessary jibes at journalists," criticized opposition politicians for putting reporters on the spot:

> Journalists work for editorial teams who in turn work for management. Journalists cannot be asked to answer criticisms against them in a forum. It is unprofessional if people do ask them to and equally unprofessional for journalists to answer questions in a forum they have come to cover.[28]

Think Centre was less measured in its response to one of its critics. S. Ramamirthan, in letters published in the newspaper *Today*, poured scorn on Think Centre's campaign for human rights, arguing that the group's very existence showed that Singapore was free enough. He advised James Gomez to:

> ... devote your precious time to more productive things in life. Sure, continue to stand up and speak up for Singaporeans, but don't go around pretending that there are human rights abuses and concerns. There are none![29]

Ramamirthan also criticized the Save JBJ Rally. In addition to sending measured responses to *Today*, Think Centre took an odd step in retaliation. Along with its reports of the Save JBJ Rally, it published on its website a photograph of an elderly Indian man at the stadium, with the caption, "S. Ramamirthan? Maybe." The accompanying story was headlined, "Anti-Think Centre man believed to have attended rally." No attempt had been made to check whether the old man really was the group's *bête noire*, and indeed a furious Ramamirthan replied that he had been nowhere near the rally. Gomez says that he and his colleagues had tried to engage Ramamirthan on the issues, but that the man had chosen to get personal in his attacks. "He belittled the work we did," Gomez argues. "That annoyed us, so we gave him a taste of his own medicine."[30] Perhaps the only benefit of Think Centre's curious stunt was that it provoked Ramamirthan into revealing himself as a sworn enemy of Think Centre. "I am decided and determined that the Think Centre has NO PLACE in Singapore," he wrote in an e-mail message to the group.

Think Centre's most controversial confrontation with the mainstream media occurred in early 2001, shortly after the government's announcement that it would gazette the group as a political organization under the Political Donations Act. The local media, Gomez says, "went into a frenzy," reporting the government's justifications of its move, and trying to discover whether Think Centre had indeed received foreign funds.[31] Gomez and his colleagues decided that if they were going to be treated as a political party, they should behave as one. They sent out a press release stating that they would field a slate of candidates to contest the coming general elections. *The Straits Times* and other media carried the story prominently the next day — April 1.[32] Close to midnight on that date, Think Centre released another statement, revealing that its earlier announcement had been an April Fool's joke.

The Straits Times was not amused. However, registering its opprobrium required some deft footwork, as the newspaper had done its own April Fool's spoof on an uncannily similar theme: it carried a made-up story that a local adventurer — a household name after having climbed Mount Everest and reached the South Pole — had decided to run for election on the ruling party ticket. On April 3, *The Straits Times* ran an article suggesting that Think Centre's joke hurt the group's credibility, while the newspaper's own story was harmless fun. The report quoted its own political editor:

I think there's a difference. It's almost a tradition for newspapers to do this, once a year, when readers expect us to do it for a laugh.... But it's different when a political organisation sends its story to all the media organisations in Singapore, the newspapers, TV and the foreign news agencies, which was what Think Centre did, to fool them all into thinking it was a serious statement.[33]

The following month, when *The Straits Times* reported Samydorai's appointment as the new executive director of Think Centre, the only past activity that the newspaper saw fit to mention by way of background information on the group was not the Save JBJ rally or the Abolish ISA campaign, but the April Fool's joke.[34]

Journalism, Think Centre Style

Anbarasu Balrasan, then the editor of ThinkCentre.org, acknowledges that public acceptance of its infamous April Fool's joke was at best "fifty-fifty," and that such stunts, while necessary, have exacted a cost. "Think Centre's main problem now is credibility," he says.[35] The dilemma is a familiar one to most social movements: sometimes, the only way activists can attract media attention is through sensational acts that live up to their stereotype as social deviants.[36] The group's unconventional methods also make it harder to persuade mainstream journalists that what it does should be considered "journalism" at all. When asked to account for their brand of journalism, Think Centre members' somewhat tentative answers show them trying to find a balance between their activist instincts and received notions of journalistic professionalism.

On the one hand, members and supporters probably get a sense of empowerment from their irreverent methods of responding to critics. Gomez argues that Think Centre's "cheeky" tone is what makes its journalism "alternative" and "innovative."[37] Melvin Tan concurs that injecting "a bit of humor, a bit of color" into their writing is now a part of their style. He adds that Think Centre's journalism must be viewed in the context of its small audience. "Not that this means we can be irresponsible, but we can afford to be more adventurous now and then," he says.[38]

On the other hand, members realize that they are operating in a media environment with powerful conventions not within their control. "It has been drummed into people's heads that 'credibility' is all-important," Balrasan says. He adds that this is especially the case for Singaporeans who have grown up under PAP rule, and have been indoctrinated to favor the officially-sanctioned over more unruly forms of political expression.[39] In fact, as noted in Chapter 4, it is not just in Singapore that journalistic professionalism is associated with a doctrine of objectivity that favors "authorized knowers" over activists. This, however, was not a mainstream trait that Think Centre intended to imitate. Part of its mission was to enlarge the democratic conversation in Singapore. The views of non-government organizations and the opposition are underreported, Melvin Tan notes. "We don't share the view that the media should cover only the government's perspective," he says.[40] Nor, clearly, does Think Centre respect the strict distinction between participation and reportage that mainstream journalism considers sacrosanct. Its members believe that the media's failure to report alternative news is only part of the problem in Singapore. The bigger challenge is to create that alternative news in the first place. Their response is a more active and participatory view of communicative practice than is normal within professional journalism. It is reminiscent of the public journalism model suggested by Jay Rosen, in which journalists take seriously their "membership in the polity as well as the fraternity," such that "the house of politics" becomes not just a place to visit and observe, but a residence that the journalist endeavors to repair.[41]

However, members readily acknowledge that there is another dimension of journalistic professionalism — that of craft skills — that they are trying to learn from the mainstream media. Balrasan notes that they have tried to "shadow" certain influential columnists in the mainstream press: they tracked the columnist's writing, and wrote responses to expose the flaws in the logic or the points of view that had been omitted. It has turned out to be much tougher than they expected, he says. Biases were sometimes too subtle and arguments too sophisticated for a group of part-time, amateur journalists to defeat, he conceded. They have also discovered what every rookie reporter finds out: that journalistic writing, while simple to read, is difficult to write. "To be fair, *ST* journalists do a good job," he says. Conscious of their lack of training, they organized coaching sessions on how to write the news. Balrasan also visited a library to read up on how to do journalism. "When we started, we had major problems with spelling, grammar, and expression," he says. He admits that they are still not as articulate as many of *The Straits Times* writers. "We still take *ST* writers as a yardstick. We're not afraid to learn how to write well."[42]

Framing the struggle

In Think Centre's efforts to become an alternative source of political information and ideas for Singaporeans, the internet did not level the playing field, but it at least let the group stay in the game. The technology has served as an indispensable resource for organizing and mobilizing. In recognition of this fact, some of Think Centre's literature describes it as an independent "web-based" political think-tank. However, there is less evidence that the group tapped the internet's potential as a cultural frame. Absent from Think Centre's discourse is the use of the internet as a symbol of liberation. Sintercom's community seemed much more inclined to refer to the internet — or a particular idea of it — as a model for political relations. In contrast, Think Centre did not frame their struggle in terms of the technology, or make claims in its name. The difference in part reflects cultural changes over the five years that separate the founding of the two websites. In 1994–5, when

Sintercom was launched, the web's early adopters were wrapping the internet in the language of liberty and transcendent change. Five years later, Think Centre was founded in the midst of the dot-com bust and other signs that the old economy — and old politics — were not about to whither away. In addition, the two groups' leaders were very different sets of individuals. Sintercom was founded by early adopters of the internet, many of whom were first and foremost advocates of the medium, and only secondarily activists with a broader political vision. Think Centre's James Gomez and his collaborators were political activists through and through. Furthermore, there was much more to Think Centre's work and self-identity than the internet. If most people are technologically promiscuous, as postulated in Chapter 1, then Think Centre was wildly so. Gomez's books were an important vehicle, as were the regular forums, rallies and even installation art.

Like a performance artist, Think Centre turned its own body into a canvas. It used the problems it encountered to publicize the political and bureaucratic restrictions on freedom of assembly and freedom of expression in Singapore. It thus turned victimhood into an asset. The result often made Think Centre appear somewhat self-serving. Early on, for example, it devoted much space to Gomez's difficulties with bookstores and distributors over his first book. On the whole, an inordinate proportion of its writing focuses on its own activities. At its worst, the group's parochial focus seemed to cloud its judgment, as when it used its site to ridicule S. Ramamirthan, who was nothing more than a member of the public with strong opinions.

At another level, the strategy was well suited to its circumstances. What with the ban on foreign donations, which denied it the funding that groups in neighboring countries were able to secure, Think Centre could not dream of hiring fulltime reporters. It did not have the resources to engage in investigative journalism. Treating its own experiences as a source of news enabled it to make an impact that belied its means. Of course, the first-person approach would have fallen flat if its experiences were uninteresting. What made it work was that many of its activities were genuinely ground-breaking, and served as test cases for democracy in Singapore. Occasionally, even the officials in charge of administering this or that regulation seemed unsure of how to handle Think Centre's requests, as they were without precedent. Operating at the edge of the system and reporting the results became an efficient way to clarify the political boundaries. This required abandoning the conventional model of disinterested journalism, and accepting a level of personal risk to which most mainstream journalists are unaccustomed.

Sometimes, the effect was to expose the coercive muscle behind the stable consensus in the country. At such times, there was little the group could do to resist. Thus, when Think Centre was directed to remove the article that was deemed to violate election advertising regulations — an offense punishable by up to a year in prison — the group dispensed with its trademark cheekiness. It was given only a few hours to comply — not an easy task for a group made up of volunteers with their own day jobs. Melvin Tan, on whose shoulders the task fell, recalls that those few hours were as pleasant as bootcamp during compulsory national service: "The pressure was tremendous, like a *tekan* session in the army."[43]

Occasionally, however, the activists showed that the boundaries were more elastic than assumed. They say they were as surprised as anyone when their Save JBJ Rally cleared one regulatory hurdle after another and actually materialized. Similarly, the website's continued existence showed that dissent was possible. Asked by an interviewer how Think Centre had changed Singapore politics, one member replied:

> By showing to Singaporeans that independent alternative views can be expressed and explored without punishment.... Our site is hosted and registered locally, in a Singapore firm.... We have expressed our fair share of alternative and differing views, and yet the site is still up.[44]

CHAPTER 7

HARAKAH: THE POWER OF PARTISANSHIP

On the desk of Zulkifli Sulong, the editor-in-chief of Harakah, stood a large photograph of a bespectacled, bearded and altogether beatific elderly man. Malaysians would recognize the portrait instantly as that of Abdul Hadi Awang, president of the country's largest opposition party, the Pan-Malaysian Islamic Party or PAS. Most mainstream journalists would regard such a flagrant display of partisan allegiance as a violation of their professional principles of objectivity and detachment. The press, according to this conventional wisdom, needs to remain above the political fray to be able to write about it truthfully. Zulkifli and his news organization do not subscribe to this vision. "We are a party mouthpiece," he says matter-of-factly.[1]

The case studies in this book illustrate different dimensions of alternative-ness that have been explored on the internet. For example, the previous chapter showed how Singapore's Think Centre blends advocacy into its journalism, breaching the mainstream's firewall between observation and participation. The present chapter is a case study in partisan journalism — which, as noted in Chapter 4, precedes the paradigm of professional objectivity in the history of journalism, though its legitimacy is today very much doubted.

From Print to Pixels

Harakah is also unique among the four case studies in having a profitable print newspaper to bankroll its forays into cyberspace. *Harakah* ("movement") was established in 1987 as the official newspaper of PAS. Confident of circulation revenue, it did not draw any start-up capital from the party coffers. Instead, distributors paid an advance. The decision to set up the paper as a self-sustaining venture was more than vindicated: indeed, *Harakah* became one of the party's main sources of income. Published twice a week, it was selling an average of about 75,000 copies in the mid-1990s. In 1998, the Anwar Ibrahim affair and the Reformasi protest movement quadrupled its circulation.[2] The reasons why PAS and *Harakah* were the main beneficiaries of these tumultuous times will be provided later in this chapter. For now, it suffices to say that the newspaper was suddenly competing head-on with the establishment press.

The paper's first internet experiment was a half-hearted attempt to post some of its content on the web. Like the mainstream press, *Harakah* was generally satisfied with the power of print. As the 1999 general election approached, however, the party recognized that in a fast-moving election campaign, the government-controlled press and broadcast stations would outpace *Harakah*, whose permit did not allow it to publish a daily edition. A week before nomination day, it launched Harakah Daily on the web as a way to provide timely counter-information to the government's inevitable assaults on PAS. Intended purely as an election tool, the website went dormant after the campaign.[3] Before long, however, the government forced PAS to take the internet more seriously.

The elections saw PAS making further gains at the expense of prime minister Mahathir Mohamed's UMNO. *Harakah* could no

longer be ignored. In the week before polling day, its circulation
had hit around 380,000 — exceeding that of the country's number
one daily, *Utusan Malaysia*. The government struck soon after the
elections. First, it demanded that the opposition paper not be sold
to non-members, since it was licensed as a party newsletter. The
irony was not lost on commentators such as Chandra Muzaffar:

> Such a condition is absurd, since the whole reason that a political
> party produces a newspaper is to influence the general public.
> While denying PAS access to the people through its newspaper,
> Dr. Mahathir's UMNO has no compunctions about using both
> public and private television channels to beam the proceedings
> of the annual UMNO General Assembly to the sitting rooms of
> millions of non-UMNO members. ... The government regards
> its monopoly over the public media and state institutions as the
> privilege and prerogative of power. In fact, for Dr. Mahathir
> electoral competition is little more than a process by which the
> ruling elite confirms its power.[4]

When *Harakah*'s publishing license expired in February 2000, the
authorities said that the new license would restrict it to publishing just
twice a month, down from nine issues per month. The government
was being kind, officials said, since it could have banned the paper
altogether. The restrictions were a massive blow to party revenue, and
constrained its ability to disseminate information in a timely manner.
The solution to the latter problem, at least, was obvious. The answer
was obvious. First, pray. "We will continue to hold mass prayers
regularly to beseech Allah to save *Harakah*," Zulkifli had said in January
when the government restricted its circulation.[5] Next, in March 2000,
the newspaper relaunched HarakahDaily.net as a daily online news
site, complete with web TV. Zulkifli acknowledges a debt to the
dozens of small Reformasi websites that had blazed the trail and
demonstrated the empowering possibilities of the internet.[6] (For
good measure, Harakah also submitted an application for a permit
to publish a daily newspaper, *Purnama*, which was never granted.)

At that point, fewer than 20 per cent of Malaysians were internet users, so the web was hardly a substitute for print. Still, the preparedness of this fundamentalist Islamic party to embrace the information revolution — so effectively mythologized in Mahathir's Vision 2020 rhetoric — demonstrated that PAS was no Taliban (a comparison that its critics occasionally make). It also represented the rise within PAS of young, educated and professional members who helped persuade the older guard of the way forward.

Harakah's deft entry into the web was viewed with some concern by government officials. Two deputy ministers issued vague threats that the online edition would be subject to regulation. Almost immediately, the government clarified that its no-censorship guarantee would be honored.[7] This was another illustration of the dynamics described in Chapter 3: at least for the time being, the government wanted to preserve its IT-friendly image more than it wanted to crack down on dissenting voices in cyberspace. Still, Zulkifli was under no illusions that cyberspace gave him any protection from the law. In January, he had already been charged with sedition for publishing a paragraph accusing the state prosecutor and the courts of acting as tools in Mahathir's conspiracy against Anwar.[8] He was found guilty three years later and paid a fine of RM5,000 in lieu of a six-month jail sentence.[9]

Like its print parent, Harakah Daily is bilingual, mainly in Malay but with substantial English content as well. Its domestic coverage is devoted mainly to politics, with an emphasis on the activities and statements of PAS leaders, news of things going wrong in the country under UMNO's leadership, and the never-ending war of words between the government and the opposition. International news tends to reflect the community's interest in events in the Muslim world, such as the Israeli-Palestinian dispute. The site also includes a regular online poll, which usually draws votes from at least 2,000 readers and sometimes more than 15,000, depending on the topic. A recent one asked in Malay, "Why do you support PAS?" Around

85 per cent of the more than 2,100 respondents chose the option "Its commitment to the Islamic state and Islamic law"; under 6 per cent identified primarily with the party's commitment to "democracy" or "the struggle for human rights" (a result that helps explain some of the party's actions — more on that later).

Harakah's fulltime staff of about 30 editors, reporters, photographers and layout artists produces content for both the website as well as the newspaper. The website has just three dedicated staff, to handle its more technical tasks. Producing a website is cheap, although not as cheap as they once assumed. "In the beginning we thought it was all free," Zulkifli Sulong notes. "With more visitors, it was free no more."[10] They started by using the free hosting service of Lycos in the United States. This was unable to cope with Harakah's volume of visits. They then paid for server space from a commercial firm in Canada. When this company wanted to raise its fees, again because of the site's high volume, Harakah decided to use its own servers. First, it tried upgrading one of its existing computers. After three months, it bought two dedicated servers. It also pays RM1,500 a month to lease a line. Thus, although amateur journalists have found that the internet has reduced the economic barriers to entry to practically zero — especially when riding on university facilities — costs are not negligible when operating on the scale of Harakah.

Harakah's board of directors, comprising party leaders, has been conscious of a potentially more serious, indirect cost. If readers stop buying the print version because they have access to the site's free content, the party organ's revenue would be reduced further. The fear of so-called "cannibalization," shared by most traditional media companies, accounts for Harakah running some special reports exclusively in its print edition.[11] At the same time, there is a clear recognition that the party's ideological goals are best served by being generous with its information. Thus, the website carries an invitation to the webmasters of other sites to take advantage of Harakah Daily's free syndication service. By the end of 2000, PAS leaders were convinced enough of the value of the technology to announce the party's IT plan. It would ensure that party leaders at all levels had individual e-mail addresses, and provide computers with internet access at all PAS offices down to the local branch level. It would also partner companies to sell computers to members and supporters, with the goal of weaning them off mainstream media entirely.[12]

The political secretary to the party president, Hatta Ramli, acknowledges the internet's value as an important avenue to respond to rumors quickly, and to circulate the "correct" news, as well as announcements and directives. Harakah Daily is now the default homepage on party organizers' web browsers, he adds. "It's a one-stop center."[13] In addition, the online capabilities that Harakah has built up have been harnessed for campaign communication. During the 2001 by-election in the rural north of the country, Harakah produced daily newsletters targeted at about 10,000 households identified by local activists as undecided voters. Reporters in the field wrote their news stories and e-mailed them from local PAS offices to Harakah's Kuala Lumpur headquarters for editing and layout. The documents were then converted into "pdf" files and e-mailed to commercial printers at the electoral battlefront, where they were printed and then hand-delivered by party workers to homes.[14] This hybrid, online-offline mode is a response to Malaysia's low internet penetration, especially away from the urban centers, and is an example of the technological promiscuity noted in Chapter 1. One related plan is to produce a printable version of Harakah Daily, with the most important stories laid out on a few pages formatted to print out easily on standard A4-sized paper. Party branches could photocopy these for local distribution, and even sell them for extra income.[15]

Islam in Motion

Like other alternative media projects, Harakah has benefited from networks of solidarity. Even before the crisis of 1998, PAS had a declared membership nudging 400,000. Its rolls have more than doubled since, and it has many more closet sympathizers. Among them are civil servants who occasionally tip off Harakah on newsworthy developments within the administration.[16] The PAS network is also a source of staff for the news organization. Many of its journalists were young idealistic party activists who joined Harakah straight out of university to contribute to the cause. This was the case with Zulkifli Sulong, the current editor. While studying plantation management in college, he was the editor of a Muslim campus magazine. His friends were active in the local PAS structure. He joined Harakah as a cadet journalist in 1987, the year it was founded.[17]

Harakah has also been able to draw on the decades-old network of smaller independent Islamic media. The first editor of its English section, P. Koya Kutty, came from such a background. A Muslim from the minority Indian community and a bank employee by profession, he had been involved in writing, editing and publishing Islamic magazines and tracts for some 20 years. In that capacity, he came to know the government's style of media management intimately. A quarterly magazine that he started in 1978, *Readings in Islam*, was stopped by the government after three years. Later, he launched the fortnightly *Muslimedia International*, and rankled the Mahathir government with an editorial arguing that UMNO was trying purge Islam from the political system. (The real reason for the government's ire on this occasion, he maintains, is that he criticized Malaysian private investments in offshore casinos in the Maldives. What look like ideological differences can often boil down to the protection of economic interests.) Koya Kutty was asked to start Harakah's English section in 1996.[18]

Besides Muslim activists, the other main group on the Harakah staff is made up of experienced professional journalists from the mainstream press. Zulkifli's deputy, for example, is a retired news editor from *Berita Harian*, the *New Straits Times* group's Malay daily.

The organization's firm business footing allows it to hire seasoned journalists at decent wages, although it is sympathy with the cause, rather than money, that would ultimately attract them to Harakah. Contributors of occasional opinion pieces come from a wider range of backgrounds, although they are generally part of the Reformasi movement. They include M.G.G. Pillai, a non-Muslim freelance journalist, and Raja Petra Kamarudin, director of the Free Anwar Campaign. Harakah also subscribes to Malaysiakini's paid syndication service, and occasionally uses the independent website's news stories. There are, however, limits to Harakah's sense of solidarity with others in the contentious journalism movement. One of the clearest signs of this is its refusal to provide links to any other site, to avoid seeming to endorse material that is not within its editors' control, as well as to keep visitors within its virtual space. So scrupulous is Harakah about maintaining a distinct identity that it does not even provide a link to the official PAS website, <http://www.parti-pas.org>.[19]

Party Roots

To understand Harakah, its mission, its successes, and its challenges, one must understand the party it represents. PAS was formed in 1951, with the ultimate goal of creating an Islamic state. Members of Malaysia's majority ethnic group, the Malays, are almost all Muslims. This has put PAS in direct conflict with the Malay nationalist party, UMNO, for influence over the majority. UMNO, the main party in the governing coalition, has been unwilling to concede the Islamic high ground to PAS, recognizing the political potency of religious rhetoric and the growing religiosity of the Malays.

In this battle to out-Islamicize PAS, one of UMNO's coups in 1982 was to co-opt a charismatic young Muslim intellectual and activist, Anwar Ibrahim, who was also being courted by PAS. Anwar rose to the position of deputy prime minister and was Mahathir's heir apparent when he was sacked in September 1998 and accused of sexual misconduct and corruption. The sordidness of his alleged misdeeds was exceeded only by that of the authorities' treatment of him. There was a growing sense "that Mahathir had overstepped the bounds of decent conduct, revealing not only a failure of justice, but a lack of social decorum."[20]

PAS reaped the benefit of the Malay discontent. UMNO's hegemony over the Malay community was based on a vision of socio-economic upliftment and modernization that coupled Western science, technology and rational learning with Islamic social consciousness. Government policies had succeeded in creating a new Malay middle class, but also a layer of super-rich crony capitalists, who inspired in the common man less admiration for the system's success than disgust at its deep corruption. In the state government of Kelantan, controlled by PAS since 1990, the party had shown itself to be relatively clean. Around the country, its activists were by most accounts more motivated and idealistic than the more cynically business-minded members of UMNO. Anwar's downfall — although nothing to do with religion — was framed by PAS as proof that Islamization could never succeed from within UMNO.

PAS was also the main beneficiary of the broad-based Reformasi protest movement, launched by Anwar himself immediately after his ouster. One scholar says of the movement:

> It attracted anyone and everyone who felt alienated and marginalised by the dominant political culture of the country. The fact that so many flocked to its cause: students, activists, academics, workers, professionals, business people and people of all races and religions suggested that here was the opportunity to create a pan-national rainbow coalition that would bring Malaysian society together. The ideals of this movement were universal and fundamentally humanistic.... Thus it did not privilege one religion over other cultural and belief systems. Its goals were likewise broad and inclusive.[21]

As with most protest movements, many of the Reformasi's constituent groups fizzled out after the initial eruption. Even Keadilan, the political party formed precisely to channel Reformasi ideals into electoral power, sputtered as the heat died down and Malaysian politics returned to its normal concerns, namely "votes and seats, money and power."[22] In contrast, the well-established organizational strength of PAS allowed it to survive the calm as well the chaos. The same is true of the Reformasi media. Most of the websites that proliferated during the crisis fell into disuse, their creators unable to sustain their enthusiasm for more than a year. *Harakah*, on the other hand, consolidated its position as the leading alternative newspaper, and Harakah Daily as the best-read alternative website.

Its organizational advantages would not have counted for much if PAS had cast its net in exclusive Islamic terms. The party was able to play a lead role in the Reformasi and its aftermath only because of its conscious effort to forge a broad multi-ethnic alliance against the ruling Barisan Nasional coalition. Accordingly, Harakah positioned itself as a focal point for the democratic movement, in addition to being a party mouthpiece.

These were not sudden decisions. By the early 1990s, Islamists in various countries were shifting towards championing democracy and participation, locating these claims in Islamic values but also finding common ground with secular democratic forces. Thus, before the Anwar crisis, PAS was already engaging in a sophisticated discourse in Islamic democracy, and attacking UMNO's authoritarian ways. It has contested every election since 1955, when it won the sole opposition seat, and has steadily increased its parliamentary presence, giving it both stakes and faith in democratic processes. "A fairly long apprenticeship of PAS as a participant in Malaysian democracy has given the party a period of habituation and experience increasingly to accept the realities of pluralistic politics," one writer has noted.[23]

The Iranian Revolution inspired a more radical turn in the early 1980s, but this was rejected firmly by voters in 1986. Since the early 1990s, therefore, the party has been influenced by moderates aware of the need to position PAS as committed to tolerance, democracy and social justice. For both the 1990 and 1995 elections, it formed coalitions with other opposition parties.[24] In 1990, it won control of the state government of Kelantan. Although the specific pacts were fragile, the principle of building coalitions with other parties — including non-Malay, non-Muslim ones — was firmly established by the mid-1990s. Syed Ahmad Hussein notes:

> The party's shift to championing democracy-related issues... was not conceived during the moment of passion following 'Anwargate'. ... But the Anwar episode, the resulting political dislocations within UMNO, the popular protests demanding democratic reforms and clean government, and an upcoming general election, provided PAS with an opportune setting to propagate its Islamic democracy platform. They also provided the catalyst to the party leadership to pursue vigorously its moderate pragmatist line that included building bridges with non-Muslim groups and parties in an attempt to build an electable alternative to the National Front.[25]

Harakah was shaped by, and was a key vehicle for, the party's twin objectives of challenging UMNO's dominance over Muslim politics, and forming an alternative alliance with non-Muslim groups. These goals were not always neatly compatible, and Harakah found itself pressured by contradictions, having to serve simultaneously as a party mouthpiece and as an open space for the broader democratic movement.

Tensions in partisan journalism

The absence of hyperlinks from harakahdaily.net to parti-pas.org notwithstanding, Harakah's ties to PAS are neither deniable nor denied. What is more difficult to ascertain is the extent to which the news organization's partisan constitution compromises its journalism. It was noted in Chapter 4 that the partisan press has deeper roots in the history of journalism than newspapers wedded to the principle of disinterestedness. Chapter 10 will develop the idea that partisan periodicals should be seen as an important ingredient in a democratic media mix. Nevertheless, within the context in which Harakah operates — contemporary Malaysian society — non-partisanship is regarded as a worthy ideal for the press. The mainstream media's independence may be recognized as a pretense, but the very effort taken to pretend reinforces the normative consensus around non-partisan journalism. For example, at one conference, the *New Straits Times* editor-in-chief retorted testily to a critic, "Can he prove UMNO's direct ownership of any newspaper?" It is unlikely that he persuaded anyone in the audience that his newspaper was truly independent, since it is well known that UMNO exercises control through cronies.[26] However, such remarks help reinforce the norm of non-partisanship, at the expense of party organs such as Harakah.

A Malaysian political beat journalist with more than 15 years' experience working for mainstream newspapers acknowledges that Harakah was at least being upfront in its partisanship, and "not hiding behind any cloak." Still, she found it hard to accept that Harakah's staff of party activists could function properly as journalists. "If you want to write with any level of comfort, you have to maintain a certain distance," she said. "That helps me to cover both the opposition and the government. I try not to like or dislike either side too much." Most of her colleagues in the mainstream press were apolitical, she added. "I think that's still better than taking sides."

This journalist's view is an example of ethical principles getting "lost in translation," as Jeremy Iggers put it.[27] Journalists start with fundamental conceptions of their responsibilities, which are then translated into ethical principles, such as avoiding conflicts of interest, which are in turn translated into operational rules for reporters — in this case, maintaining "a certain distance" from newsmakers, and trying "not to like or dislike" them too much. As well-meaning as these journalists may be, this kind of translation typically lets publishers off the hook. Iggers notes:

Why are these ethical principles (like avoiding conflict of interest) translated into procedural rules that govern the conduct of employees, but not into rules governing the economic relationships that corporate media entities may enter into? ... [W]hat is filtered out in the process of translation are those issues that could present a challenge to the prerogatives of ownership (and particularly the pursuit of profits) or the institutional interests of the medium.[28]

Predictably, Harakah defends its partisanship partly by attacking the mainstream press. "The reality is that they are more controlled than Harakah. They are controlled not just by the parties, but also by factions within the parties," Zulkifli Sulong says, in a reference to how establishment editors close to Anwar Ibrahim were purged to lay the ground for the deputy prime minister's sacking. In addition, Zulkifli argues that partisanship is not incompatible with the journalistic mission of truth-telling: "We have professional values, but our priorities are different from the mainstream." Harakah's first priority is to the truth, he says: "The news must be truthful." Second, they have a responsibility to write the news in a way that is easy for readers to understand. This is where experienced editors come in, editing stories to increase their appeal to the public. Third, Harakah is a mouthpiece of the party: "We must portray a good image of the party and of our religion."[29]

Zulkifli recognizes that there is an apparent conflict between the first and third missions, but maintains that when criticism of the party is warranted, Harakah has the freedom — and the duty — to do it:

This freedom is evident if we go back to the days of the Caliphs who succeeded the Holy Prophet (peace be upon him). Saidina Abu Bakar As-Siddiq upon his appointment as the first Caliph called upon the people to correct him should he make mistakes during his rule. The second Caliph Saidina Umar Al-Khattab was once challenged in the open by the lowest level of followers regarding his administration. Instead of putting him in jail, when challenged, the Caliph thanked the All-Mighty as there was still a servant of Allah who was prepared to remind him of his duty."[30]

Some of the examples he cites of Harakah's role as an in-house critic are not particularly impressive. For example, he recalls that it carried a letter complaining about the poor standard of toilets in the party's headquarters in Kuala Lumpur; the party secretary-general was angry, but the sub-standard toilet was duly demolished and a new one built. A more interesting case arose in early 2002. The association representing the conservative religious scholars, the *ulama*, complained to the state that several individuals had been denigrating Islam. The individuals on the blacklist were mainly outspoken Muslim writers and activists pushing for more progressive interpretations of holy texts, and criticizing the *ulama* for their literalist bent. These people did not have the authority to criticize the *ulama*, the association protested.[31]

The *ulama*'s witch-hunt was criticized by the individuals concerned, officials of the government and ruling party, and a *New Straits Times* editorial. What was more surprising, given that the scholars are closely aligned with PAS, is that *Harakah* also came out in an English editorial, penned by Koya Kutty, to argue that the *ulama* were wrong to have claimed that their Koranic interpretations were the only valid ones and above criticism. *Ulama* were not a separate class, like the priestly Brahmin caste in Hinduism, he noted. The PAS Youth chief was so stunned by *Harakah*'s stand, he alleged "sabotage" by elements within the party organ.[32] The mainstream press gleefully reported that PAS was in disarray. A few days later, an editorial by Zulkifli in Malay appeared on Harakah Daily, making clear that the earlier piece had not been a lapse. He reiterated that while the *ulama* as an institution had to be respected, their judgments were open to criticism.[33] Zulkifli says that it is only those with misconceptions about Islamic democracy and PAS who would be surprised by Harakah's boldness in this incident. "In fact, it is nothing unusual," he says.

There is, however, another possible interpretation of the affair. It is plausible that although the editorials angered some in PAS, they were published in the knowledge that the top party leadership would approve. In defending Harakah's stand to the party faithful, Zulkifli's Malay editorial argued that *ulama* who were intolerant of criticism would play into "mad mullah" stereotype, to the detriment of PAS. It also suggested that the *ulama* should learn from the PAS leader, Abdul Hadi Awang, who readily accepted criticism of his state government in Terengganu, it said. One can also speculate that if the *ulama* were to succeed in cultivating an aura of infallibility, they would be able to claim authority over the movement's political leaders — a risk that had already materialized in theocratic Iran, and to which PAS politicians could not have been blind.

Perhaps, the Harakah editorials were published with the tacit approval or active instigation of its political masters. Or, perhaps Zulkifli as an astute functionary needed no signals to help him determine what would please them. Outsiders are not privy to such details. However, irrespective of how he came to the decision, it was publicly endorsed by PAS leaders soon after. Nik Aziz Nik Mat, the most revered of PAS leaders, told reporters outside a mosque: "I do not think that editorial has done something that is against Islam. It is a fact that *ulama* can be criticized."[34]

If Harakah is well-tuned to PAS thinking, it seems to be equally the case that the party leadership has a sophisticated understanding of mass media. Hatta Ramli, the PAS president's political secretary, says that they appreciate the fact that journalists need to "sensationalize" the news if they are to get the attention of readers.[35] He offers another example of Harakah being able to give party leaders "a piece of its mind." In May 2002, an article criticized the then PAS president, the late Fadzil Noor, for sharing the stage with prime minister Mahathir during a conference on Palestine. The writer claimed that the event turned into a sham, and argued that the PAS leader should have walked out.[36] Hatta readily acknowledges, however, that there are limits to what Harakah can say about the party and its leaders. Personal attacks are out, for example.[37] Koya Kutty adds: "We cannot insult Islamic fundamentals."[38] Of course, given the religious convictions of Harakah's staff, it is unlikely that they would ever want to anyway.

Problems of success

The case for party and civic media is usually stated in terms of providing a space for the members of small and marginalized communities to deliberate among themselves, free of domination by elites. From this perspective, which will be developed in Chapter 10, these arenas are essential for communities to elaborate "alternative styles of political behavior and alternative norms of public speech," and to construct their "interests, objectives, and strategies."[39] By these standards, Harakah can be judged a stunning success.

The question is whether these are the only standards by which to assess the organ of a party that is no longer so small and so marginal. PAS is mounting the most serious counter-hegemonic challenge to Malaysia's ruling elite, and by 2000 was in power in two of the federation's 13 states. Therefore, some Malaysians rightly look to Harakah for clues about what a PAS-controlled Malaysian public sphere might be like. Their concern is that Harakah would be no more open and democratic than the current mainstream press, if and when PAS comes to power.

One independent journalist, Fathi Aris Omar, says that Harakah would not publish any exposé of "KKN" (corruption, cronyism and nepotism) within the PAS-controlled state governments of Terengganu and Kelantan. When he wrote such a piece, he sent it to Malaysiakini instead. Similarly, criticism of factionalism within PAS would be off-limits, he believes. "I doubt whether PAS would respect press freedom when they are in power," he says.[40]

Equally skeptical is Farish Noor, a progressive public intellectual who had been among those blacklisted by the *ulama*. Farish has argued that Harakah is as guilty as its nemeses of slavishly serving as propaganda vehicles for their political masters. Furthermore, Harakah is encouraging a popular political discourse that is full of Islamist terms, metaphors and symbols, and which will inevitably alienate many Malaysians. He notes:

> To talk of the present political crisis as a "jihad against the forces of kafir (non-believer) and kezaliman (injustice)" may well strike a chord with some sections of the Malay-Muslim community, but it also risks the danger of excluding others who do not share (or do not want to share) that kind of religious-political discourse.[41]

No issue has exposed the schism between PAS and its anti-Mahathir allies more than that of *hudud*, the punishments specified by conservative interpretations of Islamic law. Delivering on an election promise, the new PAS government in Terengganu state released a draft of its Hudud Bill in April 2002. It would empower the authorities to, for example, amputate a thief's right hand after his first offense. The most controversial provisions covered sexual offenses. Under the proposed law, it would be a crime for a woman to cry rape without evidence. She would have to present four witnesses, all adult Muslim males of good character and sound mind. Unsubstantiated allegations would make her liable for 80 lashes. A woman who was impregnated by someone other than her husband would be guilty of *zina*, illicit sex, which was punishable with death by stoning. Rape victims were excused — but would have to prove that they were indeed raped by presenting the required witnesses.

The party's protests that the Bill was being misrepresented, and that there would be sufficient checks to protect the innocent, could not stem the rising tide of outrage among Malaysians. Women's groups led the campaign against the Bill, and PAS duly watered down its most controversial sections before tabling it in July. In any case, there was little chance of *hudud* actually being applied in the state, since it would require federal government assent, which UMNO had declared it would not give. The same thing had happened in Kelantan, the first state taken by PAS. Indeed, it is quite likely that PAS was using the *hudud* issue as a political tool. Forcing Kuala Lumpur to block the will of voters in PAS-controlled states exposes UMNO's lack of commitment to conservative Islamic values, as well as "saves PAS from the embarrassment of having to actually chop off hands and feet, whip and stone people to death in public."[42]

Whatever gain PAS thus made with its conservative Muslim ground was at the expense of its ambitions to lead a broad alliance against the Mahathir government. The Chinese-based Democratic Action Party (DAP), a key opposition ally, pulled out of the already-fragile Barisan Alternatif in September 2001 because of irreconcilable differences over the PAS goal of an Islamic state. In the midst of the *hudud* debate, DAP went public with its unhappiness. Its chairman, Lim Kit Siang, appealed to PAS to withdraw the Bill to demonstrate its moderate agenda. His media release revealed that he had sent an e-mail to Hadi Awang, as the new PAS president and the chief minister of Terengganu, to say that the Bill would strengthen public perceptions that PAS policies were incompatible with the Constitution, pluralism, human rights, women's rights, development and modernity.[43]

DAP's attacks on the Islamic state vision were downplayed by *Harakah*. Critics see this as a clear symptom of the leading alternative publication's Achilles heel. Fathi Omar believes *Harakah* should have kept its readers informed of how other opposition parties and non-government organizations were responding to the PAS agenda. Zulkifli Sulong does not conceal his unhappiness at DAP's public attacks. "We felt DAP should understand. They have their own philosophy of struggle, we have our own philosophy of struggle. We felt we shouldn't oppose each other," he says. However, he denies that he suppressed the DAP statements in order to mislead

his readers, who would know about the controversy from the mainstream media anyway. He explains the decision in terms of propriety.
"Our leaderships must settle it in the backyard of the house, not
in front of the people," he says. For the same reason, he censored
PAS leaders' off-the-cuff remarks against DAP.[44]

> We made a stand: we won't criticize DAP, and we won't entertain
> their criticism. Every DAP criticism would be published in the
> daily papers. If we publish it, we must also publish the PAS
> reply. Then, we would be quarrelling in our own paper.[45]

The PAS position on *hudut* even tested the loyalty of some
of its own. Koya Kutty, who had been editor of Harakah's English
section since 1996, says he left the organization in 2002 partly because
of his health, but also because he disagreed with the way PAS was
interpreting Islamic texts in its *hudut* policy.[46]

A question of autonomy

Certain features of Malaysia's PAS-led Islamic movement — in
particular, the intolerance of some religious scholars, and the male
chauvinism of some leaders — have proved to be incompatible
with the values of the broader Reformasi movement. Still, in other
respects, PAS shares common ground with the rest of the opposition
and the NGO community. The party has been firmly against the
Internal Security Act, which allows detention without trial, and for
the repeal of repressive press laws. Koya Kutty is convinced that PAS
will honor its pledge to expunge these laws when it is in power.
"PAS and Islam are committed to freedom. Without freedom, Islam
cannot develop," he says.[47]

These are the values that place Harakah firmly within the
ranks of Malaysia's contentious journalism movement. It is a full
partner in the campaign for greater press freedom. However, it
is not a partnership that is without strains and contradictions, as
should be clear from the foregoing discussion. These are in a sense

the problems of success. Traits that would be dismissed as harmless idiosyncrasies in, say, the blog of an unknown amateur journalist, are treated more seriously when they are in the country's leading alternative publication. Expectations are high for *Harakah*, and rightly so. Whether it can meet those expectations depends, first, on whether PAS meets its own challenge of negotiating a common position with other opposition parties, and, second, whether PAS sees value in granting *Harakah* greater autonomy to serve the broader public interest.

Perhaps the most hopeful sign that PAS is prepared to let *Harakah* decide on how to pursue its journalism — and its profits — is the existence of an entirely separate official party website, parti-pas.org. The latter is no less professionally produced than *Harakah Daily*. It is updated daily with news from several sources (including *Harakah Daily*, naturally). It is more obviously a promotional and organizational tool, with a prominently displayed calendar of party events, seemingly endless lists of streaming audio and video of PAS speeches, and links to the sites of the various state headquarters. With parti-pas.org playing the role of an internal party newsletter, PAS may allow *Harakah* to reach out to the Malaysian public with more autonomous journalism.

CHAPTER 8

MALAYSIAKINI: INDEPENDENCE AT A PRICE

One Monday in January 2003, ten policemen visited the offices of Malaysiakini.com. As they passed through the front door, they would have faced a "Press Freedom Wall": a display in the lobby commemorating more than a dozen Malaysian newspapers and magazines that had been banned or otherwise restricted through the decades. The exhibit was meant to inspire solidarity with Malaysian journalists who have suffered injustices at the hands of the state. It does not appear that the Press Freedom Wall had the desired effect on Malaysiakini's ten visitors. When they left, the policemen took with them 19 computers, unplugged from the website's newsroom. After more than three years on a rollercoaster ride through the nation's politics, Malaysiakini came to an abrupt halt that Monday afternoon, robbed even of the satisfaction of publishing the scoop on the raid. There was, however, no shortage of messengers. E-mail lists and wire agencies spread the word, followed by local and foreign newspapers. Agence France-Presse reported:

> Police Monday raided the office of popular Internet newspaper Malaysiakini and took away its computers in a probe into

complaints that it had published a seditious letter, editor Steven
Gan said. Gan denounced the police move and said it appeared
to be an attempt to shut down the operations of Malaysiakini,
which claims a daily readership of about 100,000. "They are
taking away all 19 computers used by the journalists and our
staffers, our operations will be affected. This is an attempt to
close down Malaysiakini," he told AFP.[1]

It would soon become clear that neither the reasons for the
raid, nor its effects, were as suggested by such initial reports. Before
long, Malaysiakini was back in operation; the big loser was not
the website, but the government. In Malaysian politics, things are
rarely as they seem. The police action was an illuminating event,
but its significance lay deep beneath the surface. It exposed the
contradictions in the state's policies, as well as in Malaysiakini's
agenda. Contentious journalism projects are often most powerful
when under visible assault, and there was some truth in critics' cynical
claim that the much-publicized raid gave Malaysiakini a fillip that
it desperately needed. Unlike other alternative websites in Malaysia
and Singapore, it had chosen to tie the fate of its journalism to
commerce, in the tradition of the mainstream press. At the time
of the raid, the website was already under serious threat, not from
men who wore uniforms or carried guns, but from the invisible
hand of the market.

Refugees from the Mainstream

Malaysiakini was the brainchild of Steven Gan and Premesh
Chandran, two Malaysians who worked together at the tabloid daily
newspaper, *The Sun*. Gan became *The Sun*'s special issues editor after
spending four years as a freelance journalist based in Hongkong.
Chandran joined Gan's team. As undergraduates in Australia, both of
them had been engaged in political activism. Together with friends
from the region who were intimately concerned with struggles in
Thailand, Indonesia and China, they developed a keen interest in

human rights. They did not study journalism in university — Gan was an economics graudate and Chandran studied physics — but warmed to journalism's social and political mission.[2]

The special issues section of *The Sun* held a lot of promise for "young, energetic, idealistic" journalists like them, Gan recalls. Its mandate was to engage in in-depth investigative reporting. However, old-school values still held sway within the organization, and they grew increasingly frustrated at the internal and external battles they had to fight. Gan's defining moment came in 1995, when his newspaper refused to publish a story he broke on the deaths of 59 inmates at an immigration detention camp. He passed the information to a Malaysian human rights activist, who was subsequently charged with spreading "false news." In 1996, he quit *The Sun* after editors spiked a column. He joined *The Nation* in Bangkok as an editorial writer. Chandran moved on to graduate school and a research post at the Malaysian Trades Union Congress, writing on economics, development and labor issues.[3]

Gan and Chandran were thus casualties of the dynamics observed in Chapter 2. They were not only subject to direct repression by the government, but also faced self-censorship by gatekeepers who were either themselves fearful of coercion or ideologically persuaded that the press should not rock the boat. Chandran would later write about the status quo:

> The Malaysian print and broadcast media has for long failed to meet international media standards. Self-censorship and biased reporting is wide-spread, stemming from ownership biases, annual renewal of licenses, government support for so-called "development journalism," editorial structures and other journalistic practices. This mediocrity occurs in all forms of mass media, although the degree of independence and slant varies. The public, while often in support of a more independent media, have generally come to accept the local characteristics, and developed their own talents to "read between the lines."[4]

In a freer country, they could have responded by starting their own small newspaper, they note. Malaysia's licensing system made this a "stillborn" idea, Gan says. While on their hiatus from Malaysian journalism, the Anwar Ibrahim affair erupted, and they watched as Reformasi activists demonstrated the internet's potential as a medium for dissent. It was "an amazing, liberating tool," Gan notes. "But we realized that this would not last, because people would need credible sources of information, from professional journalists."[5] The two friends decided that they would attempt a Malaysian first: they would bring high-quality independent journalism to the web. A February 1999 proposal paper led with the following vision statement:

> To use Information Technology and the Internet to provide fresh, free, fair and fast news to the Malaysian public so as to set new standards of journalism and to support the development of freedom of speech, social justice and democracy in Malaysia.[6]

Gan returned to Kuala Lumpur from Bangkok in October 1999 to start Malaysiakini. He took the post of editor-in-chief, while Chandran served as chief executive officer. To announce Malaysiakini's arrival with a bang, they decided they would have to launch in time for the next general election, when Malaysians would be hungry for alternative news. The election was due by June the following year. To their shock, the government announced on November 11 that the polling date would be November 29, less than three weeks away. Rushing to meet their deadline, Malaysiakini went live on nomination day, November 20, 1999.[7] It got its first scoop within its first week. It received word that the Chinese-language newspaper *Sin Chew Jit Poh* had digitally manipulated a group photograph of ruling party politicians. The five-year-old file picture originally included the then deputy prime minister Anwar Ibrahim, but the newspaper removed his face and replaced it with that of the current deputy. This was apparently done by over-anxious staff without the editor's knowledge. Malaysiakini showed the two versions side by side. It compared the photographic manipulation to the practice in communist countries of expunging from history all traces of out-of-favor leaders.[8]

Professional Values

Within the contentious journalism movement in Malaysia and Singapore, Malaysiakini stands out as the project most closely tied to the norms of modern journalism as embodied by the profession's standard bearers internationally. While Think Centre and Harakah, for example, have tried in various ways to reinterpret the canons of their craft with their more activist and partisan approaches, Malaysiakini represents a return to fundamentals that its founders believe have been corrupted by Malaysia's mainstream media. They refer to touchstones such as credibility, independence, fairness and accuracy. Thus, at one interview, Gan revealed that he had just sacked one reporter the day before for making up quotations. "We hold ourselves up to a high standard," he said.[9]

Gan and his staff have tried to negotiate a middle ground that is neither politically-engaged to the point of being obviously biased, nor detached to the point of being apathetic. Getting the balance right has entailed long discussions. They debated the stand they should take towards the Mahathir government, for example. Some argued that the website should be the "mirror image" of the traditional media, taking an anti-government and pro-opposition line. Gan has rejected this approach, in favor of an "independent" stance.[10] To the question of why the site never seems to have anything good to say about the government, Gan replies:

> That's not our job. Our job is to highlight problems. Not because we are anti-government *per se*, but because we want to be different from the traditional media. If we had no competition out there, we would provide both the positive and negative. But, as things stand, our mission is to highlight the negative.[11]

With just seven journalists, he notes, it makes sense to focus on those perspectives that are not covered adequately by the mainstream press. He adds: "We don't say anything good about the opposition either." One highly publicized example was the revelation of internal criticism within the website of the opposition party Keadilan and other Reformasi sites, directed at two of the party's leaders. Malaysiakini reported this case of dissent within the opposition ranks just before a by-election in 2000, angering opposition leaders and supporters.[12] Indeed, Gan notes that all the complaining phone-calls he has received have come from opposition members who believe that Malaysiakini should play the role of a pro-opposition medium.[13]

Independence, in Malaysiakini's eyes, does not mean indifference. "We are not partisan, but we are not apolitical, either. We take strong, clear stands on political issues," Gan says. Achieving this political but non-partisan brand of independent journalism has been a challenge that Gan has had to think carefully about. He notes that some of his journalists come from activist backgrounds. This gives them a "feel" for politics, but also greater difficulty conforming to the conventional style of news writing because they see issues in terms that are too black-and-white. "I tell them, you can take positions, but you must include the other positions, even in opinion pieces," he says.[14]

He and Chandran credit the internet for allowing them to pursue their professional ideals. Chandran notes that the licensing requirement imposed on print publications has produced newspaper editors who are "programmed" to self-censor. "We are free of that," he says:

> We don't have the self-censorship mentality because we are not worried about losing a license. The psychology in our organization is to push. There's a feeling of liberation — let's go do things. In the mainstream, even writers censor themselves. This kills their energy, their enthusiasm, and idealism. How can you grow good journalism in that sort of context? We want to have an

organization that is liberated, that takes pride in someone who does something unique. We celebrate that. It's about liberating the mind.[15]

The Commercial Challenge

To realize their vision of independent journalism, Gan and Chandran had to find a way to sustain the operation. Malaysiakini's struggle for financial self-sufficiency shows the limits of the internet advantage. The internet has low economic barriers to entry if the goal is irregular, amateur journalism in the style of Sintercom and Think Centre. Daily journalism by professional journalists is a costlier proposition, whatever the medium. Harakah Daily met this cost by sharing resources with, and receiving a cross-subsidy from, its profitable print parent. Malaysiakini, on the other hand, had no such cushion.

Chandran's original business plan, for a service tentatively called "Daily Diet," displayed an optimism that would soon prove unfounded. The project would have the advantages of "low start-up costs, minimum running costs" and was "likely to be self-sufficient within a year and return a profit within two years."[16] The next iteration, "Business Plan for Internet Based News Service," noted that the internet was cheaper than traditional media, as it would "not incur any printing or distribution costs — a million dollar saving." Its costs could be met fully from advertising revenue, he wrote. The site would contain an estimated 176 slots for banner advertisements. Advertising rates would be pegged to the number of readers. This business plan projected advertising revenue to exceed RM10,000 per week in the first quarter of operation, reaching RM80,000 per week at the end of two years. By that time, he expected that the company would rake in another RM1,000 per week in fees for hosting advertisers' web pages, and RM4,000 from classified advertising. If necessary, it would solicit sponsorships and donations. Initial development expenses were estimated at RM40,000, including

RM15,000 for computers and RM3,000 to build the website. Initial staff salaries, covering 14 editorial and administrative staff, were budgeted at RM24,000 per month.[17]

By the time the idea had been crystallized into a project proposal to be pitched to potential investors, the founders had scaled back their expectations, but only slightly. They decided to start with a smaller staff, and cut their manpower budget to just RM15,000 per month. It also decided to focus on "hard" political and economic news, and dispense with lifestyle features. However, they were still hopeful that advertising revenue would allow the site to be self-financing in a couple of years.[18] The company obtained much of its start-up capital from abroad. The Bangkok-based South-East Asian Press Alliance (SEAPA) gave a grant of US$100,000. The Media Development Loan Fund (MDLF), based in New York, paid the company RM188,000 to build a software application. In 2002, MDLF invested RM1.3 million for a 29 per cent equity stake.

International foundations supportive of democratic media were thus an indispensable source of funds for Malaysiakini. However, these injections were a political liability, as the company soon discovered. In its second year, Malaysiakini was embroiled in a controversy over its source of funds. A disgruntled former employee revealed that the website had received money from the American financier, George Soros. The link was slim and indirect: Soros' Open Society Institute was one of the groups behind MDLF. Nevertheless, in Malaysian eyes, the revelation was scandalous because the speculative activities of hedge funds such as Soros' had been blamed by the government for the collapse of the currency, the ringgit, in 1997. Mahathir had gone so far as to say that Soros was acting out a Jewish conspiracy against Malaysia: "The Jews robbed the Palestinians of everything, but in Malaysia they could not do so, hence they do this, depress the ringgit."[19]

For Malaysiakini's critics, the disclosure of its link to Soros was a windfall: the perfect opportunity to tar the troublesome website as a tool of Malaysia's enemies. Officials duly plugged this line. Asked for his comments, Mahathir questioned the website's loyalty, and said, "People who love Malaysia will not support Malaysiakini."[20] Gan and Chandran protest that the company's backers have no influence over editorial content. They made MDLF sign a pledge of non-interference, which, Gan rightly points out, is a condition the mainstream press has not required of its own shareholders. They also voluntarily limited foreign ownership to under 30 per cent, in line with the finance ministry's rule for other sectors of the economy.

While Malaysiakini appeared to exercise due diligence in ensuring no foreign interference in its operations, it was unable to choose the ideological terrain on which it was forced to do battle with the establishment. That terrain was strongly nationalistic even in the best of times, and, after the financial crisis that had decimated the country's wealth, was not unreasonably suspicious of global fund managers. Even Malaysians who did not believe Mahathir's conspiracy theory were aware that financial traders were at the very least amoral and unmoved by the harmful social effects of their deals. Malaysiakini's clarifications about its links to MDLF were no match for these deeply held attitudes. Thus, when the company announced the MDLF investment in 2002, *New Straits Times* reported it as an admission, under the headline "Malaysiakini admits receiving funds."[21] Although Malaysiakini's readers familiar with the government's scapegoating tactics are resistant to such campaigns, the smear has made it harder to gain the cooperation of establishment newsmakers and advertisers, Chandran says.[22]

From advertising to subscription

The foreign funds enabled Malaysiakini to rent premises, hire full-time staff and keep going in the short term. However, donations and grants could not be a long-term solution, Gan said, as it would mean spending a lot of time raising money instead of doing journalism. The long-term plan had been to depend on advertising revenue, which would make the site self-sustaining after two years. This never materialized. Only a handful of banner ads were sold. A multinational corporation that was among the site's first advertisers pulled out its ad, apparently under pressure from the government.[23]

In early 1999, Malaysiakini's business plan had stated:

> The reduced costs of publishing allows the news site to be made available to the public at no cost. At the time when paper prices continue to spiral and in an era of environmental conservation, the news site is a free breath of fresh air.[24]

Two years later, the company had to concede that its advertiser-supported model had failed, and that it would have to start charging readers. This was a worldwide trend in online journalism. As advertisers became less convinced that banner ads worked, and investors lost patience, many commercial online publications folded. Those that did not, like the pioneering American online magazine Salon.com, began charging for access. The ones that remained free were those cross-subsidized by print or broadcast operations, such as the websites of mainstream media companies, or by non-media activities, such as Microsoft's Slate.com.

In Malaysiakini's revised business model, half of its income would come from subscriptions. It would count on advertisements for only 20 per cent of its revenue. Technology services, such as managing the content of other companies' websites, would provide another 20 per cent, and the remaining 10 per cent would be derived from *Analysis Malaysia*, its new intelligence service for high-end clients paying US$1,000 a year. Chandran says that a readership survey showed that people had come to understand that they could not expect the news service for free, and that "hardcore readers" were willing to pay. In February 2002, it began charging for access to its opinion pieces. News and letters remained free. By late March, it had fewer than 800 subscribers, about 20 per cent below its expectations.[25]

In August of the same year, Malaysiakini became a by-subscription-only site. Visitors could view the front page and peruse letters, but to read any story or column in full, they would have to log-in with their user name and password. Standard subscription rates are RM10 per month or RM100 a year. (For comparison, the newsstand price of *New Straits Times* is RM1.20.) The premium subscription rate of RM300 a year provides access to the archives in addition to current content.

Gan's editorial announcing the end of free content was a plaintive appeal to readers to chip in to support independent journalism. He noted that most online publications were in dire straits, unless they were bankrolled by print operations. However, the print option was out of the question because of the government's licensing barrier.

> [W]e are now forced to face a Hobson's choice: Lock up the website [giving the key only to paying subscribers] and stand to lose our readers — and there is no guarantee we can still survive — or continue to keep malaysiakini free until we bite the dust in the coming months. The journalists in malaysiakini have made our choice. We now leave it to our readers to make theirs. And when all is said and done, we get the media we deserve.[26]

A month later, Malaysiakini had under 1,500 subscribers, and Gan acknowledged that it was unlikely to reach its year-end target of 5,000.[27] In early 2003, it had around 2,000. It needed 10,000 to be fully self-financing. As at mid-2003, practically the only subscription news sites internationally that turned a profit were those offering specialized industry news or business intelligence. The news media industry had yet to find a way to persuade readers to pay for political or general news on the web. Malaysiakini was no exception.

The Political Challenge

While their original business plan said that the internet was subject to "no legal controls," Chandran and Gan themselves probably did not believe this claim.[28] "I've never believed the hype. I got into the internet because it was the only avenue I had," Gan says. He adds that they warned new recruits that they would probably face harassment from the authorities, and urged them to get their families' support before joining the project.[29] The first Malaysiakini writer to feel the government's wrath was a columnist, Hishamuddin Rais, who was arrested under the Internal Security Act in April 2001. Although the police interrogated him about some of his articles, his detention was not the result of anything he wrote for the website, but was connected to his role as a Reformasi protest organizer. Although officials occasionally leveled threats in the press against Malaysiakini, they generally kept their distance. "We never get threatening phonecalls from the authorities, perhaps because they know the moment they do that, we'll report it," Gan said in 2002.[30]

Gan and Chandran knew the reprieve had nothing to do with any sincere liberalization in the government's stand towards its critics. Rather, it was trying to impress potential investors in its Multimedia Super Corridor. Not all branches of government were in tune with this mission; some officials expressed their frustration with online dissent by threatening to intervene. There were evident tensions between ministries over the right approach to take. "So far it looks like the multimedia ministry has been able to talk some sense into the others," Gan said in 2001. Chandran adds that the culture in the Multimedia Development Corporation is different from the "feudalistic" older ministries. It is more open and has younger people. The multimedia agencies were "quite friendly," he says. The National IT Council has invited him to discussions along with opposition politicians and NGOs.[31]

The Malaysian police has been the least tolerant department, maintaining a blanket ban preventing Malaysiakini reporters from attending its press conferences. Its ill-will could be due to the journalists' record — dating back to when Malaysiakini's founders were at *The Sun* — of investigating police treatment of people in custody. The website is also handicapped by the authorities' refusal to give press passes to its reporters. The government's logic is simple. Accreditation is the privilege of organizations with media licenses. As Malaysiakini operates without a license, it is not entitled to press passes. Whether it can attend government functions thus depends on the issue and the minister. Some ministers, such as Mahathir's deputy and eventual successor Abdullah Badawi, were known to wave-in Malaysiakini reporters refused entry by civil servants.[32] Abdullah's special assistant, Khairy Jamaludin, said he would usually tell the minister's press secretary to grant access. There are exceptions, as when US Secretary of State Colin Powell called on the deputy prime minister in 2002. Thus, while Malaysiakini's existence is tolerated, "it doesn't mean we like them or have to make life easy for them," Khairy says.[33]

The authorities' sliver of toleration finally snapped in early 2003. A debate had been raging in the website's letters section over whether it was time to dismantle the special privileges of ethnic Malays. Although sparked by the prime minister's own remarks a few months earlier that Malays should get off their "crutches," the temperature of the exchanges on the website began to rise. One letter attacked the youth wing of the ruling Malay nationalist party, UMNO Youth, likening it to the Ku Klux Klan in the United States. The writer went by the pen name, Petrof. On Friday, January 17, incensed leaders of UMNO Youth lodged a police report against Petrof, accusing him or her of sedition. The following Monday, a 10-man police team arrived at Malaysiakini's offices, demanding to know Petrof's e-mail address. The editors refused, explaining that they had assured contributors that their anonymity would be protected. Officers and editors sat in the company's conference room to discuss the impasse. The police said that if the writer's identity was not revealed, they would have no choice but to confiscate all of Malaysiakini's computers for further investigation. The editors replied that there was no need to take all the hardware, as only one computer was related to their investigation. According to Gan, the officer in charge at the scene, from the local computer crime unit, was initially amenable to this idea. "But eventually it appeared that the decision was not theirs to make. The directive from the top was to take it all," Gan said.[34]

They seized 19 computers in all, effectively shutting down the site. Malaysiakini's technical team was able to use a back-up server at another location to get the site up again within 10 hours. Following widespread and almost instantaneous protests, police returned six computers two days later. The same day, however, Malaysiakini was dealt another blow. Its landlord served the company with an eviction order, because the website "had been found to be involved in activities which contravene the laws of the country." The building was owned by PC Suria, a computer distributor with links to the government. The landlord backed down in the face of additional protests.

Although the raid on Malaysiakini was characterized by its journalists, supporters and foreign media as a dark day for press freedom in Malaysia, its significance remains shrouded in doubt. It is unclear whether it represented a reversal of the government's no-censorship commitment. One theory is that neither UMNO Youth nor the police cleared their actions with Mahathir, who was abroad at the time. A columnist in the establishment *New Straits Times* took this view, describing the affair as a "debacle" and criticizing UMNO Youth for its "lack of maturity."[35] The national news agency, Bernama, later carried a report quoting a western author who cited the incident as an example of poor public communication, pinning the blame on junior officials too eager to impress their seniors.[36]

It is also possible that the top leaders did approve of the crackdown initially, but quickly distanced themselves from it once its effects became clear. It was, in short, an unmitigated public relations disaster. In addition to being reported widely in the region, the raid earned a scathing article in *The Economist*, and briefs in *The New York Times* and *The Wall Street Journal*.[37] One of the region's

most influential business papers, *The Asian Wall Street Journal*, hit
Mahathir where it hurt — his beloved Multimedia Super Corridor.
It led its report with the line, "Malaysia's commitment to avoid
censoring the Internet, part of its bid to lure high-tech investment,
faces scrutiny after police raided the offices of independent online
news site Malaysiakini.com this week."[38]

Whatever the inside story, the incident confirms two of the key
points made in Chapter 3. First, most practitioners of contentious
journalism in Malaysia and Singapore are fully within the reach of
the authorities, whether they operate offline or in cyberspace. Second,
the authorities' decisions are fundamentally political calculations, and
not dictated by the technology.

Mobilizing Social Networks

One of the most remarkable aspects of the police raid on Malaysiakini
was the speed and intensity of the internet-assisted protests that
arose in response. This was one of the clearest manifestations of
the power of contentious journalism as a social movement. Gan
and Chandran had been aware from the start that they were part
of something larger that they could draw sustenance from as well as
contribute to. "We are very much part of a movement," Chandran
says. They were linked to multiple networks. Intellectually and
emotionally, they identified with Malaysia's human rights NGOs,
environmentalists, drama groups, and progressive public intellectuals.
Chandran describes their shared values:

> We believe Malaysia is ripe for a cultural change, a change in
> thinking. We're ready to confront issues that have hidden in
> the shadows, serving the status quo. We're entering a new era
> of nation-building.[39]

In addition, they were closely tied to other Malaysians engaging
in contentious journalism and advocating press reform. They were
involved in Charter 2000, an alliance for media reform, and KAMI,

an alliance of independent journalists. This does not mean that there was a perfect coincidence of agendas. Chandran notes that Harakah, the Islamic party's organ, was "not necessarily in the same boat — they tend to skirt around some issues."[40] Nonetheless, it was an important ally. Even at the business plan stage, Chandran was counting on *Harakah* to help publicize their project.[41]

The third network that Malaysiakini plugged into was international: it developed close links to overseas groups that championed press freedom. Gan's Bangkok stint had put him in contact with the South-east Asian Press Alliance, which provided start-up funding. In his days at *The Sun*, he had been adopted as a prisoner of conscience by the London-based Amnesty International during a brief period in detention. After launching Malaysiakini, he was named by the Committee to Protect Journalists in New York as one of four recipients of its International Press Freedom Award in 2000.

On the afternoon of January 20, 2003, with the police officers in their offices, all it took was a few phone-calls for this elaborate and far-flung network to be activated. Before the police left, a producer at RadiqRadio, an independent web radio station, had already alerted everyone on its mailing list. Steven Gan's own message was out on the Charter 2000 mailing list by evening. Well-wishers came forward immediately to donate computers. Hours after the raid, 200 people held a candlelight vigil outside the Malaysiakini office.[42]

Before the day's end, Amnesty International, Paris-based Reporters Without Borders, and Malaysia's own Aliran had issued statements condemning the raid. From Thailand the same day, the chairman of SEAPA wrote to prime minister Mahathir, warning that "the country's international reputation would be gravely tarnished" unless the government apologized for the raid, returned the computers, and spared Malaysiakini any legal sanction. The next day, the Committee to Protect Journalists also wrote to the prime minister, protesting that Malaysiakini was only "upholding the internationally accepted standards of a free press in facilitating public discussion of controversial issues."

Within a week, Aliran and two other local human rights groups launched a joint appeal "to all concerned Malaysians to support urgently and generously the nation's only independent newspaper, malaysiakini.com in its hour of need." The NGOs asked the public to donate directly to Malaysiakini's bank account, or purchase subscriptions. By March, the donation drive had raised more than RM35,000.

Surviving the Calm

The month that Malaysiakini turned to full-subscription mode, Khairy Jamaludin, special assistant to the deputy prime minister and a rising star in UMNO, recalled that the government had been "annoyed" by the website the year before. It had resisted the temptation to do anything, because it wanted to preserve its IT-friendly reputation.[43] In a chilling reminder of the censoring power of the free market, Khairy noted with wry amusement the website's commercial troubles:

> We read Malaysiakini, but decided that we couldn't do anything about it. Now, you're seeing a process of natural selection in IT. Malaysiakini has been dying. It's moved to a subscription model, and it's fighting for its survival. I'm glad we didn't do anything to close down the site. The market may do it for us.[44]

Five months later, Khairy, an office holder in UMNO Youth, would find himself embarrassed by the police raid. A column in *New Straits Times* pointed out what he already knew:

> It would... have helped if Umno Youth had done some background research on Malaysiakini, which, financially, was in dire straits. ... What Umno Youth did by lodging the report that led to the police raid was to give Malaysiakini a lifeline. A Malaysian working for a foreign mission said: 'Now, given the attention it is getting from the international community, Malaysiakini will probably win some award, apart from getting

financial support from those sympathetic to its cause. If Umno Youth had not been so hasty, Malaysiakini would have, in the not-too-distant future, died a natural death.' Looking at the way Malaysiakini has managed to use the raid to its advantage, it is getting back quite a lot of support.[45]

Despite this surge in interest, in the middle of its fourth year, it remained unclear whether Malaysiakini's ambition to be a commercially viable independent news source would ever be achieved. If the company folds, it would support some scholars' contention that journalism is a case of "market failure." C. Edwin Baker says that the market fails because:

> ... the products that prevail in the unregulated market often do not adequately serve intense political and informational interests, especially of smaller groups. It also fails because it does not take account of huge positive externalities in speech's contribution to democracy, an institution or practice whose proper functioning people value. And the unregulated market fails because it does not appropriately identify, and is too inegalitarian in weighing, people's desires for democratically relevant speech.[46]

The internet has not altered that reality. Subsidies — in the form of massive investments in network infrastructure and software development by governments, research agencies and private corporations — have reduced the individual web publisher's cost of distribution to almost zero. However, to maintain a staff of fulltime journalists remains expensive, whether online or offline, and the cost of even a small team like Malaysiakini's seems to be more than readers are willing to bear. People's willingness to pay for contentious journalism rises during times of crisis, as when overt government repression activates their political senses. In Malaysia's hegemonic politics, however, most people's memories are short and their lives invariably return to an apolitical calm after even after the most tumultuous of times. Paradoxically, therefore, Malaysiakini's greatest challenge has not been how to survive the attacks, but how to endure the truce.

CHAPTER 9

CONTENTIOUS MEDIA IN COMPARATIVE PERSPECTIVE

In 2002, Harvard University's Center for International Development released the results of a study ranking 75 countries' preparedness and potential to participate in a networked world. The "Networked Readiness Index" placed Singapore at number 8, the only country outside North America and Europe in the top 10. Malaysia was ranked number 36 out of the 75.[1] Neither Singapore's sterling showing nor Malaysia's middling rank was surprising. Their relative standings in the survey reflected the income gap between them — Singaporeans earn five times more than Malaysians on average — and were in line with previously published hard data. For example, in 2000, Singapore had 32 internet users and 48 personal computers per 100 inhabitants, while Malaysia had 17 and 9, respectively. In absolute terms, Malaysia was five times as populous as Singapore but had only three times the number of internet users: 4 million versus 1.3 million.[2] Based on aggregate data, Singapore's technological superiority over Malaysia is obvious and unambiguous.

Now, the paradox: It is Malaysia, not Singapore, that is home to the more developed contentious online journalism. Malaysia's main alternative websites reach more than 100,000 people; Singapore's measure their visitors in the thousands, or hundreds. Malaysia has at least three alternative sites employing fulltime staff; Singapore has none. Malaysia's leading sites produce daily news updates; in Singapore, a website can consider itself on a roll if it adds a new article once a week. These striking differences between the two countries add up to a participation/penetration paradox: On every conceivable yardstick, the intensity of participation in contentious online journalism is inversely related to the technology's penetration. Explaining this paradox will be one of the goals of this penultimate chapter.

While this study has treated contentious journalism projects as belonging to an identifiable social movement, there are significant differences within the movement that need to be explored. This should not be surprising, as every social movement is marked by internal diversity. In addition to differences between the two countries, there are also major differences among the four groups, as should have become obvious from the case studies. In some instances, those differences are fundamental enough to threaten the groups' solidarity — a theme that will be picked up in the concluding chapter. This should not be surprising. Contentious journalism, this book has argued, occurs in a network akin to a social movement, and every social movement is marked by internal diversity as well as coherence. In this chapter, we explore the differences between the groups, comparing them in the light of the concepts introduced in Chapter 4. The reader will recall from that chapter that the scholarship on alternative media and on social movements provides useful heuristics with which to understand contentious online journalism. The alternative media literature suggests that there are different dimensions of alternativeness, and that various combinations of these may yield quite different outcomes. The social movements literature offers the political process perspective as a way to think about how movements emerge and develop, focusing not only on environmental factors but also on the actual work done by activists. These concepts provided a loose framework for the case studies, but the preceding four chapters have been driven by narrative and an attention to the details of each group's unique history. Here, we engage in more systematic comparison. Drawing on the case studies, we can try to arrive at some generalizations about contentious journalism and the internet.

Alternative Strategies for Alternative Media

The four groups examined in this book challenge the status quo not only through what they say, but also in the ways they say it. They organize themselves differently from mainstream media, in some cases because they have no choice, in others because they appreciate that form should follow function, and that their internal structures and norms should be congruent with their mission to democratize communication. In Chapter 4, it was suggested that alternative media could differentiate themselves by radically abandoning or reinterpreting the mainstream norms of professionalism, hierarchical organization, and capitalization. However, it is clear that questions of strategy and structure have no easy answers. There is no obvious form that alternative media should take, even if there is agreement about the functions they should serve. Each approach has costs as well as benefits; every group must contend not only with external opponents but also with the limitations and contradictions of their chosen strategies. In a sense, these groups are grappling with unresolved issues that have plagued journalism from the start. The following pages focus on three of these issues, stated in the form choices that publishers and journalists must make. The first is the choice of journalistic principles, in particular between objective disinterest on the one hand, and a commitment to particular causes or parties on the other. Second, they must choose their level of dependence on capital, and whether to meet that requirement through internal resources, the market, or institutional sponsors. Third, there are various alternative internal arrangements to pick from, affecting the degree of internal democracy within the organization, and the independence of editors from owners. These choices are closely related. For example, partisan journalists would be more comfortable with the idea of ceding some autonomy to, and accepting funds from, the organizations representing their chosen cause. On the other hand, the ideal of disinterestedness is logically associated with a wariness of external funding and influence — although in practice, the influence of capital is often a blind spot among journalists who adhere to this principle.

Disinterested or cause-driven?

Objectivity and disinterestedness have become part of the core values of professional journalism worldwide. The news is supposed to be reported free of bias, with journalists observing reality from a distance, striving for factual accuracy, and keeping their own opinions out of their stories. Among the four groups studied, Malaysiakini operates closest to these norms. It does not challenge conventional notions of professionalism, but instead aspires to beat the mainstream press at its own game, by being more objective, more balanced, more accurate. Sintercom, which is less news-driven, also nods at convention by maintaining a certain neutrality in its editorial position. Think Centre and Harakah follow different traditions. Harakah, although stylistically indistinguishable from mainstream news media, calls itself a party mouthpiece — a label that would make most mainstream journalists cringe. Think Centre follows the advocacy model, championing a slate of progressive issues. Not only do its reports drip with their writers' opinions about the reality out there, they reflect the writers' deliberate interventions in that reality. They break down the barriers between news and commentary, and even between news reporter and news maker.

A neutral stance has important merits. Heterogeneous, divided societies need common spaces for discussion of common concerns.

News media that strive for disinterested journalism are more likely to be accepted as honest brokers between groups. However, trying to sit on the fence can seem almost irresponsible in situations where societal problems are acute and urgent. In such circumstances, it could be argued that the point is not to report on the world, but to change it. In that light, journalists subscribing to the advocacy or partisan model appear more conscious of their civic duty. On the down side, Think Centre and Harakah show the risks of such an approach. Think Centre has sometimes appeared self-indulgent, as if its main cause is its own institutional interests rather than some larger principle. Such tendencies would have been filtered out by the instinct of professional objectivity, which imposes self-restraint on journalists and a focus on the perspectives and interests of people other than themselves. Harakah, meanwhile, can be accused of not reporting critically enough on PAS. This would be less of an issue if its parent organization were relatively small and unimportant. PAS, however, has shown that it is capable of gaining control of Malaysia's state governments, at the very least. Harakah's partisanship is a problem to the extent that it prevents it from speaking truth to the power that is PAS.

Dot-com or dot-org?

The choice of business model has far-reaching consequences. Sintercom consciously opted for a non-commercial strategy, deciding that it did not want to be held hostage by the market. Its vow of abstinence in an increasingly profit-driven medium was especially a burden in Singapore, which, unlike other industrialized societies, does not have a tradition of grant-giving or philanthropy towards politically-oriented or advocacy-type work. Its dot-org strategy thus confined it to an increasingly marginal existence in the fast-expanding internet in Singapore. As long as it remained small, however, it had the merit of being easily sustainable. Both Sintercom and Think Centre are sporadically updated. Their resource requirements are therefore minimal compared with Malaysiakini and Harakah, which are daily news media with a high proportion of original content. While most readers would probably say that they are more impressed by the latter two sites, few seem prepared to put their money where their mouths are by paying for content. This is especially so with the internet, which has spoiled audiences with free content. The strategy of Sintercom and Think Centre is one rational response: keep costs so low that they can be borne out of the group's own resources.

The two Malaysian sites have taken the more ambitious route. The Harakah model is viable as long as its parent organization considers the cross-subsidy from its profitable operations to be money well spent. Malaysiakini aims to be self-sustaining — a goal that has so far eluded it. Traditionally, the main concern about accepting commercial sponsorship and advertising is the influence those corporations may exert over editorial operations. Malaysiakini's concern is less subtle: it is simply not getting enough revenue to survive for long. Its financial woes are an example of the market failure that plagues the news media industry worldwide. Despite Malaysiakini's drawing more than 100,000 readers, the market may be unable to sustain its existence.

Institutionalization or informality?

The issue of internal governance was handled differently by the four sites, as their leaders tried to find the right balance between internal democracy and control. Sintercom had the flattest structure. At one stage, there were more than 20 editors independently running sections of the website, and it had a minimally moderated discussion board. The absence of central control was modeled on the founders' understanding of what the internet itself was like. Informality had its costs. Unwilling to conform to the conventional structure of an organization, it could not register itself as a society, which in turn meant that it could not raise funds from the public.[3] Furthermore, without an institutionalized leadership structure, the site went through long stretches of inactivity, as editors slipped away to do other things. The tragedy of the commons, after all, is that instead of everybody taking responsibility for what is collectively owned, nobody does. On the other hand, it could be said that a spirit of openness was what enabled Sintercom to obtain a new lease of life overseas: no complicated negotiations or transactions were required to transfer Sintercom's content to new managers. In contrast, when commercial web publications die — as many did in the dot-com crash — their content usually disappears into a black hole, along with their corporate existence.

Think Centre adopted a strategy of gradual but steady institutionalization. Starting out as a sole proprietorship owned by James Gomez, it took on four additional partners in 2000. Gomez then removed himself as a partner, after which Think Centre de-registered itself as a business firm and registered as a society run by committee. It was necessary to "de-James-Gomez" the organization, the founder himself says. There are signs that it has successfully transformed itself from a personality-driven to a more institutionalized group, with a regular turnover of positions. Management by committee is of course not as swift as a one-man-show, and the website is not as responsive as it could be to current events, Gomez notes. To address this problem, all executive committee members can independently update the site.

Malaysiakini and Harakah have more traditionally organized newsrooms, with clear lines of authority. Both editors maintain that their reporters enjoy more autonomy than they would in a mainstream newspaper. Steven Gan says that some of his reporters have activist backgrounds that — with his blessings — influence their choice of stories to chase. His own radical background has meant that he expects his staff to "ask tough questions out there, but also internally."[4] Based on their staff sizes alone, it is not difficult to believe that a cub reporter would have a greater say within Harakah or Malaysiakini than in *New Straits Times* or *Utusan Malaysia*, for example. The two alternative media organizations are small enough for their entire newsrooms to participate in editorial meetings.

Another institutional factor is editors' degree of independence from publishers or owners. Sintercom and Malaysiakini can be described as self-governing media, their editors answering to nobody but themselves, since they also own the publications. Thinkcentre.org and Harakah Daily editors serve at the pleasure of the Think Centre executive committee and the PAS leadership respectively. There are trade-offs either way. The latter two sites enjoy institutional resources that arguably compensate for their lack of editorial independence.

Comparing Political Processes

In the political process perspective, social movements are said to depend on, first, favorable shifts in political opportunities; second, the mobilization of resources; and, third, cultural framing work by activists. These three concepts help to explain the dynamics of contentious online journalism.

Political opportunity structure

In Chapter 3, we saw that the internet's introduction precipitated a shift in political opportunities for media activists, because it was less amenable to narrowly tailored political controls than were earlier media technologies. Attracted by its value as economic infrastructure, the two governments reconciled themselves to a more liberal internet policy regime. The internet became the only mass medium for which producers did not need a permit. Thus, the internet has been a boon for contentious journalism. By the early 2000s, it has become somewhat unfashionable to say this. The intellectual trend is to bemoan the internet's lost innocence, constrained by government controls on one side, and corrupted by commercial values on the other. Fortunately, however, there still remains space for alternative media on the internet, not to dominate but at least to exist. The medium's potential for alternative communication has been more resilient than that of radio, whose limited spectrum has been more completely colonized by the powerful.

It is important to emphasize that the activists' expectations of the medium were modest. Malaysiakini, when appealing to readers to support its subscription drive, made this point abundantly clear: it was forced to use the internet because the options were even worse. In an editorial, Steven Gan related the plight of a fellow independent publisher, Ahmad Lutfi Othman, who had chosen the print route instead.[5] After his news magazine, *Detik*, lost its publishing license, Lutfi ingeniously explored a loophole in the press law. Since licenses were required for periodicals but not one-off publications, Lutfi began producing a series of what looked like one-time tabloids, each with a different masthead. They were recognizable as his work because of their uniform layout. Selling around 50,000 copies per issue, his publications were able to support him and the staff of the banned *Detik*.

> But loophole or not, the authorities eventually stepped in. Vendors who sold Lutfi's publications were harassed. A number were hauled to court for selling 'illegal' printing materials. Lutfi offered to pay their fines — totalling between RM20,000 and RM30,000 — as a gesture of goodwill. Still, many vendors were spooked. The death blow came last October when Home Ministry officials raided the printing plant and confiscated truckloads of his latest edition. Lutfi lost RM50,000 and slipped into debt. Soon after, he ceased publication. On every May 3 — World Press Freedom Day — Lufti made it a point to visit the Human Rights Commission, or Suhakam, to lodge complaints against the government's harassment. Last year, he was accompanied by his 30-odd staff. This year, he had only two with him — the rest were retrenched. 'Next year, there could be no one left to make the complaints,' he lamented.[6]

Gan still maintains that he would have preferred to start a newspaper than a website. People are more prepared to pay for print than for online content. However, the political opportunity was greater in cyberspace than in print. Even as the governments in Malaysia and Singapore show themselves increasingly willing to crack down on online dissent, the internet continues to be relatively more hospitable to contentious journalism, compared with print and broadcast platforms.

One of the advantages of the internet was that its arrival was associated with the emergence of allies within the elite: officials who championed new technology and recognized the activists as techno-entrepreneurs to be encouraged and nurtured. As we saw in the Malaysiakini case, this was the case with officials of the multimedia ministry and the National Information Technology Council in Malaysia. In Singapore, Sintercom's founder acknowledged the godfather role played by Philip Yeo. One of Singapore's highest-ranking civil servants, and more influential than some ministers, Yeo was an information technology pioneer. In the early 1980s, he built up the IT capabilities of the defense ministry, which eventually became the prototype for Singapore's public sector computerization program. One of his legendary stunts in the early days was buying the defense ministry's first IBM mainframe computer under the guise of an "intermediate business machine" because only the finance ministry at the time was allowed to have a mainframe or its own IT department.[7] Yeo does not bother to conceal his contempt for his stuffier colleagues in the public sector. A maverick by temperament and a technologist by conviction, he was a natural ally when Sintercom moved from the US to Singapore, and when it was staving off the regulators in 1996.

Political opportunities are never absolute or permanent. As highlighted in Chapter 3, the legal loophole that activists exploit in Malaysia and Singapore — the unique absence of prior restraints in the form of discretionary government permits or licenses — is a function of regulators' political assessments, and not inherent in technology of the internet. Government calculations can change, making repression more attractive. Elite allies can lose interest, or lose influence. Activists in Malaysia and Singapore also know that elections are always preceded by a tightening of controls. Ruling parties' concern for their international reputation takes a back seat; their priority becomes hemming in challengers and dissenters in the months running up to an election. Thus, in the six months prior to Singapore's November 2001 general election, the government insisted that Sintercom register itself as a political site, and introduced new regulations on election advertising, which it immediately targeted at Think Centre's site.

Mobilization

Resource mobilization is the second main ingredient for social movement emergence and growth. All four case studies underscore the value of networks for the mobilization of resources. Comparing the groups' experiences, a few other tentative conclusions can be offered. First, virtual and real communities both play important roles, although it cannot be assumed that both are equally effective. It is true that Sintercom grew out of the online community of soc.culture. singapore participants, and was itself mainly an online phenomenon. Its founders' wonderment at the power of the virtual connections was not misplaced. To sustain a project across three continents, with hardly any face-to-face interaction, was no mean feat. But, perhaps that was one reason why it was *not* sustained, at least not in its original form. When Tan Chong Kee decided to abandon the site in August 2001, the community murmured sympathetically, but there was no concerted rescue bid. The anonymous individual who took over Sintercom's content a month or two later and relaunched it as New Sintercom was not a member of the SGDaily mailing list, where discussions about the site's fate were taking place.

> I just happened to visit the site. I had visited it a couple of times
> before that, but I was never an active member of the community.
> I found it rather disappointing initially that for all the 'strength'
> of the Sintercom community, it had to take an 'outsider' like

myself in order to come and attempt to revive it. I don't know why no one else of the original community had the guts, the moral courage, (or maybe the web skills) to do it themselves.[8]

Compare Sintercom with Harakah Daily — embedded within the network of one of the region's most highly mobilized opposition parties — and the relative weakness of the former's virtual community is plain to see. Harakah's writers and readers may adhere to some other-worldly, transcendent beliefs — in that sense, all religious groups are virtual communities — but their loyalty and drive also derive from regular face-to-face interactions at mosques and meetings, and the door-to-door, village-to-village struggles of a grassroots political party. Of course, few readers would be surprised by the conclusion that, all other things being equal, people's commitment to online communities is not as high as to face-to-face ones. It bears emphasizing only because of the tendency in the literature to conflate the internet's value as a tool of political dissent with its role in virtual communities. As noted in Chapter 1, most case studies of radical internet use have focused on how activists and dissidents employ the technology to transcend space, either to stay clear of the police's physical reach or to coordinate their actions with partners far away. In such cases, the internet user's relationships with others are primarily and necessarily virtual. Face-to-face interactions threaten the underground dissident's security, and are impractical for the transnational activist. In Malaysia and Singapore, however, contentious online journalism is largely practiced in the midst of real communities. In such contexts, activists are more successful when they develop and exploit offline social networks, instead of getting seduced by virtual communities.

A related observation is that networks of individuals may not be as effective or resilient as networks of networks. Contentious journalism projects appear most promising when their supporting networks comprise pre-existing organizations rather than isolated individuals. Organizations bring superior ideological as well as material resources to the table. It is not for nothing that authoritarian regimes abhor independent organizations, as Adam Przeworski has noted. People power is not about the massing of disaffected individuals or the breakdown of state legitimacy. It is about the "organization of counterhegemony" through "collective projects for an alternative future": "Only when collective alternatives are available does political choice become available to isolated individuals," Przeworski says.[9] Our case studies have provided several examples of how contentious journalism has benefited from supportive organizations. Aliran, Malaysia's human rights NGO, has not only served as an important source of alternative news and comment, but also lobbied on behalf of independent journalists. In Singapore, Socratic Circle, Roundtable and the Open Singapore Centre were key institutional partners for Think Centre's programs.

Working with political parties can be especially advantageous. Not only do parties tend to have more material resources than civil society organizations, their members also possess stronger ideological commitments. In Malaysia and Singapore, joining an opposition party is an invitation to closer scrutiny and possible harassment by the state. This limits the size and influence of opposition parties, but also means that those who actually do join them tend to be intensely committed and resilient. On the one hand, the fear factor can make opposition links a liability for media activists. When Think Centre announced that its members were going to put up candidates for the coming general election (an April Fool's joke, it said later), several individuals demanded to be removed immediately from its mailing list — such is the fear of being seen to support in any way an opposition-linked site. On the other hand, while a media organization may thus lose the fickle and the feckless, it may gain in quality of support what it gives up in quantity. James Gomez appeared to recognize this, shifting Think Centre's alliances away from non-partisan groups and towards political parties. Malaysiakini, which has stuck resolutely with its independent non-partisan model, has also discovered the strength of opposition party loyalties the hard way. "When we ran articles critical of an opposition party, we would get party members calling for a boycott of our website," said its former news editor, Fathi Omar.[10]

A final observation on the theme of resources and mobilization has to do with the degree of dependence on the internet. As noted in Chapter 1, the case-study literature suggests that internet users are technologically promiscuous, though this fact is seldom acknowledged by the authors and has yet to be worked into theory-building. The four case studies in this work confirm that technological promiscuity pays. The two most robust projects among the four are Think Centre and Harakah, both of which engage in contentious communication through multiple channels. Diversification helps because contentious journalism is threatened constantly by both the state and the market. Both Sintercom and Malaysiakini have suffered from being internet "pure plays," to borrow dot-com jargon. A change in internet regulations caused Sintercom to wind up its operations, while Malaysiakini was silenced for half a day when police seized its computers. Even if left alone by the authorities, Malaysiakini's survival is under severe threat from market forces. Most news sites in Malaysia and the world are cross-subsidized by profitable print and broadcast parent media. Like Salon.com in the US — and countless others that have already died — Malaysiakini struggles as a standalone website.

Cultural framing

In addition to providing alternative news and views, contentious media also engage in a second level of communicative praxis. As predicted by the political process perspective, the four groups had to work hard to frame their struggles in a way that would inspire and motivate both insiders and followers. The internet emerged as an important symbol, though to varying degrees and with varying meaning. It was especially important to Sintercom, some of whose members argued in terms of libertarian values that they associated with the technology. Although several writers have challenged the assumption that the internet has an inherent affinity to libertarianism — or any ism — the point here is that activists made rhetorical use of that image to further their goals, especially to argue against government intervention. Indeed, the political opportunity structure analyzed above was affected by this particular cultural frame: the two governments had to factor the symbolic power of the internet into their policy calculations.

For Think Centre and Harakah — which were not exclusively, or even mainly, internet organizations — using the internet helped to enhance their sense of efficacy, and their image as active, forward-looking organizations. For Harakah in particular, the embrace of the latest technology helped to signal to Malaysians and the world that the brand of fundamentalist Islam championed by PAS was modern and open. PAS was not prepared to concede to Mahathir the mantle of Malaysian modernizer. Therefore, even if most of its supporters did not use the internet, it was with some satisfaction that it announced that Harakah Daily would be the first news site in the country to incorporate web TV, for example.

The strategic use of internet hype by media activists has an important implication for research. One needs to distinguish between their rhetoric and their private beliefs. Take Malaysiakini as an example. At no time did its founders really believe that the internet would give them immunity from government retribution. They knew they were personally at risk, and warned the individuals they hired that they would have be prepared for punishment. In their public communication, however, it was in Malaysiakini's interest to milk the hype about the internet's power. The world's media at the time were hungry for examples of how the internet was undermining authoritarian regimes. "We rode the publicity wave," Gan says. "The exposure helped a lot."[11] (The contrast with Lutfi Othman's print titles is telling. Lutfi's experiment was at least as bold and ingenious as Malaysiakini, but it has received little international media attention, partly because he did not work in English, but also because print was not as sexy as the internet.) When research takes media activists' marketing pitches at face value, it risks making them out to be more naïve than they really are. It also contributes to the pendulum-like assessments of the internet's impact. The hype, strategically encouraged by activists, fueled exaggerated predictions of revolutionary change, which were followed — when revolution did not materialize — by equally sweeping claims that everything had stayed the same. When one discounts the rhetoric, it becomes clear that the reality on the ground has always been and will continue to be one of struggle and uncertainty.

The case studies also suggest that the internet had depreciating value as a cultural frame. It was most powerful in the early years, when it was novel, exciting, almost magical. As its use proliferated, it became normal, mundane, even taken for granted. This, of course, was what the prophets and early adopters had predicted: that the technology would eventually be woven invisibly into the fabric of life. As this happened, the internet was dropped from activists' rhetoric. Increasingly, their struggle was framed in the language of democracy and human rights. An example is Malaysiakini's editorial appealing for subscriptions, quoted above, which spoke of the internet as a medium of last resort.[12]

The editorial was also an example of another frame used by all four groups: that of the righteous underdog. All the groups realized that if they could not avoid repression, they had might as well milk it to draw sympathy for themselves and their cause, rather than suffer in silence. The underdog frame is, of course, the one that is most readily available to any social movement, and contentious media are no exception. Until they succeed in their insurgency and become the mainstream, they can always count on the fact that they are marginalized and weaker than establishment institutions. Even if a group fails to stay afloat, it can at least go down in a way that makes a point on behalf of the larger cause. Thus, Tan Chong Kee says his last-gasp public exchange with the regulators was intended in part to expose the government's insincerity in inviting Singaporeans to participate in national affairs.

It is, to me, clearly absurd to demand that a webmaster take full personal responsibility for all content while refusing to answer enquiries as to what content authorities deem unacceptable. This is the crux of that matter because it demonstrates that self-censorship is state-induced. Before and after Sintercom, the Singapore state continues to chant, 'speak up, get involved, don't be a quitter.' Sintercom took up that challenge at face value. And it is the state that made it impossible for us to continue with any integrity. If the closing of Sintercom accomplishes nothing else, it should be a marker for this crucial point. Only if the problem is clearly marked can we ever hope to begin addressing it.[13]

Ideally, of course, most groups would want to survive rather than suffer martyrdom. For such groups, making effective use of the underdog frame is not a straightforward matter. Two conflicting objectives come into play. On the one hand, social movement leaders need to convince their followers and bystander publics that the status quo is unjust and a cause for moral indignation. This goal is well served by portraying themselves as a downtrodden lot. On the other hand, leaders need to demonstrate efficacy, showing that theirs is not an utterly futile cause, that determined and diligent contention can make a difference. The role of helpless victim is incompatible with this objective. A David *v.* Goliath image is a powerful one, but only because David won against the odds. If he *had* been favored to win — or if he had lost — his battle with Goliath would not have been mythologized as an inspirational tale. That, in a nutshell, is the social movement activist's Catch-22 dilemma when framing its struggle: how to demonstrate potency while still drawing sympathy.

Think Centre's unusual approach is probably the most interesting response to this challenge. Deliberately cheeky in many of its confrontations, it adopted the attitude that even if you are a victim, you don't need to act like one. Its "watching the watchers" stunts were a product of such thinking. By turning cameras on surveillance agents, it achieved a number of things simultaneously. First, it reminded Singaporeans of what many prefer to forget: that the state spies on its citizens with impunity. Second, it suggested that its own activities were making enough of an impact for them to become targets of surveillance. And, third, it showed that, instead of cowering under the state's scrutiny, it could answer back — not on equal terms, by any means, but at least enough to break a psychological barrier.

The Penetration/Participation Paradox

The checklist of questions suggested by the political process perspective can help us understand why contentious online journalism is more developed in Malaysia than in Singapore. At first glance, differences in internet content regulation seem to provide a sufficient explanation. Malaysia has a no-censorship guarantee; Singapore does not. However, on closer inspection, it does not appear that this discrepancy amounted to a significant difference in the political opportunity structure for online dissent. To suggest that Malaysian journalists were more active because of a more liberal policy regime is to grossly underestimate the political risks they took. They knew that some officials were itching to act against them. Note that Zulkifli Sulong, the Harakah editor who launched its website, had a charge of sedition hanging over his head throughout the period of this research. Only in mid-2003, three years after he was charged, did he know he would not have to serve a prison sentence — he was fined instead. The Malaysian government's rhetoric may have been more in keeping with what American investors wanted to hear, but Malaysian internet activists were no strangers to police questioning, raids on their premises, and credible threats of arrest. Across the border, Singapore's content regulations dispensed with liberal niceties, but in practice the regulatory environment was not much different from Malaysia's. Like Malaysia, the Singapore government refrained from blocking websites and limited itself mainly to highly selective and infrequent action against writers and editors of content that had already been published.

A more plausible explanation for the penetration/participation paradox may be found in the second dimension of the political process framework, that of resource mobilization. Our case studies have shown that online journalism projects rely on at least two kinds of network. Computer networks are, by definition, indispensable for online projects — but clearly do not determine the level of activism. The second type of network, the social kind, may play a much more decisive role. These networks provide manpower, funds, ideas, and moral support. While the two countries are similar in many respects, Malaysia has an appreciably broader political society and thicker civil society than Singapore. Media activists in Malaysia can therefore plug into social networks that their counterparts in Singapore can only dream of. For example, Malaysia's 25-year-old human rights NGO, Aliran, has no peer in Singapore. Thus, when Malaysiakini wants to report on human rights, it can turn to Aliran and other informed, articulate sources within the country. When Singapore's Think Centre wants to do the same, it has to rely on less detailed and less frequent reports from overseas, or try to double up as newsmaker and reporter. Similarly, Singapore does not have a website like HarakahDaily.net because it does not have a newspaper like *Harakah*, which is in turn because the country does not have an opposition party like PAS — formidably organized, well endowed, and strongly ideological.

Singapore under the PAP also has less of a tradition of alternative journalism — in any medium — than Malaysia. Other than one or two small and infrequent opposition newsletters, Singapore had virtually no independent political periodicals before the internet was introduced. They existed under the British, but died out under the PAP. Pre-internet Malaysia had several, published by opposition parties, NGOs, and independent journalists. Note that some of the most significant political websites did not start from scratch, but were online versions of pre-existing newspapers and magazines repressed by the government. Contentious online journalism was therefore able to draw on these print media's resources, including writers, editors and allied groups. One important resource that should not be overlooked is sheer imagination and gumption. Creative thinking and willpower are cultural resources that are transportable across media channels. The social movements literature refers these resources as "repertoires of contention" — collective memories of how to use limited resources to challenge more powerful opponents.[14] Again, Lutfi Othman's contentious print journalism is an interesting example. His tactic of serial monographs could in theory also work in Singapore, but has never been attempted there. Lutfi was driven at least in part by the practical need to keep him and his *Detik* staff employed. Thus, contentious journalism begets contentious journalism.

Another telling contrast emerged in civil society efforts to lobby for media reform. In Singapore, a small group of concerned citizens gathered in August 2000 at the home of Sintercom's Tan Chong Kee to launch such an initiative.[15] The following month, an unrelated group met in Malaysia for a similar purpose.[16] Their subsequent trajectories were strikingly divergent. The Singapore project, dubbed the Media Watch Committee, progressed far enough along for the group to hold a press conference to announce their plans, and to register as a non-profit company in June 2001. However, in September 2001, before moving beyond the planning stages, the group announced that it was giving up; partly because it had failed to raise money from foundations, but also because key individuals were no longer available to play leadership roles.[17] In contrast, the Malaysian initiative, called Charter 2000, took off immediately and has not looked back. By March 2003, Charter 2000 had been endorsed by 29 organizations, including the Malaysian Trades Union Congress, the Human Rights Society of Malaysia, Sisters in Islam, and professional groups such as the Independent Media Activists Group, an alliance that includes Malaysiakini and Harakah. Charter 2000 has lobbied for the repeal of repressive press laws, and protested against cases of government intervention. It has helped organize an annual petition calling for greater press freedom, which in 2002 carried the signatures of more than 900 mainstream and independent journalists.[18]

Charter 2000's momentum, compared with Singapore's stillborn effort, is perhaps best explained by the involvement of established organizations. Aliran initiated the project, and drew on its experience in lobbying for reforms in other fields. The existence of so many other likeminded organizations meant that the movement for media reform could progress with much longer strides than Media Watch's individual-by-individual approach. Chandra Muzaffar notes that this is a significant difference between the two neighboring countries. Singapore has a more monolithic political structure, with a handful of "NGIs" or non-governmental *individuals*, while in Malaysia there is a rich variety of organized groups.[19] As for the next obvious question — why Malaysia has a thicker civil society layer than Singapore — only the outlines of an answer are suggested here, as a fuller explanation would be beyond the scope of this work.

One possible reason is Singapore's lesser reliance on overt coercion, which in turn lessens the degree of public outrage that mobilizers can count on. This is not to suggest that the PAP is any less control-minded than Malaysia's ruling party. The difference lies in the ways in which controls are exercised. Both governments rely heavily on prior restraints on political expression, including media licenses, permits for public meetings, and the registration of societies. Effective prior restraint, it was noted in Chapter 2, reduces the need for after-the-fact punishment, which is invariably uglier and more public. Leaders on both sides know this, but Singapore applies behind-the-scenes prior restraints more systematically and more efficiently than Malaysia, which has more dissident activity but is also more overtly repressive. Since the 1990s, there have been fewer instances of brutal repression in Singapore than in Malaysia. The point is illustrated most poignantly by Lee Kuan Yew's comments about the Anwar affair, which, it will be remembered, was probably the single most important catalyst for online dissent in Malaysia. Mahathir's harsh actions against his former deputy had been severely criticized by western and even neighboring governments. Asked for his opinion, Singapore's senior minister (SM) did not join the chorus of condemnation or question Mahathir's motives, but instead put it down to a tactical error. According to *The Straits Times*:

> SM Lee said that Dr Mahathir had made several errors of judgment in handling his former protégé's case. Among these was arresting the politician under the Internal Security Act shortly after his dismissal from government in September 1998.

> When they met in Davos in January 1999, SM Lee asked Dr Mahathir: "Why did you arrest him under the ISA?"

> "And he told me he did not know that Anwar was going to be arrested under the ISA. The Police chief had acted on his own authority."

> "It never should have been that way, it should have been a straight-forward criminal charge."

> The next disaster was the assault on the jailed politician by former top police officer Tan Sri Rahim Noor. The Malaysian leader said that he would not have obtained any benefit from an assault on Anwar.

> "I agreed, but these are things that have been done and I am afraid he has paid very dearly for it. My sympathies are with him."[20]

The spectacle of two authoritarian leaders having a heart-to-heart on how best to handle their political enemies is both chilling and revealing. The exchange shows their common appreciation of the need for restraint in the exercise of repression, but also the Malaysian regime's relative lack of success in achieving the required finesse. Chandra Muzaffar agrees that there is an efficiency gap between Singapore and his own country. "Here, they are not as efficient in control, which works to the advantage of dissidents," he says.[21] Independent journalist M.G.G Pillai, a Malaysian who has also worked in Singapore, puts it more colorfully: "Singapore civil servants know how to push the buttons. Malaysian civil servants don't know where the buttons are."[22] The police raid on Malaysiakini, which may have been carried out without Mahathir's go-ahead and which has strengthened support for the website, is a case in point.

In addition to differences in state capacity, William Case sees differences in elite structure: Singapore has a stable and cohesive elite, which has systematically channeled social forces into non-contentious grooves; while Malaysia's elite is more internally competitive — note that the government is run by a coalition, and not a single party; and witness the periodic contests at the very top, most dramatically the Mahathir-Anwar rift. As elite factions jockey for power, they are more inclined to concede some democratic space and organizational autonomy to the opposition and civil society.[23]

Whatever the reasons for the differences between Malaysia and Singapore, what is clear is the limited explanatory power of technological availability. As important as the internet has been for contentious journalism, it does not explain significant features of the movement. Of course, online journalism cannot develop in the total absence of the technological infrastructure. However, once the technology has reached a certain threshold, every additional computer, modem or user does not translate into a greater quantity or quality of contentious use. Beyond this threshold — which wider cross-national studies could help determine with more quantitative precision — human ingenuity and mobilization takes over. At that point, the critical factors seem to be the motivation for radical applications of the technology, and the involvement of social networks of organizations and individuals.

CHAPTER 10

A DEMOCRATIC CASE FOR MEDIA DIVERSITY

Everybody, it seems, believes in Democracy. Think Centre certainly does: much of its website's content is aimed at promoting democratic choice by publicizing alternatives and encouraging popular participation in public affairs. The Singapore government's Elections Department also says it does. In line with its mission to conduct free and fair elections, it once directed Think Centre to remove from its site an article by an opposition politician, saying that it violated new regulations on campaign advertising.[1] Those regulations, which ban non-party websites from carrying election advertising during the campaign period, can be found on the Elections Department's official site, beneath the banner "Democracy@WORK."[2]

The irony of this situation reflects the contemporary reality of democracy. Everyone believes in it — but belongs to a different denomination. And, inter-denominational disputes, in politics as in religion, can be as fierce as clashes between entirely different faiths. Intellectually, the simplest way to resolve such a conflict is to label one side as hypocrites or heretics. It is easy to justify such a conclusion in the cases of Malaysia and Singapore. After all, the two countries appear to fit the classic profile of hybrid, pseudodemocratic states that have taken democracy's name in vain, manipulating the political structure in order to benefit from the legitimacy conferred by elections, while minimizing the risk of losing power.[3] To let the argument rest there, however, would oversimplify matters. Even sincere believers differ in their understanding of democracy's tenets. One symptom of this lack of consensus is the interminable debate in liberal democracies over press reform. In the United States, for example, not even the oracle of press freedom, the First Amendment, has been able to settle fundamental questions about the news media's democratic roles and responsibilities. Should the media facilitate democratic rule by helping society arrive quickly at a national consensus, or should they provide maximum opportunity for democratic expression of diverse views that may delay a consensus? Is democracy better served by a few large, well-resourced media corporations or many small publishers? Should journalists affect an objective and disinterested stance, or try to activate public life by adopting a more interventionist role? Such questions remain open. C. Edwin Baker has pointed out that even the deceptively simple principle of "freedom of the press" begs the question, "Freedom for whom?" The answer could be "for the public," or "for the press professionals," or "for the owners." Each of these constituencies can back its claim with a reasonable case, and each of these answers corresponds to a different kind of media.[4] The wellspring of democracy produces divergent streams. Some are more nourishing of media diversity and contentious journalism than others.

Privileging the Mainstream

Operational definitions of democracy contain two indispensable aspects: competition among political actors, and participation by the citizenry.[5] Theorists differ in how they interpret these two aspects, and the relative importance attached to them.[6] There are a number of democratic narratives that are not particularly enthusiastic about "the public" as something constituted by active citizen participation. As such, they have little room for the idea of contentious journalism and its mobilizing role. For a start, libertarian philosophy, while upholding the right to free speech, is suspicious of the community-building impulse that drives many alternative media projects, especially when they do not share libertarians' respect for capitalism. In the libertarian view, press freedom is justified on the basis of the gratification it accords to the individual writer. No higher principle than individual freedom is necessary for the press, because in the free contest of ideas, the truth will emerge, thanks to the self-righting principle. Oliver Wendell Holmes' use of the marketplace metaphor to describe this principle in *Abrams v. United States* — "the best test of truth is the power of thought to get itself accepted in the competition of the market" — sealed the association between a free market economy and a free press.[7] The libertarianism of Friedrich Hayek further argued for a minimal role for the state and maximum freedom for the market economy, on the assumption that market mechanisms are more open to individual initiative and will than state institutions.[8]

Classic liberalism emerged to fight political censorship and repression at a time when the press was small and weak, making it easier to equate press freedom with individual rights. In modern times, the press is organized mainly as large media corporations, with operations and interests that are quite distinct from those of the proverbial lone pamphleteer. One democratic narrative that is sympathetic towards the institutional press is the competitive elitism of Joseph Schumpeter and Walter Lippmann. Schumpeter, in search of a more realistic vision of democracy than classic liberalism, decided that modern society was too complex, and most citizens too limited in intellect, for the "will of the people" to serve as a guiding light for government.[9] Instead, it is the governing elite's job to establish the common good, and voters' job to pick the most competent leaders. The function of democracy is thus reduced to providing periodic elections for changing the ruling elite, and effective checks against tyranny. Lippmann's *Public Opinion*, predating Schumpeter's ideas by more than 20 years, argued that to imagine public opinion directing public affairs was a "false ideal," and as futile as expecting "a fat man to try to be a ballet dancer." Mahathir Mohamad and Lee Kuan Yew could hardly have put it better. While it would be an injustice to Lippmann and Schumpeter to say that they provided a justification for authoritarian rule — both called for more checks on power than exist in either Malaysia or Singapore — they certainly show that it is not only authoritarian leaders who are skeptical of the public's potential.

Lippmann argued that it was foolhardy to expect the press to realize the fiction of citizens with "a competent opinion about all public affairs".

> If the newspapers, then, are to be charged with the duty of translating the whole public life of mankind, so that every adult can arrive at an opinion on every moot topic, they fail, they are bound to fail, in any future one can conceive they will continue to fail.[10]

The public's realistic democratic role was to serve as a "reserve of force" mobilized to support or oppose the elites who actually govern, he said. Within this elitist formulation of democracy, the proper and reasonable mission of journalists is to facilitate publicity — helping to keep the powerful honest by shedding light on their actions and motives — and to serve as translators between experts and the public. When the democratic function of the press is framed in this way, media diversity becomes a non-issue. Indeed, oligopolistic media might be preferred. They would have brighter spotlights to point at governing institutions, and the resources to translate the complexities of key issues into stories that ordinary people can begin to understand.

The highly influential pluralist narrative shares the elitist view that most people are — and will remain — uninterested in political affairs. However, it allows for a more competitive and more representative form of politics. Starting with Robert Dahl, pluralists argued that intermediary interest groups such as community associations and trade unions formed a layer of social life that ensured enough competition and dispersion of influence to prevent any one group from dominating the others in any important decision.[11] This sounds at first like a promising platform from which to launch a case for media diversity. Appreciating the value of multiple interest groups is only a small step away from acknowledging the value of multiple media, to represent those diverse interests. However, classic pluralism does not take that step. Dahl favored a strong national consensus around basic norms. This would require that the airing of differences be subject to a certain self-restraint. The American system worked, he said, because citizens are "indoctrinated" to believe in the "democratic creed," the elements of which include a belief in democracy as the best form of government, the desirability of rights, and the legitimacy of key political institutions. These beliefs, produced through formal schooling, are reinforced in adult life, "articulated by leading political figures and transmitted through the mass media," he said in a rare reference to the press.[12] Lance Bennett makes a similar observation when he argues that the news "provides a daily refresher course on the grand rule systems of constitutions, legal codes, elections, and legislative procedures that set the boundaries of the imagined — or at least the legitimate — political universe."[13] Pluralism sees the news media (like the state) as reflecting — rather than constructing — the social structure, and helping to maintain the boundary between constructive, legitimate expression and illegitimate political action. It assumes that the prevailing consensus in a working democracy already embodies the myriad competing, legitimate interests. In this paradigm, contentious politics and their media are unnecessary, and exist only because some people are irrational and do not share their society's healthy norms and values. Dahl himself would later abandon this highly conservative form of pluralism, but it remains an influential model of democracy.

In Defense of the Margins

Another set of democratic narratives rejects the assumption that decisions about the common good are best left to elites or the institutionalized routines of interest-group politics. While these theories accept that the public has not lived up to democratic expectations, they blame not the layman's lack of intellect, but the ways in which he has been conditioned to disengage from public affairs. Contrary to the libertarian worldview, people are not individuals first and foremost, but social beings innately adept at deliberation, a skill they would apply if given the chance. These narratives also hold that the popular will that emerges through deliberation is qualitatively superior and more democratic than that which emerges through opinion polling of individuals, or which is led by elites.[14] The most thorough and systematic argument for the deliberative ideal is contained in the writings of Jurgen Habermas. He argues for reviving the "public sphere" — the domain of life in which authorities are engaged in debate through the "people's public use of their reason."[15] The public sphere ideal stands in sharp contrast to marketplace notions of communication, which celebrate the privately-held, individual right to be heard. The formation of a collective will, according to Habermas, is intersubjective and "cannot be correctly construed as individual will formation writ large."[16] This is because moral questions can only be settled by the "intermeshing of the perspective of each with the perspectives of all."[17]

John Dewey similarly viewed the public as not extinct, but merely inactive.[18] People have lost track of their shared interests. The challenge is therefore to prod people's awareness of their inter-dependence, partly by nourishing communication at the local level: "Unless local communal life can be restored, the public cannot adequately resolve its most urgent problem: to find and identify itself."[19] Political parties and their media also play an important role in cultivating a more active public. Habermas notes that the decline of the partisan press is paradoxically associated with the establishment of the constitutional state and the legalization of the political public sphere. Now that the press no longer had to fight for its political space, "it could abandon its polemical stance and concentrate on the profit opportunities for a commercial business."[20]

Seen in the light of the deliberative ideal, the public becomes a genuine possibility that journalists have the opportunity to help form, rather than a phantom that they try in vain to *in*form. "The public will begin to reawaken when they are addressed as a conversational partner and are encouraged to join the talk rather than sit passively as spectators before a discussion conducted by journalists and experts," James Carey argues.[21] In the US, the most elaborate and sustained attempt to engage readers in such a democratic dialogue has been the public journalism movement, under which local newspapers have, for example, organized town hall meetings to get citizens talking about issues. While traditional journalists believe that "it would be nice if public life worked, but it's beyond our role to make it work and it's dangerous to think we can," public journalists believe "public life should work, and journalism has a role in making it work."[22]

These deliberative democrats believe that citizens' silence in the public sphere is not to be equated with consent. If citizens cannot or do not access the public sphere, there can be no genuine democratic consensus. From this perspective, mainstream journalism's detachment from the public, and its framing of politics as a spectacle performed by elites, has contributed to the decline of the public sphere. The alternative media help to reawaken community life. They provide spaces where groups can express their interests and deliberate on their concerns. These, the deliberative model suggests, will reactivate the public sphere. Another narrative, that of radical pluralism, is not as optimistic that discourse within small communities can be extrapolated to democratize the whole society. With an increase in scope and scale comes greater complexity and incommensurability of interests, as well as more barriers to free participation. Therefore, radical pluralists caution that the dream of an overarching consensus or a unitary public, contained in other models of democracy, inevitably privileges some groups and excludes others. Instead, democratization requires the proliferation of autonomous spheres.

Nancy Fraser makes this case in her critique of Habermas.[23] Even the bourgeois public sphere that he idealized practiced a form of discourse that marginalized women and plebeians through protocols of gentility. This is why a number of competing public spheres arose at the same time, comprising nationalists, peasants, elite women, and others. Without these counterpublics, Fraser says, members of subordinated groups would have no venues where they can deliberate among themselves about their interests, goals, and strategies. Conversely, "the proliferation of counterpublics means a widening of contestation, a condition that, in stratified societies, is desirable."[24] Habermas himself acknowledges the value of what he calls "informal" or "procedurally unregulated" public spheres, that reflect the social complexity of subcultures:

> Here, new problem situations can be perceived more sensitively, discourses aimed at achieving self-understanding can be conducted more widely and expressively, collective identities and need interpretations can be articulated with fewer compulsions than is the case in procedurally regulated public spheres.[25]

David Morley applies this perspective to his critique of mass media. He notes that a national broadcasting system, for example, can create a sense of unity within a country, by serving as a "symbolic home for the nation's members."[26] However, such a project is always and inevitably incomplete, as some groups will always be excluded from the mediated public sphere. No matter how it is constituted, the public sphere will be more hospitable to some forms of expression than others.

> To this extent, an egalitarian multicultural society depends on the creation and maintenance of a plurality of public arenas in

which a wide range of groups, with a diverse range of values
and rhetorics, can effectively participate.[27]

It is in this light that John Downing's frustration with mainstream media, and his tribute to radical alternative media, make
sense. Although small and generally unimpressive, alternative media
are, he says, "the chief standard bearers of a democratic communication
structure."[28] Alternative media, as described in Chapter 4, lower one
or more of the barriers — skills, capital and controls — blocking
public access to media. By abandoning or reinterpreting professional
codes, choosing low-cost technologies for production and distribution,
and flattening internal hierarchies, alternative media democratize
journalism in ways that the mainstream press has been unable or
unwilling to do.

Multiple Democratic Visions, Multiple Journalisms

The various perspectives on democracy have their respective adherents
among scholars, journalists, publishers and policy-makers. There
are few purists: the deployment of democratic rhetoric is invariably
strategic, selective and self-serving. Mainstream media and their
defenders, for example, use liberal or libertarian arguments to fend
off criticism and calls for reform. Although, conceptually, it is
difficult to think of large and powerful corporations as having
"natural" rights, or as embodying the individual's freedom of
expression, libertarianism is routinely wielded to protect and further
the economic interests of media enterprises, against arguments
for public service principles such as diversity and responsibility,
and — more recently — against antitrust regulation. Thus, some
authors argue that the public journalism movement must be resisted
because it compromises the god-given natural rights of the individual
journalist.[29] However, when the mainstream media are challenged by
radical practitioners claiming those libertarian rights, the same authors
shift to an elitist argument for professionalism and credibility. They

warn that the internet's "megapluralism or cacophony of uncontrolled voices" will elicit a public backlash, and that the internet "in its haste to democratize journalism, will have, in effect, destroyed the institutional autonomy of the press."[30]

Such contradictions may be inevitable. None of the democratic denominations outlined above is either all right or all wrong. Each gets at a partial truth about democracy's promise and problems. Michael Schudson acknowledges this when he suggests that journalists' superficial knowledge of political theory may not be a bad thing.[31] Rather than try to decide which theorists to believe, it is better that news media be "self-consciously schizophrenic" in their efforts to perform a democratic political function.[32] There are times when an informed and involved electorate does not exist, and Lippmann's realist prescription makes sense: the press can act as a stand-in for the public, using the searchlight of publicity to hold authority responsible to publicly agreed-upon goals. At other times, the press could champion the kind of public sphere that deliberative democrats say does not exist but should be built. "The virtue of schizophrenia is that *both* things are true under different circumstances," Schudson says.[33]

James Curran has proposed a different kind of schizophrenia. Instead of a unitary press with multiple personalities, he suggests a diverse media *system*, with different sectors serving different democratic functions.[34] No single institutional form or professional code can straddle these various roles effectively, he says. Each has its own strengths and limitations. What is important is that the system as a whole serves essential democratic functions. First, democracy needs media that provide a common forum for individuals and groups to take part in public dialogue about the direction of the whole society. This form of journalism aims to expose people to competing definitions of the common interest, and through a process of deliberation, allows individual interests to coalesce into a public interest. Based on his British experience, Curran argues that a healthy public service broadcasting sector can play this role. Organizationally, this sector must be insulated from state or market interests through funding and control structures that are independent in law and in fact.

Second, commercial news media are important, as they have a strong incentive to respond to audience demand, thus balancing the almost inevitable elitism of public service broadcasting. Although Curran does not make this point, commercial journalism's heavy subsidy from advertising revenue also gives it resources that public funding cannot match (although whether these deep pockets are actually used for democracy-enhancing journalism is another question altogether). Rooted in libertarian ideology and funded by private enterprise, this sector is also less likely to succumb to direct government pressure. While it is naïve to think that commercial media can act as a wholly independent watchdog, Curran argues that commercial media and public service corporations are vulnerable to government influence in different ways — "And in this difference, there is a modest measure of security," he says.[35]

Curran's third sector comprises "civic media," similar to what others would call alternative media. These media respond to the need for self-expression, representation and deliberation within groups that, for want of numerical strength or political power, are excluded from the dominant discourse in both the public service and commercial sectors. This category would include party-controlled newspapers aimed at sustaining and promoting particular, and usually adversarial, viewpoints; media relating to sub-cultural constituencies such as gays and lesbians; and organizational newsletters serving as internal channels of communication. Fourth, are self-governing media, another kind of alternative media. This sector comprises unaligned journalists, working autonomously of any corporation or organized interest, and answering only to their professional calling of "truth-seeking." This professional sector would serve as a "bedrock of independence and... can be relied upon to maintain a critical surveillance of all power centres in society, and expose them to the play of public opinion."[36]

The contentious media analyzed in the present study may be unimpressive when judged by the standards of mainstream commercial media, but they do serve Curran's third and fourth goals. All are examples of civic media, sustaining an alternative discourse under pressure from dominant ideologies; additionally, Malaysiakini seems to be a case of self-governing media, run by professional journalists answering to the values of their chosen vocation. According to Curran, such diversity in the media system can strengthen democracy, by addressing genuine differences in democratic goals. This mixed media perspective represents an important advance over arguments in favor of one or another system. Given the varying denominations of democracy — and the fact that each sector is more than likely to fall short of its own democratic ideals — it makes sense for a society to hedge its bets as Curran suggests. From this perspective, democratic reform of the press should focus not only on the performance of each sector, but also on attaining a healthy balance of sectors. Striking that balance may require creative institution-building and public intervention to prevent whole sectors from collapsing out of neglect or careless policy.

Enhancing the alternative sector

Politicians in Malaysia and Singapore sometimes point to internet dissent as evidence that their countries are not as un-free as critics allege. However, it is one thing to note the empirical fact that insurgents are exploiting available democratic space, and quite another to concede the normative point that they are beneficial for democracy. The latter admission has not been forthcoming from officials, and only rarely from mainstream journalists and intellectuals. This miserliness with praise is probably the result of the all-or-nothing mindset that typifies discussions of this sort. People wonder if it would be a good thing if today's alternative media became tomorrow's dominant mainstream, and if the answer is "no" — and there are good reasons for a negative answer — people conclude that alternative media are something society can do without. Curran's mixed media perspective reminds us that alternative media are not substitutes for the mainstream and need not be judged in the same terms. The right questions to ask are instead, first, whether and why alternative media as such are worth having, protecting and nurturing as a niche within a society's media mix; and, second, what can be done to improve their performance. The first set of questions has been answered in the course of this study by the practitioners themselves. Their responses are very much in line with the arguments that Curran, Downing, Chris Atton and others have made. Such media provide opportunities for counter-hegemonic discourse, playing with and keeping alive alternative ways of looking at the world, challenging the consensus and churning public opinion.

As for what would help them, Curran and others have suggested that public funds be made available to support civic groups' media activities. It is an idea that, in Malaysia and Singapore, practitioners of contentious journalism would consider laughable. A goal that is more within reach is the removal of administrative and institutional barriers that hinder their work. One that affects independent journalists even in liberal democracies is the authorities' denial of accreditation, and, with it, access to some sources and certain legal protections. Malaysiakini's failed attempts to obtain press passes from the Home Ministry were noted in Chapter 8. In Singapore, alternative media's pariah status in the eyes of the government is institutionalized in election laws, which do not cover independent online media under the definition of "news" — a privilege confined to licensed organizations — and therefore do not exempt them from regulations on election advertising. "Virtual" media organizations are further disadvantaged. Sintercom could not register itself as a society because Singapore law does not recognize annual general meetings held online. Registration would have also required establishing an organizational hierarchy, which Sintercom did not want.[37] Thus, existing administrative rules militate against radical forms of organization that the internet enables.

Governments are not the only institutions with the power to affect alternative media's fate. Commercial organizations play a rarely acknowledged role in shaping the architecture of the internet in ways that help or hurt content providers. For example, most internet users' experience in cyberspace is mediated by third parties such as search engines, internet service providers, and portal sites, which add convenience by making various choices for the user. Like any good tour guide, internet companies that claim to show users through the streets of cyberspace have a special responsibility to point out the less obvious local color, but this is not always the case. In an early-2003 check, Yahoo!'s "Politics" category under its Malaysian "News and Media" directory listed just three sites, including Malaysiakini and the human rights group Aliran. None of the political parties' organs were listed. Yahoo!'s editors, apparently, subscribe to the mainstream belief that partisan journalism is an oxymoron.[38] As for the popular Google search engine, when asked to find "Singapore news," it filled screen after screen with mainstream sources, commercial and governmental. The first alternative source was 26th on the list. The Singapore government's own SGNews service, managed by the information ministry, was number two.[39] So much for the internet as a great equalizer. If alternative media are to gain ground, portal sites and directory services need to recognize this sector's contribution to the media system.

More direct assistance is already being given by some international organizations such as the Media Development Loan Fund. As shown in the Malaysiakini case study, western funding can be a political liability. Money is not the only kind of help needed. Malaysiakini has benefited from moral support and shows of solidarity from groups overseas. The swift mobilization of Amnesty International, Reporters Without Borders and the Committee to

Protect Journalists when police seized Malaysiakini's computers in early 2003 may have embarrassed the government enough to make it back down. International public opinion is probably not as influential in Malaysia and Singapore as outsiders think, but it is unlikely to hurt. Unfortunately, international NGOs, like editors at portal sites, may use selection criteria that are not entirely transparent. Malaysiakini's cause has been adopted by western advocates of human rights and press freedom, while Harakah has not attained as high an international profile. Partly, this is by choice. Harakah, with its solid domestic constituency, does not need international publicity to the same extent as Malaysiakini. Even if it did, however, it is far from certain that it would have received positive press. There is much about Harakah and PAS that the global human rights industry would find difficult to swallow. Unlike Malaysiakini, it is mainly in Malay rather than English, it is not independent but a party organ — that of a fundamentalist Islamic party, to boot — and it rejects certain key articles of faith in the basket of progressive issues, notably the western interpretation of women's rights.

Both Downing and Fraser have warned us not to expect alternative media to conform to some agreeable, consistent, progressive standard. They are "not tidily segregated into a radical political reservation," as Downing puts it.[40] They are mixed: radical in some respects but not in others. Historically, for example, women suffragists in the US failed to oppose slavery, while organized labor did little for women and minority workers. Fraser similarly acknowledges that among the multiple public spheres that she advocates, some may be explicitly anti-democratic and anti-egalitarian.[41] They are nevertheless emancipatory moments, their very existence representing an enlargement of discursive space. This is not merely to say that they demonstrate that democratic space exists (like the official view mentioned in the introduction to this section). Rather, Fraser argues that going public requires that one's claims be subject to challenge in ever-widening circles: "In principle, assumptions that were previously exempt from contestation will now have to be publicly argued out."[42] This argument relates to Habermas' discourse ethics: regardless of one's political beliefs, the decision to enter into an argument and make claims of others requires that one accept the logic of accountability through open, impartial and honest discourse.

Implications for the mainstream press

For professional journalists and mainstream news organizations, the most significant aspect of Curran's model is that it denies them exclusive rights to the high ground that they tend to claim whenever "media" and "democracy" are uttered in the same breath. This study suggests two necessary responses if they are to retain their status. The first applies especially to Malaysia, Singapore and other societies where the press is subject to obvious political controls. The mainstream media there must become more resistant to government pressure and take fewer liberties with their credibility. They need to convince their political masters that the national media's survival is at stake. When the press purveys grossly distorted, unbalanced and unrepresentative coverage, their audiences drift to alternative media. Although alternative media have been conceptualized here in complementary rather than competitive terms, the Reformasi period showed that in periods of crisis, readers may indeed turn to them as substitutes for the mainstream press. Malaysia's establishment media paid the price during the Reformasi protests, losing as much as one-third of their circulation. In the tens of thousands, readers turned to websites that gave them undoubtedly more, and occasionally better, coverage of the dramatic political turmoil. It is unclear how much autonomy Malaysian gatekeepers had during the crisis. Certainly, the departure of Anwar loyalists prior to the deputy prime minister's sacking was a clear signal to other editors that Mahathir expected their total support. Some insiders say, however, that gatekeepers went above and beyond the call of political duty. Some of their reporters and columnists were so frustrated, they took to sending articles secretly to the alternative websites, which published them under pseudonyms. One senior journalist says she even advised her colleagues to do so — such was the depth of the mainstream media system's loss of legitimacy among even their own staff.

Even without government control, professional journalists are finding it difficult to preserve their status and identity. Traditionally, their claim was simple if somewhat tautological: they were journalists because they worked for the press; the press was the purveyor of journalism; and journalism was what journalists did. Increasingly, however, others are entering the journalism business. They include not only unaffiliated individuals who use the internet to report and comment independently on public affairs, but also the entertainment divisions of media corporations that produce the hybrid genres of infotainment and docudrama, recognizing that what's newsworthy is often highly marketable. The predictable response from mainstream journalists is to try to set themselves apart on the basis of their professionalism, and in particular their standards of objectivity. This hardly settles the matter. After all, alternative media can, if they wish, adopt the same standards — as Malaysiakini has done. Furthermore, it is doubtful whether the public values objectivity, in the form in which it is practiced, as much as journalists do. In theory, objectivity was supposed to ensure that the press served the public interest instead of its own. In practice, it has been translated into a set of operational procedures that turns journalism away from independent truth-seeking and towards the factual reproduction of what others — especially official sources — claim the truth is. This version of objectivity has turned journalists into "passive recipients of news instead of aggressive explainers and analyzers of it."[43] Worse, this procedural approach to objectivity — in which professionalism is equated with the methods applied rather than the substance of what is reported — is used to limit newsrooms' liability for what they report, and reduce their accountability to the public.[44] While honoring objectivity in this limited form, news organizations have generally refused to pin themselves down to professional codes and creeds to which the public could hold them accountable — although those are precisely the kinds of assurance that readers would find most meaningful. Downing notes:

> We still must face up to the fact that mainstream media make no pretense of offering themselves up to any form of public control, short of consumers' letters or consumers' refusal to buy them or switch them on. As means of public leverage of democratic influence, these various responses are either feeble or indiscriminately blunt. … Consumer sovereignty, often blazoned as a democratic fix-all, bears no relation to practical media realities.[45]

Mainstream news media have preferred to define their mission in value-neutral terms, such as to inform, educate and entertain. The profession needs to be more articulate in explaining what is special about it. It needs to engage in what some journalism reformers have called "branding by values."[46] One scholar has argued that since journalism cannot claim to be a profession based on esoteric knowledge, and does not want to distinguish itself through tight self-regulation, its claim to professionalism has to be based on its "sacred" aspect, which it shares with other professions such as priests and doctors: a certain altruism and a unique responsibility to the general public.[47] From this perspective, if the profession is to retain its status, it may have to take on the unfamiliar task of arguing its case in terms of its intimate link to democracy — or whatever its interests may be. Objectivity is but a fig leaf in such a discussion. Theodore Glasser notes:

> The folly of believing that journalism can detach itself from what it covers leaves journalists unaware of their interests and thus unprepared to examine them. And without an examination of their interests, without good reasons for accepting, rejecting or revising them, journalists relinquish the right to claim the very independence of judgment that presumably distinguishes news

from what journalists ordinarily regard as less trustworthy forms of public communication.[48]

A normative turn in journalism's self-definition need not entail a total abandonment of its professional values. Curran's model recognizes this in his inclusion of a self-governing professional sector. Indeed, professional journalism could be viewed as a formal, institutionalized public sphere where Habermas' "discourse ethics" is approximated.[49] Many basic newsroom procedures for objectivity — such as interviewing all affected parties in a story — strive at fairness and impartiality within their constraints of time and space. However, by focusing almost exclusively on ritualized operational procedures and ignoring their underlying ethical principles, journalism misses the wood for the trees. Both public accountability and democratic values are lost in translation.[50] These need to be reintroduced into professional discourse and practice. In the west, this would entail abandoning the naïve pretence of detachment, a principle that in a society rife with inequalities of power and privilege translates into reinforcing the status quo. In countries such as Malaysia and Singapore, a commitment to fairness might require courageously correcting the imbalance in a public discourse that is overly dominated by state elites.

Contentious journalism

This book has been largely sympathetic to the practitioners of contentious journalism. Its writer's professional career has been entirely within mainstream journalism, playing by professional rules that the alternative media violate with impunity. Nancy Fraser's warning has been taken to heart: to understand those on the fringe, one must examine critically the formal barriers and the informal codes that serve to marginalize them — even if one has personally benefited from being on the privileged side of the tracks. In writing this book, I have therefore tried to suspend my conditioned preference for several hallowed professional standards: non-partisanship, objectivity, factual accuracy, and the idea that journalism should be a career, not a part-time hobby. By framing contentious journalism as a social movement, as alternative or civic media, and as complementary to rather than substitutes for mainstream media, this study has argued for more tolerant and inclusive standards than are applied to the mainstream press. This writer sympathizes with Herbert Gans' conclusion about the need for multiple perspectives in a country's media. Gans argues: "Different perspectives lead to different questions and different answers, thereby requiring different facts and different news."[51]

> For those who believe that cohesion and order are prime national and societal goals, multiperspectivism would be objectionable. For those who feel, as I do, that the interests of diverse groups have priority over the needs of nation and society, multiperspectival news and some decentralization of the national media are preferable. Even so, if more people obtain news relevant to their interests, and if that news helps them achieve their own goals, they may feel themselves to be part of a larger whole. In the long run, then, the country would be more cohesive in fact if not in symbol.[52]

Practitioners of contentious journalism tend to argue that they are dealing in a "different news," as Gan puts it, when questioned about their performance. There were telling exchanges of this sort during a discussion in Singapore organized in the course of this project. The participants included representatives of both the mainstream and alternative media. The first question was from Peter Lim, a former editor-in-chief of The Straits Times group. Anbarasu Balrasan, editor of ThinkCentre.org, and Tan Chong Kee, founding editor of Sintercom, responded:

> Peter Lim: The traditional media measures success in terms of circulation, revenue and so on. How does one measure the reach of alternative media? Is it being done? How should it be done?

Anbarasu Balrasan: [The government] gazetted us. That's importance.... They felt they had to gazette us.... If the government sees us a threat, I think we've got a reach. And that actually gave us the resolve to do more, rather than less....

Tan Chong Kee: ... The real test is not how many people read you, but how much impact you have on individuals. The biggest satisfaction comes from people who say their eyes were opened by something you published.[53]

Asked by a mass communication educator and researcher whether political or cause-driven organs such as Think Centre and Sintercom qualified as "news" media at all, Tan responded that the distinction between mainstream and alternative boiled down to the difference between "reporting what happened versus reporting what we think *really* happened."[54] In these and other ways, practitioners of contentious journalism position themselves as being engaged in a separate but equal form of journalism. Such a stance is essential for developing any sense of self-efficacy. Most media in this category do not have the resources for daily news reporting, for example. Looking at Malaysiakini's struggles to survive, it is not even clear that all of them should try. Comment-driven, cause-oriented journalism is a viable and valuable niche.

There is a danger, however, that the sheer breadth of the "alternative" umbrella ends up rationalizing all the shortcomings and failures of those who take ideological shelter beneath it. There is a hint of this in Fraser's conceptualization of multiple public spheres, when she says that they may include groups that are explicitly illiberal and undemocratic. Downing states a similar caveat, observing that radical alternative media are likely to be flawed and sometimes in opposition to each other, since they are "part of popular culture and of the overall societal mesh and not tidily segregated into a radical political reservation."[55]

Within the movement that has been the subject of this study, the clearest signs of such trouble are the breaks in ideological coherence between the various groups. Although their leaders have readily identified themselves as belonging to the same broad movement, and have cooperated in concrete ways, there are definite limits to their camaraderie. One interesting episode involved Sintercom's Tan Chong Kee and James Gomez, who later founded Think Centre. Both were leading figures in The Working Committee (TWC), a network of civil society organizations and individuals. The initiative came to the brink of total breakdown over Gomez's proposal to invite an opposition politician to speak at an inaugural TWC event. Tan, who had offered Sintercom as TWC's web home, was among those who opposed the idea, on the grounds that some member organizations feared associating themselves with the opposition and would have backed out of the network as a result. Also in conflict were competing definitions of civil society. Gomez's belief that political parties were part of civil society was not shared by most of the others, and he quit TWC amidst some acrimony.[56] He established Think Centre shortly after as an explicitly *multi*-partisan rather than *non*-partisan group.

In Malaysia, the relationship between Malaysiakini and Harakah is also an uneasy one. They are allies but "not in the same boat," Malaysiakini co-founder Premesh Chandran says.[57] Both were opposed to many aspects of the Barisan Nasional government, but Malaysiakini's refusal to adopt a pro-opposition editorial policy distinguishes it from the partisan Harakah. While both stand for the abolition of discretionary powers contained in the Internal Security Act and the Printing Presses Act, one draws its inspiration from western liberal democratic thought, while the other grounds its position in Islamic theology. As the relationship between religion and politics is one of the most important issues facing Malaysian society, the limits that Harakah places on open discussion of Islam and PAS are hardly trivial. Significantly, one of Malaysia's main progressive Muslim intellectual voices, Farish Noor, writes his column in Malaysiakini, not Harakah. "Malaysiakini has been a forum for

Progressive Islam — Harakah has never given the same space or opportunity," he says. Critical of PAS as well as of the government, Farish was one of the writers blacklisted by religious scholars close to PAS. Harakah, it was noted in Chapter 7, was critical of the religious establishment in that instance, and cites the episode as an example of its editorial independence. "But this had more to do with PAS's internal politics," Farish notes. "At no point did Harakah defend people like me. In fact in that same editorial there was a barbed accusation of me as *fasiq* (evil)."[58]

Differences within the contentious journalism movement need to be debated if it is to develop. Of course, among alternative media are those serving communities that just want to be left alone. This is the case with several cultural and religious groups using the web as an enclave for their members, free of domination by the state. The websites studied in the preceding pages, however, are not just sites of resistance; they are sites of contention, trying to reshape public discourse and making claims on the state and other groups. For media as large and as influential as Harakah, it is reasonable to expect a level of accountability close to what they demand of the mainstream press. Even smaller projects such as Think Centre profess to have qualitatively better visions of democracy, and of journalism. Those claims need to stand up to public scrutiny. Therefore, lack of internal coherence within the movement cannot be glossed over. This is not to suggest that the movement should be judged by the internal consistency of its moral vision. Habermas warns us that, given the pluralism of values, the rush to settle questions of the good life is bound to exclude the perspectives of some. The goal is instead to practice a just process — free, open, fair — through which differences can be discussed in the search for common ground.[59] It is the quality of this deliberative process rather than the coherence of its positions that the contentious journalism movement should exemplify in its internal dynamics. There are some encouraging models for this. After Gomez's dispute with TWC, for example, the

organizers he had fought with invited him to contribute a chapter
to a book documenting the initiative. The editors of the volume,
who included Tan Chong Kee, explained that they wanted to record
TWC's experience in dealing with the dynamics of difference. Gomez
was thus given an opportunity to explain his version of events, and
to articulate his more explicitly political vision for civil society, which
by then was embodied in Think Centre.[60]

Calling as they do for more democratic discourse in the public
sphere, contentious media thus need to live by the same values in
their dealings with each other. Their most urgent challenge, however, is to live at all. The reader should not underestimate the
strength of the coercive and hegemonic powers arrayed against these
groups. Ten years after the internet was made available to the public,
this technology can be said to have transformed the way Malaysians
and Singaporeans communicate, but without rearranging the structures of power. While this study has so far scrupulously resisted the
temptation to assess the overall impact of the internet on democracy
in the two countries, it is worth touching on this big question now,
if only to emphasize the elusiveness of its answers. The internet
would spark a revolution, according to some predictions. It did not.
In Malaysia, Mahathir's successor, Abdullah Badawi, led the Barisan
Nasional to another general election victory in 2004, gaining ground
against PAS. In Singapore the same year, the ruling People's Action
Party was able to celebrate the 50th anniversary of its founding, as
sure of its grip on power as at any time in its history. Even after
embracing perhaps the most decentralized communication technology in history, it transpires that the center can hold.

In each country, control of the mainstream media remains
part of the government's strategy for longevity. Mohamed Rahmat,
who was Malaysia's information minister when the internet was
introduced, told this writer that as long as broadcasting was in
government hands, the internet would not pose a political problem.[61]
Singapore's information minister in 2003 enunciated the role of

the press in terms no different from the government's position
10 years earlier:

> Your role is to inform and educate Singaporeans without
> compromising the nation's overriding need for social and political
> stability.... It is the duty of Singapore's media to do its part for
> national education and values. This will help to build a strong
> national consensus and social resilience to enable Singaporeans
> to respond cohesively and rationally to challenges.[62]

In addition to emphasizing consensus and cohesion, the
minister reminded the mainstream press to observe the traditional
separation between commentary and news reporting — evidence
that governments, and not just media scholars, can see that the
professional norm of objectivity has a conservative bias. In no
uncertain terms, advocacy and partisanship — the bread-and-butter of
contentious media — was declared as incompatible with journalism:
"When journalists want to campaign for political viewpoints or
issues, they should not do so from their media positions which
give them unique opportunity to influence the public. They should
enter the political contest, declare their intention and campaign
as politicians."[63]

Within this panoramic picture of stability, however, there are
also signs of change. Things are not falling apart; the center holds
— but things are getting interesting at the margins. Thanks partly
to the internet but mainly to the irrepressible human spirit, there are
now new options for self-expression, organization and mobilization.
Less clear is to what extent these activities on the margins color
public discourse at the center. It is quite possible, though this has
been outside the scope of this study, that the alternative media
have influenced the mainstream. They represent the perspectives of
marginal groups in ways that are easily accessed by other journalists,
increasing the likelihood that at least a glimmer of these viewpoints
will be reflected in the mainstream media. Contentious journalism
may also increase the room for maneuver of mainstream journalists

trying to produce more critical and independent work, through a kind of "radical flank" effect — compared with the radical journalism of a Harakah or a Think Centre, even critical stories by *The Star* or *The Straits Times* may pass the authorities' scrutiny as relatively harmless. The action on the margins may also have prodded the state to adapt to a more diverse and critical audience. In Malaysia, one of Abdullah Badawi's first moves as prime minister was to launch an inquiry into police conduct, to address accusations of corruption and brutality. When Anwar Ibrahim, the catalyst of Reformasi, was released from prison in 2004, some observers interpreted this move as an attempt by the new prime minister to repair the ruling party's relationship with the Malay ground, and Malaysia's reputation among Western nations. As recounted in this book, contentious online media had played an important role in keeping alive such issues as Anwar's arrest and police misbehavior. In Singapore, the new prime minister Lee Hsien Loong surprised many with his assurances that the government would encourage debate and value diversity. "We don't mind if you have different views, but you must have some views," he said when describing the kind of Singaporean he hoped would step forward to serve the country.[64] Perhaps, the persistence of contentious media has persuaded such leaders to accept that the ideological landscape has become more diverse, and that they have no choice but to adapt to a new world where the state's dominance will never be total, even at the center. This claim must remain at the level of speculation, as it is impossible to parse out the independent effect of alternative media relative to other social changes, such as rising education levels, more frequent travel, a growing middle class, and the spread of democratic values. One can only surmise that contentious online journalism is part of a mix of forces that is pressuring the old basis of consensus. In theory, this could destabilize the state, but in the cases of Malaysia and Singapore it is quite possible that intelligent, incremental changes at the center will succeed in preserving the status quo.

As for contentious journalism, there is no reason to doubt that it will continue to exist as a lively and resilient species of media on the margins of the polity in Malaysia and Singapore. After all, even in less hospitable and more repressive environments, alternative journalism surfaces to challenge the hegemonic dominance of the mainstream. However, the fate of any individual organism of this diverse species remains tenuous. For those who, in reading these pages, have come round to rooting for these underdog activists, there is no happy ending here. None of the groups has found a formula free of internal contradictions or external pressures. Neither, however, is theirs a lost cause. These groups keep alight what Downing calls a "mnemonic flame."[65] In societies that have tended to reward blinkered conformity, they remain flickering reminders of alternative possibilities.

NOTES

Chapter 1

1. "Weed out the Roots," *New Straits Times*, 6 January 2002; "Cohesion above all," *The Straits Times*, 8 January 2002. *New Straits Times* and *The Straits Times* are the main broadsheet newspapers of Malaysia and Singapore respectively. Their similar names are due to the fact that they were once the same paper, serving both territories.

2. Cherian George, "Framing the fight against terror: order versus liberty in the mainstream and alternative media." Paper delivered at the International Communication Association Annual Conference, San Diego, 27 May 2003.

3. Susan Loone, "Gov't Rapped for Latest ISA Arrests, Urged to Show Evidence," *Malaysiakini*, 5 January 2002.

4. Anbarasu Balrasan, "ISD Arrests: Take Political Realities into Account," ThinkCentre, 7 January 2002 [cited January 2003]; available from <http://www.thinkcentre.org>.

5. Note that this definition of journalism incorporates practitioners' acceptance of certain responsibilities. This is in the spirit of, for example, the Committee of Concerned Journalists' "Statement of Concern;" available from <http://www.journalism.org>.

6.   *Information and Communication Technology Statistics* [web page].
     International Telecommunication Union [cited March 2003]. Available
     from <http://www.itu.int/ITU-D/ict/statistics>.

7.   See, for example, Putnam.

8.   See, for example: Peter Dahlgren, "The Public Sphere and the
     Net: Structure, Space and Communication," in *Mediated Politics:
     Communication in the Future of Democracy*, ed. W. Lance Bennett and
     Robert M. Entman (Cambridge: Cambridge University Press, 2001);
     Z. Papacharissi, "The Virtual Sphere: The Internet as a Public Sphere,"
     New Media and Society 4, no. 1 (2002); S. O'Donnell, "Analysing the
     Internet and the Public Sphere: The Case of Womenslink," *Javnost
     – The Public* 8, no. 1 (2001); Bruce Bimber, "The Internet and Political
     Transformation: Populism, Community, and Accelerated Pluralism,"
     Polity 31, no. 1 (1998); Lincoln Dahlberg, "Cyberspace and the Public
     Sphere: Exploring the Democratic Potential of the Net," *Convergence*
     4, no. 1 (1998): 70–84.

9.   Kevin A. Hill and John E. Hughes, "Computer-Mediated Political
     Communication: The Usenet and Political Communities," *Political
     Communication* 14, no. 1 (1997). See also Flaherty, Lisa M., Kevin J.
     Pearce, and Rebecca B. Rubin, "Internet and Face-to-Face Com-
     munication: Not Functional Alternatives," *Communication Quarterly*
     46, no. 3 (1998): 250–68.

10. For example: Kenneth L. Hacker, "Missing Links in the Evolution
     of Electronic Democratization," *Media, Culture and Society* 18 (1996);
     Barry N. Hague and Brian D. Loader, eds., *Digital Democracy: Discourse
     and Decision Making in the Information Age* (London and New York:
     Routledge, 1999).

11. For example: John V. Pavlik and Steven S. Ross, "Journalism Online:
     Exploring the Impact of New Media on News and Society," in
     *Understanding the Web: Social, Political, and Economic Dimensions of
     the Internet*, ed. Alan B. Albarran and David H. Goff (Ames, Iowa:
     Iowa State University Press, 2000).

12. Bill Kovach and Tom Rosenstiel, *Warp Speed: America in the Age of
     Mixed Media* (New York: Century Foundation, 1999).

13. Elihu Katz, "The End of Journalism? Notes on Watching the War,"
     Journal of Communication 42 (1992).

14. See, for example: Thomas Johnson and Barbara K. Kaye, "Cruising Is Believing? Comparing Internet and Traditional Sources on Media Credibility Measures," *Journalism and Mass Communication Quarterly* 75, no. 2 (1998): 325–40; Thomas Johnson, Mahmoud A.M. Braima, and Jayanthi Sothirajah, "Doing the Traditional Media Sidestep: Comparing the Effects of the Internet and Other Nontraditional Media with Traditional Media in the 1996 Presidential Campaign," *Journalism and Mass Communication Quarterly* 76, no. 1 (1999): 99–123.

15. Colin Sparks, "From Dead Trees to Live Wires: The Internet's Challenge to the Traditional Newspaper," in *Mass Media and Society*, ed. James Curran and Michael Gurevitch (New York: Oxford University Press, 2000).

16. H.M. Cleaver, Jr., "The Zapatista Effect: The Internet and the Rise of an Alternative Political Fabric," *Journal of International Affairs* 51, no. 2 (1998); Tamara Villarreal Ford and Geneve Gil, "Radical Internet Use," in *Radical Media: Rebellious Communication and Social Movements*, ed. John D.H. Downing (Thousand Oaks, Calif.: Sage, 2001); O. Froehling, "The Cyberspace 'War of Ink and Internet' in Chiapas, Mexico," *Geographical Review* 87, no. 2 (1997); Jerry W. Knudson, "Rebellion in Chiapas: Insurrection by Internet and Public Relations," *Media, Culture & Society* 20, no. 3 (1998). A. Russell, "Chiapas and the New News: Internet and Newspaper Coverage of a Broken Cease-Fire," *Journalism* 2, no. 2 (2001).

17. Knudson, "Rebellion in Chiapas: Insurrection by Internet and Public Relations," p. 507.

18. Kasun Ubayasiri, "A Virtual Eelam: Democracy, Internet and Sri Lanka's Tamil Struggle," in *Asian Cyberactivism: Freedom of Expression and Media Censorship*, ed. Steven Gan, James Gomez, and Uwe Johannen (Bangkok, Thailand: Friedrich Naumann Stiftung, 2004).

19. Tedjabayu Basuki, "Indonesia: The Web as a Weapon," *Development Dialogue* 2 (1998); David T. Hill and Krishna Sen, "The Internet in Indonesia's New Democracy," *Democratization* 7, no. 1 (2000).

20. Peter Ferdinand, "The Internet, Democracy and Democratization," *Democratization* 7, no. 1 (2000).

21. Craig Warkentin and Karen Mingst, "International Institutions, the State, and Global Civil Society in the Age of the World Wide Web," *Global Governance* 6, no. 2 (2000).

22. S. O'Donnell, "Analysing the Internet and the Public Sphere: The Case of Womenslink," *Javnost – The Public* 8, no. 1 (2001): 39–57; Susanna George and Luz Maria Martinez, "Digital advocacy and the women's movement: global success, grassroots challenge," in *Asian Cyberactivism: Freedom of Expression and Media Censorship*, ed. Steven Gan, James Gomez, and Uwe Johannen (Bangkok, Thailand: Friedrich Naumann Stiftung, 2004).

23. Michael Whine, "Cyberspace — a New Medium for Communication, Command, and Control by Extremists," *Studies in Conflict and Terrorism* 22, no. 3 (1999); Peter Chroust, "Neo-Nazis and Taliban on-Line: Anti-Modern Political Movements and Modern Media," *Democratization* 7, no. 1 (2000); James David Ballard, Joseph G. Hornik, and Douglas McKenzie, "Technological Facilitation of Terrorism," *American Behavioral Scientist* 45, no. 6 (2002). Brian Levin, "Cyberhate: A Legal and Historical Analysis of Extremists' Use of Computer Networks in America," *American Behavioral Scientist* 45, no. 6 (2002); John J. Stanton, "Terror in Cyberspace," *American Behavioral Scientist* 45, no. 6 (2002). Whine, "Cyberspace — a New Medium for Communication, Command, and Control by Extremists;" John Arquilla, David Ronfeldt, and Michele Zanini. "Information-Age Terrorism," *Current History* 99, no. 636 (2000): 179. Zafarullah Khan, "Cyber jihad: Fighting the infidels from Pakistan," in *Asian Cyberactivism: Freedom of Expression and Media Censorship*, Steven Gan, James Gomez, and Uwe Johannen (Bangkok, Thailand: Friedrich Naumann Stiftung, 2004).

24. Geoffry Taubman, "A Not-So World Wide Web: The Internet, China, and the Challenges to Nondemocratic Rule," *Political Communication* 15 (1998): 268.

25. Jonathan Zittrain and Benjamin Edelman, *Empirical Analysis of Internet Filtering in China*, Berkman Center for Internet & Society, Harvard Law School, 2003 [cited May 2003]. Available from <http://cyber.law.harvard.edu/filtering/china>.

26. S. Kalathil and T.C. Boas, "The Internet and State Control in Authoritarian Regimes: China, Cuba, and the Counterrevolution," in *Carnegie Endowment Working Papers 21* (Washington, DC: Carnegie Endowment for International Peace, 2001). See also Jason P. Abbott, "Democracy@InternetAsia? The Challenges to the Emancipatory Potential of theNet: Lessons from China and Malaysia," *Third World Quarterly* 22, no. 1 (2001): 99–114; Nina Hachigian, "China's Cyber-Strategy," *Foreign Affairs*, March/April (2000): 118–33; Hao, Xiaoming, K. Zhang and H. Yu, "The Internet and Information Control: The Case of China," *Electronic Journal of Communication* 6, no. 2 (1996); Georgette Wang, "Regulating Network Communication in Asia: A Different Balancing Act?" *Telecommunications Policy* 23, no. 3/4 (1999): 277–87; Deibert, Ronald J. "Dark Guests and Great Firewalls: The Internet and Chinese Security Policy," *Journal of Social Issues* 58, no. 1 (2002): 143–59.

27. "The Internet's New Borders," *The Economist*, 11–17 August 2001.

28. Lawrence Lessig, *The Future of Ideas* (New York: Vintage, 2002). Also: J.H. Saltzer, D.P. Reed, and D.D. Clark, *End-to-End Arguments in System Design* (1981 [cited February 2003]); available from <http://web.mit.edu/Saltzer/www/publications>.

29. Robert Keohane and Joseph S. Nye Jr., "Power and Inter-dependence in the Information Age," in *Governance.Com: Democracy in the Information Age*, ed. Elaine Ciulla Kamarck and Joseph S. Nye Jr. (Cambridge, Mass.; Washington, D.C.: Brookings Institution Press, 2002), p. 165. See also: Nazli Choucri, "Introduction: Cyberpolitics in International Relations," *International Political Science Review* 21, no. 3 (2000): 243–63.

30. Martin Spinelli, "Democratic Rhetoric and Emergent Media: The Marketing of Participatory Community on Radio and the Internet," *International Journal of Cultural Studies* 3, no. 2 (2000): 276–7.

31. C.S. Fisher, "Studying Technology and Social Life," in *Technology, Space and Society: Emerging Trends*, ed. M. Castells (Beverly Hills, Calif.: Sage, 1985). Francois Fortier, *Virtuality Check: Power Relations and Alternative Strategies in the Information Society* (London and New York: Verso, 2001).

32. Lawrence Lessig, *Code* (New York: Basic Books, 1999), p. 6.

33. M. Blumenthal and D. Clark, "Rethinking the Design of the Internet: The End to End Arguments vs. The Brave New World," in *Communications Policy in Transition: The Internet and Beyond*, ed. S. Greenstein and B. Compaine (Cambridge, Mass.: MIT Press, 2001).

34. Lessig, *The Future of Ideas*, p. 146.

35. Robert W. McChesney, *Rich Media, Poor Democracy: Communication Politics in Dubious Times* (Urbana and Chicago: University of Illinois Press, 1999). Ben H. Bagdikian, *The Media Monopoly*, 5th ed. (Boston: Beacon Press, 1997).

36. Lessig, *Code*, p. 44.

37. Ibid., p. 25.

38. John Bray, "Tibet, Democracy and the Internet Bazaar," *Democratization* 7, no. 1 (2000).

39. David L. Richards, "Making the National International: Information Technology and Government Respect for Human Rights," in *Technology, Development, and Democracy: International Conflict and Cooperation in the Information Age*, ed. Juliann Emmons Allison (Albany, New York: State University of New York Press, 2002).

40. Kevin A. Hill and John E. Hughes, "Is the Internet an Instrument of Global Democratization," *Democratization* 6, no. 2 (1999).

41. Tim Jordan, "Language and Libertarianism: The Politics of Cyberculture and the Culture of Cyberpolitics," *The Sociological Review* 49, no. 1 (2001).

42. Ibid., p. 8.

43. C. Nass and L. Mason, "On the Study of Technology and Task: A Variable-Based Approach," in *Organization and Communication Technology*, ed. J. Fulk and C. Steinfeld (Newbury Park: Sage, 1990). J.S. Steuer, "Defining Virtual Reality: Dimensions Determining Telepresence," *Journal of Communication* 42, no. 4 (1992).

44. J.D. Bolter, *Turing's Man: Western Culture in the Computer Age* (Chapel Hill: University of North Carolina Press, 1984).

45. Paul C. Adams, "Cyberspace and Virtual Places," *Geographical Review* 87, no. 2 (1997).

46. Ibid., p. 155.

47. Ibid., p. 157.

48. Ibid., p. 168.

49. Papacharissi, "The Virtual Sphere: The Internet as a Public Sphere."
50. Gary King, Robert Keohane, and Sidney Verba, *Designing Social Inquiry: Scientific Inference in Qualitative Research.* (Princeton, New Jersey: Princeton University Press, 1994), p. 43.
51. Paul DiMaggio *et al.*, "The Internet's Impact on Society," *Annual Review of Sociology 2001* 27 (2001).
52. Philip Howard, "Can Technology Enhance Democracy? The Doubters' Answer," *Journal of Politics* 63, no. 3 (2001): 952.
53. Charles C. Ragin, *The Comparative Method* (Berkeley and Los Angeles, Calif.: University of California Press, 1987).
54. Ibid., p. 167.
55. C. Gershman, "The Internet and Democracy Building — the N.E.D. Experience," Paper presented at The Internet and Democracy Building International Workshop, the U.K. Foreign and Commonwealth Office, Wilton Park, U.K., 27–28 April 2001.

Chapter 2

1. Fred S. Siebert, Theodore Peterson, and Wilbur Schramm, *Four Theories of the Press: The Authoritarian, Libertarian, Social Responsibility and Soviet Communist Concepts of What the Press Should Be and Do* (Urbana: University of Illinois Press, 1956).
2. John C. Nerone, ed., *Last Rights: Revisiting 'Four Theories of the Press'* (Urbana: University of Illinois Press, 1995).
3. Larry Diamond, "Thinking About Hybrid Regimes," *Journal of Democracy* 13, no. 2 (2002).
4. Philippe C. Schmitter, "More Liberal, Preliberal, or Postliberal?," in *The Global Resurgence of Democracy*, ed. Larry Diamond and Marc F. Plattner (Baltimore and London: The Johns Hopkins University Press, 1996), p. 329.
5. Diamond, "Thinking About Hybrid Regimes."
6. Ibid., p. 25.
7. John C. Merrill, Peter J. Gade, and Frederick R. Blevens, *Twilight of Press Freedom: The Rise of People's Journalism* (Mahwah, New Jersey: Lawrence Erlbaum, 2001), p. 2.
8. Eric Kit-Wai Ma, "Rethinking Media Studies: The Case of China," in *De-Westernizing Media Studies*, ed. James Curran and Myung-Jin

Park (London: Routledge, 2000), Colin Sparks, "Media Theory after the Fall of European Communism: Why the Old Models from East and West Won't Do Anymore," in *De-Westernizing Media Studies*, ed. James Curran and Myung-Jin Park (London: Routledge, 2000).

9. Nerone, ed., *Last Rights: Revisiting 'Four Theories of the Press'*.

10. Daniel Hallin and Paolo Mancini. "Speaking of the President: Political Structure and Representational Form in U.S. And Italian Television News," *Theory and Society* 13, no. 6 (1984): 829–50.

11. Ibid., p. 846.

12. Daniel Hallin and Paolo Mancini, *Comparing Media Systems: Three Models of Media and Politics* (Cambridge, UK: Cambridge University Press, 2004).

13. Gade Merrill and Blevens, *Twilight of Press Freedom: The Rise of People's Journalism*.

14. Ibid., p. 6.

15. An example is Adam Przeworski *et al*'s study, *Democracy and development: political institutions and material well-being in the world, 1950–1990* (Cambridge: Cambridge University Press, 2000).

16. Max Weber, *Economy and Society: An Outline of Interpretive Sociology*, ed. Guenther Roth and Claus Wittich, 2 vols., vol. 1 (Berkeley: University of California Press, 1978).

17. Ibid., p. 56.

18. James Scott, *Seeing Like a State: How Certain Schemes to Improve the Human Condition Have Failed* (New Haven: Yale University Press, 1998).

19. Michel Foucault, "Governmentality," in *The Foucault Effect: Studies in Governmentality*, ed. Graham Burchell, Colin Gordon, and Peter Miller (Chicago: University of Chicago Press, 1991), p. 92.

20. Weber, *Economy and Society: An Outline of Interpretive Sociology*, p. 314.

21. Stephen Krasner, "Approaches to the State: Alternative Conceptions and Historical Dynamics," *Comparative Politics* (1984): 227.

22. Barry Weingast, "The Political Foundations of Democracy and the Rule of Law," *American Political Science Review* 91, no. 2 (1997).

23. Ronald Wintrobe, *The Political Economy of Dictatorship* (Cambridge University Press, 1998), p. 38.

24. Mancur Olson, *Power and Prosperity: Outgrowing Communist and Capitalist Dictatorships* (New York: Basic Books, 2000).

25. David Held, *Political Theory and the Modern State* (Stanford, Calif.: Stanford University Press, 1989), p. 101.

26. Diamond, "Thinking About Hybrid Regimes," p. 24.

27. Andreas Schedler, "The Menu of Manipulation," *Journal of Democracy* 13, no. 2 (2002): 37.

28. Ibid., p. 36.

29. Perry Anderson, "The Antinomies of Antonio Gramsci," *New Left Review*, no. 100 (1997).

30. Raymond Williams, *Marxism and Literature* (Oxford, New York: Oxford University Press, 1977), p. 110.

31. Stuart Hall, "The Rediscovery of 'Ideology': Return of the Repressed in Media Studies," in *Culture, Society and the Media*, ed. Michael Gurevitch *et al.* (London and New York: Methuen, 1982).

32. Ralph Miliband, *The State in Capitalist Society* (London: Weidenfeld and Nicolson, 1969), p. 238.

33. Colin Gordon, "Government Rationality: An Introduction," in *The Foucault Effect: Studies in Governmentality*, ed. Graham Burchell, Colin Gordon, and Peter Miller (Chicago: University of Chicago Press, 1991), p. 3.

34. Ibid., p. 48.

35. Quoted in ibid., p. 5.

36. Theda Skocpol, "Bringing the State Back In: Strategies of Analysis in Current Research," in *Bringing the State Back In*, ed. Peter Evans, Dietrich Rueschemeyer, and Theda Skocpol (Cambridge University Press, 1985), p. 9.

37. James C. Scott, *Domination and the Arts of Resistance: Hidden Transcripts* (New Haven: Yale University Press, 1990).

38. Ibid., p. 120.

39. Sidney Tarrow, *Power in Movement: Social Movements and Contentious Politics*, 2nd ed. (Cambridge University Press, 1998), p. 67.

40. Miliband, *The State in Capitalist Society*, p. 54.

41. Akhil Gupta, "Blurred Boundaries: The Discourse of Corruption, the Culture of Politics, and the Imagined State," *American Ethnologist* 22, no. 2 (1995).

42. Singapore Infomap, <http://www.sg>.
43. Malaya — the western, peninsular portion of what became Malaysia — was a British colony until 1957. Singapore, together with Malaysia's eastern states on the island of Borneo, was under the British until 1963.
44. For general historical and critical reviews of politics, see, for example: Robert Milne and Diane Mauzy, *Malaysian Politics under Mahathir* (London; New York: Routledge, 1999); Francis Loh and Khoo Boo Teik (eds.), *Democracy in Malaysia: Discourses and Practices* (Richmond, Surrey: Curzon, 2002); Diane Mauzy and Robert Milne, *Singapore politics under the People's Action Party* (London: Routledge, 2002); Cherian George, *Singapore: The Air-conditioned Nation. Essays on the Politics of Comfort and Control, 1990–2000* (Singapore: Landmark Books, 2000).
45. Diamond, "Thinking About Hybrid Regimes."
46. Adam Przeworski, *Democracy and the Market: Political and Economic Reforms in Eastern Europe and Latin America* (Cambridge: Cambridge University Press, 1991), p. 58.
47. See, for example, Beng-Huat Chua, *Communitarian Ideology and Democracy in Singapore* (London, New York: Routledge, 1995); John Hilley, *Malaysia: Mahathirism, Hegemony and the New Opposition* (London; New York: Zed Books, 2001).
48. The phrase is borrowed from the literature on democratic consolidation, such as Juan J. Linz and Alfred Stepan, *Problems of Democratic Transition and Consolidation* (Baltimore and London: The Johns Hopkins University Press, 1996).
49. William Case, "Semi-Democracy in Malaysia: Withstanding the Pressures for Regime Change," *Pacific Affairs* 66, no. 2 (1993): 204. See also William Case, *Politics in Southeast Asia* (Richmond, Surrey: Curzon Press, 2002).
50. See also Alvin Gouldner, *The Dialectic of Ideology and Technology: The Origins, Grammar, and Future of Ideology* (New York: The Seabury Press, 1976). Gouldner argues that the mass media, or "consciousness industry," operates within a profit-maximization framework that is integrated with the state apparatus, seeking to avoid overtly political acts.

51. Overviews of media regulations in the two countries can be found in Kean Wong, "Malaysia: In the Grip of the Goverment," in *Losing Control: Freedom of the Press in Asia*, ed. Louise Williams and Roland Rich (Asia Pacific Press at the Australian National University, 2000); Garry Rodan, "Singapore: Information Lockdown," in *Losing Control: Freedom of the Press in Asia*, ed. Louise Williams and Roland Rich (Asia Pacific Press at the Australian National University, 2000); Zaharom Nain, "Globalized Theories and National Control: The State, the Market, and the Malaysian Media," in *De-Westernizing Media Studies*, ed. James Curran and Myung-Jin Park (London: Routledge, 2000); Wang Lay Kim, "Media and Democracy in Malaysia," *Javnost – The Public* 8, no. 2 (2001). Francis T. Seow, *The Media Enthralled: Singapore Revisited* (Boulder, Colorado: Lynne Rienner Publishers, 1998); William Hachten, "Media Development without Press Freedom: Lee Kuan Yew's Singapore," *Journalism Quarterly* 66, no. 4 (1989): 822–27.

52. Wong, "Malaysia: In the Grip of the Goverment."

53. Diane Mauzy and Robert Milne, *Singapore Politics under the People's Action Party* (London; New York: Routledge, 2002).

54. In Malaysia, the relevant law is the Houses of Parliament (Privileges and Powers) Act 1952. Singapore's is the Parliament (Privileges, Immunities And Powers) Act 1962.

55. Newspaper and Printing Presses Act 1974.

56. Rodan, "Singapore: Information Lockdown."

57. Leslie Fong, "A time to cheer, a time to dissent," *The Straits Times, 150 Years* anniversary supplement (15 July 1995).

58. Ben H. Bagdikian, *The Media Monopoly*, 5th ed. (Boston: Beacon Press, 1997), Robert W. McChesney, *Rich Media, Poor Democracy: Communication Politics in Dubious Times* (Urbana and Chicago: University of Illinois Press, 1999), Robert G. Picard, "Media Concentration, Economics, and Regulation," in *The Politics of News, the News of Politics*, ed. Doris Graber, Denis McQuail, and Pippa Norris (Washington, D.C.: C.Q. Press, 1998).

59. Edmund Terence Gomez and K.S. Jomo, *Malaysia's Political Economy: Politics, Patronage and Profits*, 2nd ed. (Cambridge University Press, 1999).

60. Drew O. McDaniel, *Broadcasting in the Malay World* (Norwood, New Jersey: Ablex, 1994), p. 85.

61. Gomez and Jomo, *Malaysia's Political Economy: Politics, Patronage and Profits.*

62. Zaharom Nain, "Rhetoric and Realities in Malaysian Television Policy in an Era of Globalization," *Asian Journal of Communication* 6, no. 1 (1996): 50, 54.

63. Gomez and Jomo, *Malaysia's Political Economy: Politics, Patronage and Profits.*

64. Nain, "Rhetoric and Realities in Malaysian Television Policy in an Era of Globalization," p. 52.

65. Zaharom Nain, "The Media and Malaysia's Reformasi Movement," in *Media Fortunes, Changing Times: Asean States in Transition*, ed. Russell Hiang-Khng Heng (Singapore: Institute of Southeast Asian Studies, 2002).

66. Nain, "Rhetoric and Realities in Malaysian Television Policy in an Era of Globalization," p. 48.

67. "A few minutes cost S'pore businessmen," *The Straits Times*, 13 February 1991: 16.

68. Satellite dishes: Temporary licences for banks," *The Straits Times*, 10 February 1991: 1.

69. Garry Rodan, "Asian Crisis, Transparency and the International Media in Singapore," *The Pacific Review* 13, no. 2 (2000): 218.

70. Ibid., pp. 236–7.

71. Ibid., p. 221.

72. Ibid., p. 219.

Chapter 3

1. Francois Fortier, *Virtuality Check: Power Relations and Alternative Strategies in the Information Society* (London and New York: Verso, 2001).

2. *Reno, Attorney General of the United States Et Al. V. American Civil Liberties Union Et Al.*, 000 U.S. 96-511, 1997.

3. Printing Presses and Publications Act (1984)

4. See Chapter 2.

5. See Chapter 2.

6. Newspaper and Printing Presses Act
7. Thomas P. Hughes, *Rescuing Prometheus* (New York: Pantheon Books, 1998).
8. Manuel Castells, *The Rise of the Network Society*, 2nd ed., vol. 1, *The Information Age: Economy, Society and Culture* (Oxford: Blackwell, 2000), pp. 16–7.
9. Ibid., p. 147.
10. W. Russell Neuman, Lee McKnight, and Richard Jay Solomon, *The Gordian Knot: Political Gridlock on the Information Highway* (Cambridge, Massachusetts; London, England: MIT Press, 1997), p. 14.
11. Michael Minges and Vanessa Gray, *Multimedia Malaysia: Internet Case Study* (International Telecommunication Union, 2002 [cited March 2003]); available from <http://www.itu.int/ITU-D/ict/cs/>. Rahmah Hashim and Arfah Yusof, "Malaysia," in *Internet in Asia*, ed. Sankaran Ramanathan and Jorg Becker (Singapore: Asian Media Information and Communication Centre, 2001).
12. John Hilley, *Malaysia: Mahathirism, Hegemony and the New Opposition* (London; New York: Zed Books, 2001), p. 4.
13. "P.M. Confident Malaysia Can Maintain Growth Rate," *New Straits Times*, 8 August 1996.
14. "Global Bridge to Information Age," *New Straits Times*, 16 January 1997.
15. "Chairmen of N.I.T.C.'s Five Working Groups Named," *New Straits Times*, 1 October 1998.
16. "Global Bridge to Information Age."
17. *About the M. D. C.* [web page]. Multimedia Development Corporation, [cited February 2003]. Available from <http://www.mdc.com.my>.
18. Michael Minges, Magda Ismail, and Larry Press, *The E-City: Singapore Internet Case Study* (International Telecommunication Union, 2001 [cited March 2003]); available from <http://www.itu.int/ITU-D/ict/cs/>.
19. M. Jussawalla, M.H. Toh, and L. Low, "Singapore: An Intelligent City-State," *Asian Journal of Communication* 2, no. 3 (1992).
20. "Singnet Will Allow Public to Access Data from July 1," *The Straits Times*, 25 June 1994.
21. Yeo Cheow Tong, "Bridging the Digital Divide — Dot-Comming the People Sector. Speech at the Launch of E-Celebrations Singapore," 1 March 2000.

22. George Yeo, "Speech at the Launch of Singapore Infomap," 8 March 1995.
23. See, for example, Kace Ong, "Michael Fay, Singapore and Internet," *The Straits Times*, 30 June 1994.
24. Ibid.
25. <http://www.sg>.
26. Stanley D. Brunn and Charles D. Cottle, "Small States and Cyberboosterism," *Geographical Review* 87, no. 2 (1997): 249.
27. Jimmy Yap, "Wrong Information on S'pore Posted on Internet," *The Straits Times*, 27 February 1995; "M.C.A. To Launch Homepage in Internet for Detailed Party Information," *New Straits Times*, 6 March 1996.
28. "Global Bridge to Information Age."
29. Ibid.
30. See, for example, "Internet to Stay Uncensored, Says Moggie," *Bernama*, 4 March 2000.
31. Khairy Jamaludin, Interview with author, Bali, Indonesia, 31 August 2002.
32. Brendan Pereira, "Police Clamp Down on Net Rumours," *The Straits Times*, 24 September 1998.
33. "Pro-Anwar Websites Closed by Us Hosting Service," *The Straits Times*, 20 March 2001.
34. Leslie Lau, "Police Query Online Paper's Staff over 'Seditious' Letter," *The Straits Times*, 23 January 2003.
35. Singapore's pioneering regulatory model has inspired other authoritarian regimes, according to Garry Rodan, "The Internet and Political Control in Singapore," *Political Science Quarterly* 113, no. 1 (1998): 63–89.
36. "A Question of Freedom," *Investor's Digest*, 16 March 1997.
37. Jason Tan, "Banning of 100 smut sites more a gesture of concern," *The Straits Times*, 2 November 1997: 27.
38. Samtani Anil, "Re-Visiting the Singapore Internet Code of Practice," *Journal of Information, Law and Technology*, no. 2 (2001).
39. *Myths and Facts About M.D.A. And the Internet* [web page]. Media Development Authority, [cited February 2003]. Available from <http://www.mda.gov.sg/medium/internet/i_myths.html>.

40. "Man Allegedly 'Encouraged Law-Breaking on Web'," *The Straits Times*, 18 November 2001.

41. Rodan argues that the internet has facilitated government surveillance, helping it to identify critics. See "The Internet and Political Control in Singapore."

42. Zulfikar Mohamad Shariff, "Fateha.com: challenging control over Malay/Muslim voices in Singapore," pp. 318–68 in *Asian Cyberactivism: Freedom of Expression and Media Censorship*, ed. S. Gan, J. Gomez, and U. Johannen (Bangkok, Thailand: Friedrich Naumann Foundation, 2004).

43. Firdaus Abdullah, "PM: Others Now Also Using ISA," *The New Straits Times*, September 30, 2001.

44. J.H. Saltzer, D.P. Reed, and D.D. Clark, *End-to-End Arguments in System Design* (1981 [cited February 2003]); available from <http://web.mit.edu/Saltzer/www/publications>.

45. M. Blumenthal and D. Clark, "Rethinking the Design of the Internet: The End to End Arguments Vs. The Brave New World," in *Communications Policy in Transition: The Internet and Beyond*, ed. S. Greenstein and B. Compaine (Cambridge, Mass.: MIT Press, 2001).

46. Lawrence Lessig, *Code* (New York: Basic Books, 1999).

47. John Perry Barlow, *A Declaration of the Independence of Cyberspace* (1996 [cited February 2003]); available from <http://www.eff.org/~barlow/Declaration-Final.html>.

48. "The Internet's New Borders," *The Economist*, 9 August 2001: 9.

49. Shanthi Kalathil and Taylor C. Boas, *Open Networks Closed Regimes: The Impact of the Internet on Authoritarian Rule* (Washington, DC: Carnegie Endowment for International Peace, 2003), p. 136.

Chapter 4

1. "N.S.P. Is First Opposition Party to Launch Own Web Site," *The Straits Times*, 9 March 1996; Ian Stewart, "Internet Curbs in the Pipeline," *South China Morning Post*, 13 March 1996.

2. <http://www.malaysia.net/lists/sangkancil/>.

3. M.G.G. Pillai, Interview with author, Kuala Lumpur, Malaysia, 23 July 2002.

4. "Websites Used to Attack Government Identified," *New Straits Times*, 9 August 1999. Among the sites named were Reformasi (<http://www.mahazalim.net/>) and Free Malaysia (<http://www.freemalaysia.com>).

5. Joceline Tan, "No-Holds-Barred Game of Malay Politics on the Net," *New Straits Times*, 23 May 1999.

6. Chandra Muzaffar, Interview with author, Kuala Lumpur, Malaysia, March 2002.

7. Zain's online journalism has been published in a book, Sabri Zain, *Face Off: A Malaysian Reformasi Diary (1998–99)* (Singapore: BigO Books, 2002). Saksi is at <http://www.saksi.com>.

8. <http://www.malaysiakini.com>; <http://www.harakahdaily.net>; <http://www.agendadaily.com>.

9. <http://www.aliran.com>.

10. <http://www.radiqradio.com>.

11. K.C. Ho, Zaheer Baber, and Habibul Khondker, "'Sites' of Resistance: Alternative Websites and State-Society Relations," *British Journal of Sociology* 53, no. 1 (2002).

12. <http://www.sfdonline and http://www.singapore-window.org>.

13. <http://www.thinkcentre.org>.

14. <http://www.fateha.com>. See Zulfikar Mohamad Shariff, "Fateha.com: challenging control over Malay/Muslim voices in Singapore," pp. 318–68 in *Asian Cyberactivism: Freedom of Expression and Media Censorship*, ed. S. Gan, J. Gomez, and U. Johannen (Bangkok, Thailand: Friedrich Naumann Foundation, 2004).

15. <http://www.bigo.com.sg>.

16. <http://www.sammyboy.com/>.

17. Glenn Carroll, "Concentration and Specialization: Dynamics of Niche Width in Populations of Organizations," *American Journal of Sociology* 90, no. 6 (1985); Glenn Carroll, *Publish and Perish: The Organizational Ecology of Newspaper Industries* (Greenwich, Conn.: JAI Press, 1987).

18. Chris Atton, *Alternative Media* (London: Sage Publications, 2002); John D.H. Downing, *Radical Media: Rebellious Communication and Social Movements* (Thousand Oaks, Calif.: Sage, 2001).

19. Downing, *Radical Media: Rebellious Communication and Social Movements*, p. v.

20. Ibid., p. 8.
21. Charlotte Morton, "The 'Arbeiter Illustrierte Zeitung' in Weimar Germany," *Media, Culture and Society* 7, no. 2 (1985): 202.
22. Elliott Shore, "Selling Socialism: The 'Appeal to Reason' and the Radical Press in Turn-of-the-Century America," *Media, Culture and Society* 7, no. 2 (1985).
23. C.C. Maslog *et al.*, eds., *Communication for People Power: An Introduction to Community Communication* (Philippines: UNESCO, Project Tambali, 1997); Frances J. Berrigan, *Access: Some Western Models of Community Media* (Paris: United Nations Educational, Scientific and Cultural Organization, 1977).
24. Colin Sparks, "The Working-Class Press: Radical and Revolutionary Alternatives," *Media, Culture and Society* 7, no. 2 (1985).
25. Shore, "Selling Socialism: The 'Appeal to Reason' and the Radical Press in Turn-of-the-Century America."
26. Mitchell Stephens, *A History of News* (New York: Viking, 1988); Michael Schudson, *Discovering the News: A Social History of American Newspapers* (Basic Books, 1978).
27. David Armstrong, *A Trumpet to Arms: Alternative Media in America* (Boston, Mass.: South End Press, 1981).
28. James K. Hertog and Douglas M. McLeod, "Anarchists Wreak Havoc in Downtown Minneapolis: A Multi-Level Study of Media Coverage of Radical Protest," *Journalism and Mass Communication Monographs* 151 (1995). See also Eric Swank, "In Newspapers We Trust? Assessing the Credibility of News Sources that Cover Protest Campaigns," in *Research in Social Movements, Conflict and Change* 22, ed. Patrick G. Coy (Stamford, Conn.: JAI Press, 2000).
29. Todd Gitlin, *The Whole World Is Watching: Mass Media in the Making and Unmaking of the New Left* (Berkeley, Los Angeles, London: University of California Press, 1980).
30. W.A. Gamson and G. Wolfsfeld, "Movements and Media as Interacting Systems," *Annals of The American Academy of Political and Social Science* 528 (1993).
31. Pamela J. Shoemaker, "Media Treatment of Deviant Groups," *Journalism Quarterly* 61, no. 1 (1984): 75.

32. Herbert J. Gans, *Deciding What's News: A Study of CBS Evening News, NBC Nightly News, Newsweek, and Time* (New York: Pantheon Books, 1979).

33. Ibid., p. 51.

34. Ibid., p. 61.

35. See, for example: W Lance Bennett, "Cracking the News Code: Some Rules That Journalists Live By," in *Do the Media Govern?: Politicians, Voters, and Reporters in America*, ed. Shanto Iyengar and Richard Reeves (Thousand Oaks, Calif.: Sage Publications, 1997); Gitlin, *The Whole World Is Watching: Mass Media in the Making and Unmaking of the New Left;* Leon V. Sigal, "Who? Sources Make the News," in *Reading the News*, ed. Robert Karl Manoff and Michael Schudson (New York: Pantheon Books, 1986).

36. Nina Eliasoph, "Routines and the Making of Oppositional News," *Critical Studies in Mass Communication* 5, no. 4 (1988); Edward S. Herman, "The Propaganda Model Revisited," in *Capitalism and the Information Age: The Political Economy of the Global Communication Revolution*, ed. Robert W. McChesney, Ellen Meiksins Wood, and John Bellamy Foster (New York: Monthly Review Press, 1998); Robert W. McChesney, "The Political Economy of Global Communication," in *Capitalism and the Information Age: The Political Economy of the Global Communication Revolution*, ed. Robert W. McChesney, Ellen Meiksins Wood, and John Bellamy Foster (New York: Monthly Review Press, 1998).

37. Raymond Williams, "Means of Communication as Means of Production," in *Problems in Materialism and Culture: Selected Essays* (London: Verso, 1980).

38. Atton, *Alternative Media.*

39. Downing, *Radical Media: Rebellious Communication and Social Movements*, p. 51.

40. Maslog *et al.*, eds., *Communication for People Power: An Introduction to Community Communication.*

41. Armstrong, *A Trumpet to Arms: Alternative Media in America.*

42. Philip F. Lawler, *The Alternative Influence: The Impact of Investigative Reporting Groups on America's Media* (Lanham, Maryland: University Press of America and The Media Institute, 1984).

43. Shore, "Selling Socialism: The 'Appeal to Reason' and the Radical Press in Turn-of-the-Century America."

44. Morton, "The 'Arbeiter Illustrierte Zeitung' in Weimar Germany."

45. Atton, *Alternative Media*.

46. Karin Wahl-Jorgensen, "The Construction of the Public in Letters to the Editor: Deliberative Democracy and the Idiom of Insanity," *Journalism* 3, no. 2 (2002).

47. Morris Janowitz, "Professional Models in Journalism: The Gatekeeper and the Advocate," *Journalism Quarterly* 52 (1975).

48. Gaye Tuchman, "Objectivity as Strategic Ritual: An Examination of Newsmen's Notions of Objectivity," *American Journal of Sociology* 77 (1972). See also Daniel Hallin and Paolo Mancini. "Speaking of the President: Political Structure and Representational Form in U.S. And Italian Television News," *Theory and Society* 13, no. 6 (1984): 829–50.

49. Mark Fishman, *Manufacturing the News* (Austin, Texas: University of Texas Press, 1980), Jeremy Iggers, *Good News, Bad News: Journalism Ethics and the Public Interest* (Boulder, Colorado: Westview Press, 1998).

50. Glenn Carroll and Michael Hannan, *The Demography of Corporations and Industries* (Princeton, NJ: Princeton University Press, 2000), pp. 273–4.

51. Hertog and McLeod, "Anarchists Wreak Havoc in Downtown Minneapolis: A Multi-Level Study of Media Coverage of Radical Protest."

52. Sidney Tarrow, *Power in Movement: Social Movements and Contentious Politics*, 2nd ed. (Cambridge University Press, 1998).

53. David S. Meyer, "Protest and Political Process," in *The Blackwell Companion to Political Sociology*, ed. Kate Nash and Alan Scott (Oxford, England: Blackwell, 2001), p. 167.

54. Doug McAdam, Sidney Tarrow, and Charles Tilly, *Dynamics of Contention* (Cambridge: Cambridge University Press, 2001).

55. Doug McAdam, "The Political Process Model," in *Political Process and the Development of Black Insurgency, 1930–1970* (Chicago and London: University of Chicago Press, 1999), p. 57.

56. D. McAdam, J.D. McCarthy, and M.N. Zald, eds., *Comparative Perspectives on Social Movements Opportunities, Mobilizing Structures, and Framing* (Cambridge: Cambridge University Press, 1996); Ron Pagnucco, "The Comparative Study of Social Movements and Democratization: Political Interaction and Political Process Approaches," pp. 145–83 in *Research in Social Movements, Conflict and Change*, ed. Louis Kriesberg, Michael Dobkowski, and Isidor Wallimann, (Greenwich, Connecticut and London, England: JAI Press, 1995).

57. Ibid., p. 27.

58. McAdam, "The Political Process Model," p. 41.

59. McAdam, McCarthy, and Zald, eds., *Comparative Perspectives on Social Movements Opportunities, Mobilizing Structures, and Framing*, p. 3.

60. McAdam, "The Political Process Model."

61. Ann Swidler, "Culture in Action: Symbols and Strategies," *American Sociological Review* 51, no. 2 (1986): 273–86.

62. Robert D. Benford and David A. Snow, "Framing Processes and Social Movements: An Overview and Assessment," *Annual Review of Sociology* 26 (2000).

63. McAdam, Tarrow, and Tilly, *Dynamics of Contention*.

64. By prominence in the public sphere, I mean mentions in the mainstream press, online discussions, and conversations among politically-aware Malaysians and Singaporeans. The most interesting *excluded* case is probably Singapore's Fateha, which rose in prominence shortly after the cases were chosen for this study, and is referred to in Chapters 3 and 4.

65. Clifford Geertz, "Thick Description: Toward an Interpretive Theory of Culture," in *The Interpretation of Cultures* (New York: Basic Books, 1973), p. 25.

Chapter 5

1. The contraction of Singapore Internet Community was originally spelt SInterCom, but this was eventually simplified as Sintercom, which is used throughout this work.

2. Robert W. McChesney, *Rich Media, Poor Democracy: Communication Politics in Dubious Times* (Urbana and Chicago: University of Illinois Press, 1999).

3. Chong Kee Tan, E-mail interview with author, January–February 2000.

4. Ibid.

5. *Who Are We?* (Sintercom, 2000 [cited February 2000]); available from <http://www.sintercom.org/editors.html>.

6. Tan.

7. Ibid.

8. *Who Are We?*.

9. *Our Philosophy* (Sintercom, 2000 [cited February 2000]); available from <http://www.sintercom.org/editors.html>.

10. Tan.

11. Wynthia Goh, E-mail interview with author, January–February 2000.

12. Tan.

13. See, for example, Howard Rheingold, "A Slice of My Life in My Virtual Community," in *High Noon on the Electronic Frontier: Conceptual Issues in Cyberspace*, ed. Peter Ludlow (Cambridge, Mass.: MIT Press, 1996).

14. Tan.

15. *Who Are We?*.

16. *Our Philosophy*.

17. *Who Are We?*.

18. Ibid.

19. Alvin Jiang, E-mail interview with author, January–February 2000.

20. Goh.

21. Tan.

22. Ibid.

23. Ibid.

24. Goh.

25. Seng Hon Wong, E-mail interview with author, February 2000.

26. Ibid.

27. Kian Jin Jek, E-mail interview with author, February 2000.

28. Ward Hanson, *Principles of Internet Marketing* (Cincinnati, Ohio: South-Western College Publishing, 2000), p. 6.

29. Tiziana Terranova, "Free Labor: Producing Culture for the Digital Economy," *Social Text* 18, no. 2 (2000): 33.

30. "Pacific Internet Brings Home Sintercom Site," *The Straits Times*, 23 September 1995.

31. Thomas Hughes, *American Genesis*, p. 138.

32. Interviews with Tan Chong Kee, Wynthia Goh.

33. Ibid.

34. Jimmy Yap, "S'poreans Overseas Find a Home Away from Home on the Net," *The Straits Times*, 4 May 1995.

35. Walter Fernandez, "Facets of S'pore Life Showcased on Sintercom," *The Straits Times*, 2 May 1996.

36. Raoul Le Blond, "Scheme Affects 2 Groups: Content, Access Providers," *The Straits Times*, 12 July 1996.

37. *Registration Form B for Class Licensable Broadcasting Services* [pdf document] (Singapore Broadcasting Authority, 1996 [cited February 2000]); available from <http://www.sba.gov.sg/work/sba/internet. nsf/pages/Doc21>.

38. Harish Pillay, *The S.B.A. Internet Regulation Fiasco* (1996 [cited March 2000]); available from <home.pacific.net.sg/~harish/fiasco.html>.

39. Harish Pillay, "Broad Phrasing of Guidelines Open to Wide Interpretation," *The Straits Times*, 13 July 1996.

40. Tan.

41. Chong Kee Tan, *What Does This Piece of Regulation Mean?* (Sintercom, 1996 [cited February 2000]); available from <http://www.sintercom. org/contradictions.html>.

42. Tan.

43. "Respect Not Regulation," Sintercom [cited February 2000].

44. Tan.

45. King Yu Chia, Letter from S.B.A. to Wynthia Goh, 24 September 1996.

46. "A Wee Bit Subversive?," *Business Times*, 16 July 1996.

47. George Yeo, "Strengthening the S'pore Network for the Web World," *The Straits Times*, 7 May 1998.

48. Stephanie Sim, E-mail interview with author, February 2000.

49. Yvonne Ann Paglar, Letter from S.B.A. to Tan Chong Kee and Wynthia Goh, 5 July 2001.

50. Ibid.
51. Chong Kee Tan, E-mail to SGDaily mailing list, 18 July 2001.
52. *Singapore Broadcasting Act*, Chapter 297 (1995).
53. Tan.
54. Felicia Toh, E-mail from S.B.A. to Tan Chong Kee, 20 July 2001.
55. Felicia Toh, E-mail from S.B.A. to Tan Chong Kee, 7 August 2001.
56. Tarn How Tan, "Sintercom Founder Fades out of Cyberspace," *The Straits Times*, 22 August 2001.
57. Angela Faye Oon, E-mail to SGDaily mailing list, 18 July 2001.
58. Yuin Chung Lok, E-mail to SGDaily mailing list, 19 July 2001.
59. Chong Kee Tan, Interview with author, Singapore, 3 September 2002.
60. <http://www.geocities.com/newsintercom>.
61. Lok.

Chapter 6

1. Anbarasu Balrasan, Interview with author, Singapore, 2 September 2002.
2. Think Centre home page, <http://www.thinkcentre.org>.
3. James Gomez, *Internet Politics: Surveillance & Intimidation in Singapore* (Singapore: Think Centre, 2002).
4. Balrasan.
5. Melvin Tan, Interview with author, Singapore, 21 March 2002.
6. Melvin Tan, "How Newspapers in Singapore Reported on the 'Abolish ISA' Event" (ThinkCentre.org, 16 January 2001 [cited March 2003]); available from <http://www.thinkcentre.org/article.cfm?ArticleID=373>.
7. Bryan Lim, "Commemorating Human Rights Day in Singapore for the First Time" (ThinkCentre.org, 15 December 2000 [cited March 2003]); available from <http://www.thinkcentre.org/article.cfm?ArticleID=273>.
8. Gomez, *Internet Politics: Surveillance & Intimidation in Singapore*, 60–1.
9. "Questions over Groups' Funding," *The Straits Times*, 31 March 2001.
10. Tarn How Tan, "Think Centre Shuts Web Forum," *The Straits Times*, 17 August 2001.
11. "Dear Elections Department..." ThinkCentre, 10 October 2001.

12. "Elections Department's 'Shy Away' Attitude," ThinkCentre, 23 October 2001.
13. "Shame Again, Elections Department!" ThinkCentre, 24 October 2001.
14. "Group to Meet Police on Rally," *The Straits Times*, 6 April 2001; "New Application to Hold 'Save J.B.J.' Rally," *The Straits Times*, 31 March 2001; "Permit Sought for Save J.B.J. Rally," *The Straits Times*, 10 March 2001; "Save J.B.J. Rally Permit Denied," *The Straits Times*, 27 March 2001; "'Save J.B.J.' Rally Looks Set for April 28," *The Sunday Times*, 22 April 2001; "'Save J.B.J.' Rally Organisers Allowed to Sell Items," *The Straits Times*, 26 April 2001.
15. Quoted in "New Application to Hold 'Save J.B.J. ' Rally."
16. G. Sivakkumaran, "Event Raises $19,000 for Jeya," *The Straits Times*, 5 May 2001.
17. "Youths Let Off with 'Warning' for Organising Public Forum," *ThinkCentre.org*, 2 February 2000.
18. Gomez, *Internet Politics: Surveillance & Intimidation in Singapore*, p. 77.
19. Ibid., pp. 76–9.
20. Ibid., p. 76.
21. "Radio Programme Re-Edited," *ThinkCentre.org*, 11 December 2000.
22. "You Got It Wrong," *ThinkCentre.org*, 19 December 2000.
23. "Media Watch Report — Update on R.C.S. Management's Re-Editing of Radio Programme," *ThinkCentre.org*, 20 December 2000.
24. "Where Is Fauziah Ibrahim?," *ThinkCentre.org*, 8 February 2001.
25. "Permit Rejected for Singaporean Press Freedom Protest," *Associated Press Worldstream*, 26 February 2001.
26. "Mediacorp Radio's Reply to Think Centre's Protest Letter," *ThinkCentre.org*, 16 March 2001.
27. Ibid.
28. "Good Forum Marred by Unnecessary Jibes at Journalists," *ThinkCentre. org*, 25 August 2002.
29. S. Ramamirthan, "No Need for Human Rights Commission," *Today*, 18 December 2000.
30. James Gomez, Interview with author, Singapore, 29 March 2002.
31. Gomez, *Internet Politics: Surveillance & Intimidation in Singapore*, p. 66.

32. "Civil Society Activist to Stand in Election," *The Sunday Times*, 1 April 2001.

33. Sharon Vasoo, "Too Serious an April Fool's Joke?," *The Straits Times*, 3 April 2001.

34. "Think Centre to Focus on Human Rights," *The Straits Times*, 25 May 2001.

35. Balrasan.

36. Pamela J. Shoemaker, "The Communication of Deviance," in *Progress in Communication Sciences*, ed. Brenda Dervin and Melvin J. Voigt (Norwood, New Jersey: Ablex, 1987).

37. Gomez.

38. Tan.

39. Balrasan.

40. Tan.

41. Jay Rosen, *What Are Journalists For?* (New Haven: Yale University Press, 1999), pp. 290–1.

42. Balrasan.

43. Tan.

44. "Think Centre's Web Master Speaks," *ThinkCentre.org*, 9 March 2001.

Chapter 7

1. Zulkifli Sulong, Interview with author, Kuala Lumpur, Malaysia, 18 September 2002.

2. Ibid.

3. Ibid.

4. Chandra Muzaffar, "Mahathir's Clampdown," *The Asian Wall Street Journal*, 17 January 2000.

5. "P.A.S. To Print Fewer Copies of Its Newspaper," *The Straits Times*, 18 January 2000.

6. Zulkifli.

7. Simon Elegant, "Malaysia — Net Gains: An Opposition Web Site Is Cleared to Continue Operating," *Far Eastern Economic Review*, 16 March 2000.

8. Satwant Singh and Patrick Sennyah, "Harakah Editor, Printer Charged," *New Straits Times*, 14 January 2000.

9. Rosnazura Idrus, "Harakah editor fined RM5,000 for publishing seditious article," *New Straits Times,* 3 May 2003.
10. Zulkifli.
11. Ibid.
12. Hamid Wan Hamidi, "Pas' Search for Alternate Media Takes It to I.T.," *The Straits Times,* 2000.
13. Hatta Ramli, Interview with author, Kuala Lumpur, Malaysia, 22 July 2002.
14. Zulkifli.
15. Ibid.
16. Ibid.
17. Ibid.
18. P. Koya Kutty, Interview with author, Kuala Lumpur, Malaysia, 4 August 2002.
19. Zulkifli.
20. John Hilley, *Malaysia: Mahathirism, Hegemony and the New Opposition* (London; New York: Zed Books, 2001), 206.
21. Farish A. Noor, "Hey! What Happened to the Pematang Pauh Declaration?," *Malaysiakini.com,* 1 June 2002.
22. Ibid.
23. Syed Ahmad Hussein, "Muslim Politics and the Discourse on Democracy," in *Democracy in Malaysia: Discourses and Practices,* ed. Francis Loh and Boo Teik Khoo (Richmond, Surrey: Curzon, 2002), p. 80.
24. Ibid.
25. Ibid., pp. 102–3.
26. Claudia Theophilus, "Political Link Issue Hits Nst Boss' Nerve at Media Talk," *Malaysiakini.com,* 24 March 2003.
27. Jeremy Iggers, *Good News, Bad News: Journalism Ethics and the Public Interest* (Boulder, Colorado: Westview Press, 1998), p. 41.
28. Ibid., pp. 42, 51.
29. Zulkifli.
30. Zulkifli Sulong, "Speech at World Press Freedom Day 2002 at Apdc Building" (3 May 2002).
31. "Ulama Submit Memo against Several Writers," *New Straits Times,* 5 February 2002.
32. "P.A.S. Disgusted with Own Editorial," *New Paper,* 5 February 2002.

33. Zulkifli Sulong, *Ulama Memang Boleh Ditegur* (HarakahDaily.net, 28 February 2002 [cited March 2003]); available from <http://www.harakahdaily.net/article.php?sid=403>.

34. "Ulama, Pas Leaders Can Be Criticised, Says Nik Aziz," *New Straits Times*, 24 February 2002.

35. Hatta Ramli.

36. "Fadzil's Participation in Forum Was Right, Say Pas Leaders," *New Straits Times*, 25 May 2002.

37. Hatta Ramli.

38. Koya Kutty.

39. Nancy Fraser, *Rethinking the Public Sphere: A Contribution to the Critique of Actually Existing Democracy*, vol. Working Paper No. 10 (Milwaukee, Wisconsin: Center for Twentieth Century Studies, 1990–1), 6, 11.

40. Fathi Aris Omar, Interview with author, Kuala Lumpur, Malaysia, 16 September 2002.

41. Farish A. Noor, "One Nation, Two Audiences?" *Malaysiakini.com*, 12 April 2001.

42. Farish A. Noor, "Why Hudud? — Why Not?" *Malaysiakini.com*, 13 July 2002.

43. Lim Kit Siang, *Hadi Should Withdraw the Controversial Terengganu Syariah Criminal Enactment Bill* (Democratic Action Party media statement, 25 June 2002 [cited March 2003]); available from <http://malaysia.net/dap/lks1676.htm>.

44. Zulkifli.

45. Ibid.

46. Koya Kutty.

47. Ibid.

Chapter 8

1. "Malaysian Police Raid Office of Internet Newspaper," Agence France-Presse, 20 January 2003.

2. Steven Gan and Premesh Chandran, Interview with author, Kuala Lumpur, Malaysia, 21 December 2001.

3. Ibid.

4. Premesh Chandran, "Business Plan for Internet Based News Service" (1999).

5. Steven Gan, Interview with author, Kuala Lumpur, Malaysia, 21 December 2001.
6. Premesh Chandran, "Project Proposal for Malaysiakini" (1999).
7. Gan.
8. Thomas Fuller, "Paper Deletes Anwar from Group Photo," *International Herald Tribune*, 23 November 1999.
9. Gan.
10. Steven Gan, Interview with author, Kuala Lumpur, Malaysia, 18 September 2002.
11. Ibid.
12. Fathi Aris Omar, Interview with author, Kuala Lumpur, Malaysia, 16 September 2002.
13. Gan.
14. Ibid.
15. Premesh Chandran, Interview with author, Kuala Lumpur, Malaysia, 28 March 2002.
16. Premesh Chandran, "Hungry for Independent and Fresh News? Daily Diet" (1998).
17. Chandran, "Business Plan for Internet Based News Service."
18. Chandran, "Project Proposal for Malaysiakini."
19. Seth Mydans, "Malaysian Premier Sees Jews Behind Nation's Money Crisis," *The New York Times*, 16 October 1997.
20. "P.M.: Those Loyal Won't Support News Portal," *New Straits Times*, 5 March 2001.
21. Shi-Ian Lee, "Malaysiakini Admits Receiving Funds," *New Straits Times*, 28 March 2002.
22. Chandran.
23. Gan.
24. Chandran, "Business Plan for Internet Based News Service."
25. Chandran.
26. Steven Gan, "Online Media's Hobson's Choice," Malaysiakini, 16 August 2002.
27. Gan.
28. Chandran, "Hungry for Independent and Fresh News? Daily Diet."
29. Gan.
30. Gan.

31. Gan and Chandran.
32. Gan.
33. Khairy Jamaludin, Interview with author, Bali, Indonesia, 31 August 2002.
34. Steven Gan, "The Day They Took Away Our Computers," Malaysiakini, 28 January 2003.
35. Shamsul Akmar, "Knee-Jerk Reaction Cost Umno Youth an Opportunity to Rise to the Occasion," *New Straits Times*, 15 February 2003.
36. "Author Explains Why M'sia Needs Better P.R.," Bernama, 21 March 2003.
37. "Going, Going, Gan — Press Freedom in Malaysia," *The Economist*, 25 January 2003. Seth Mydans, "Internet Newspaper Raided," *The New York Times*, 23 January 2003. "World Watch," *The Wall Street Journal*, 23 January 2003.
38. Cris Prystay, "Malaysia Tries to Swat Online Gadfly," *The Asian Wall Street Journal*, 23 January 2003.
39. Chandran.
40. Ibid.
41. Chandran, "Business Plan for Internet Based News Service."
42. Gan, "The Day They Took Away Our Computers."
43. Jamaludin.
44. Ibid.
45. Akmar, "Knee-Jerk Reaction Cost Umno Youth an Opportunity to Rise to the Occasion."
46. C. Edwin Baker, *Media, Markets, and Democracy* (Cambridge: Cambridge University Press, 2002), p. 246.

Chapter 9

1. Geoffrey S. Kirkman, Carlos A. Osorio, and Jeffrey D. Sachs, *The Networked Readiness Index: Measuring the Preparedness of Nations for the Networked World* (2002 [cited March 2003]); available from <http://www.cid.harvard.edu/cr/pdf/gitrr2002_ch02.pdf.>
2. *Information and Communication Technology Statistics* [web page]. International Telecommunication Union, [cited March 2003]. Available from <http://www.itu.int/ITU-D/ict/statistics.>

3. Tan Chong Kee, E-mail to author, 8 April 2003.

4. Steven Gan, Interview with author, Kuala Lumpur, Malaysia, 18 September 2002.

5. Steven Gan, "Online Media's Hobson's Choice," *Malaysiakini.com*, 16 August 2002.

6. Ibid.

7. Khaw Boon Wan, *Speech at the Singapore Computer Society Gala Dinner and the I.T. Leader Award 2003 Presentation Ceremony, 22 February 2003* (2003 [cited 2003]).

8. New Sintercom Editor, E-mail to author, 14 January 2003.

9. Adam Przeworski, *Democracy and the Market: Political and Economic Reforms in Eastern Europe and Latin America* (Cambridge: Cambridge University Press, 1991), pp. 54–5.

10. Fathi Aris Omar, Interview with author, Kuala Lumpur, Malaysia, 16 September 2002.

11. Steven Gan, Interview with author, Kuala Lumpur, Malaysia, 21 December 2001.

12. Gan, "Online Media's Hobson's Choice."

13. Tan, E-mail to author, April 2003.

14. Sidney Tarrow, *Power in Movement: Social Movements and Contentious Politics*, 2nd ed. (Cambridge University Press, 1998).

15. The author attended this meeting as an adviser.

16. Anil Netto, *Charter 2000: We Can Make a Difference* (Aliran, 2001 [cited March 2003]); available from <http://www.malaysia.net/aliran/charter/background.html>.

17. G. Sivakkumaran, "Independent Media Watchdog to Fold," *The Straits Times*, 12 September 2001.

18. "Charter 2000," Aliran.com [cited April 2003]. Available from <http://www.aliran.com/charter/index.html>.

19. Chandra Muzaffar, Interview with author, Kuala Lumpur, Malaysia, March 2002.

20. Brendan Pereira, "'Some Errors in Judgment Were Made'," *The Straits Times*, 18 August 2000.

21. Chandra Muzaffar.

22. M.G.G. Pillai, Interview with author, Kuala Lumpur, Malaysia, 23 July 2002.

23. William Case, *Politics in Southeast Asia: Democracy or Less* (Richmond, Surrey: Curzon, 2002).

Chapter 10

1. "Shame on Elections Department," ThinkCentre, 20 October 2001.
2. Parliamentary Elections (Election Advertising) Regulations (Singapore Elections Department, 2001 [cited February 2003]); available from <http://www.elections.gov.sg/democracy/electionsSingapore/appendix_A.html>.
3. Andreas Schedler, "The Menu of Manipulation," *Journal of Democracy* 13, no. 2 (2002): 37.
4. C. Edwin Baker, *Human Liberty and Freedom of Speech* (Oxford: Oxford University Press, 1989).
5. Beata Rozumilowicz, "Democratic Change: A Theoretical Perspective," in *Media Reform: Democratizing the Media, Democratizing the State*, ed. Monroe E. Price, Beata Rozumilowicz, and Stefaan G. Verhulst (London: Routledge, 2002).
6. See Margaret Scammell and Holli Semetko, eds., *The Media, Journalism and Democracy* (Aldershot: Ashgate, 2000).
7. *Abrams Et Al. v. United States*, 250 U.S. 616, 1919.
8. F.A. Hayek, *The Constitution of Liberty* (London: Routledge & Kegan Paul, 1960).
9. Joseph A. Schumpeter, *Capitalism, Socialism and Democracy*, 3rd ed. (New York: Harper & Row, 1950).
10. Walter Lippmann, *Public Opinion* (New York: Macmillan, 1922).
11. Robert Dahl, *Who Governs?* (New Haven: Yale University Press, 1961).
12. Ibid., pp. 316–7.
13. W. Lance Bennett, "Cracking the News Code: Some Rules That Journalists Live By," in *Do the Media Govern?: Politicians, Voters, and Reporters in America*, ed. Shanto Iyengar and Richard Reeves (Thousand Oaks, Calif.: Sage Publications, 1997), p. 104.
14. Simone Chambers and Anne Costaine, eds., *Deliberation, Democracy and the Media* (Lanham, Maryland: Rowman & Littlefield Publishers, 2000).
15. Jurgen Habermas, *The Structural Transformation of the Public Sphere* (Cambridge, Mass.: MIT Press, 1991), p. 27.

16. Jurgen Habermas, *Justification and Application: Remarks on Discourse Ethics* (Cambridge, Mass.: MIT Press, 1993), p. 16.

17. Ibid., p. 12.

18. John Dewey, *The Public and Its Problems* (Henry Holt, 1927).

19. Ibid., p. 216.

20. Habermas, *The Structural Transformation of the Public Sphere*, p. 192.

21. James W. Carey, "The Press and Public Discourse," *The Center Magazine* 1987, p. 14.

22. A. Charity, *Doing Public Journalism* (New York: Guildford Press, 1995), 10. See also Theodore Glasser, "The Idea of Public Journalism," in *The Idea of Public Journalism*, ed. Theodore Glasser (New York: Guilford Press, 1999).

23. Nancy Fraser, *Rethinking the Public Sphere: A Contribution to the Critique of Actually Existing Democracy*, vol. Working Paper No. 10 (Milwaukee, Wisconsin: Center for Twentieth Century Studies, 1990–91).

24. Ibid., p. 11.

25. Jurgen Habermas, *Between Facts and Norms* (Cambridge, Mass.: MIT Press, 1996), p. 308.

26. David Morley, *Home Territories: Media, Mobility and Identity* (London: Routledge, 2000), p. 105.

27. Ibid., p. 118.

28. John D.H. Downing, *Radical Media: Rebellious Communication and Social Movements* (Thousand Oaks, Calif.: Sage Publications, 2001), p. 43.

29. Merrill, Gade and Blevens, *Twilight of Press Freedom: The Rise of People's Journalism*.

30. Ibid., p. 181.

31. Michael Schudson, *The News Media and the Democratic Process* (New York: Aspen Institute, 1983).

32. Ibid., p. 12.

33. Ibid., p. 30.

34. James Curran, "Mass Media and Democracy: A Reappraisal," in *Mass Media and Society*, ed. James Curran and Michael Gurevitch (London: Edward Arnold, 1991). Herbert Gans comes to a similar conclusion in his call for "multiperspectival news," in *Deciding What's News* (New York: Pantheon, 1979). However, Gans does not quite argue that

the media system requires fundamentally different *journalisms*. His proposal is based on the concern that national news media will not have the time and space to tell the news from different perspectives, rather than that any one model of journalism would be inadequate, which is Curran's point.

35. Ibid., p. 110.
36. Ibid., p. 110.
37. Tan Chong Kee, E-mail to author, 8 April 2003.
38. <http://dir.yahoo.com/Regional/Countries/Malaysia/News_and_Media/>[cited February 2003].
39. <http://www.google.com> [cited February 2003].
40. Downing, *Radical Media: Rebellious Communication and Social Movements*, p. 8.
41. Fraser, *Rethinking the Public Sphere: A Contribution to the Critique of Actually Existing Democracy*.
42. Ibid., pp. 11–2.
43. Brent Cunningham, "Re-thinking Objectivity," *Columbia Journalism Review* July/August 2003.
44. Gaye Tuchman, "Objectivity as Strategic Ritual: An Examination of Newsmen's Notions of Objectivity," *American Journal of Sociology* 77 (1972).
45. Downing, *Radical Media: Rebellious Communication and Social Movements*, p. 43.
46. Bill Kovach and Tom Rosenstiel, *Warp Speed: America in the Age of Mixed Media* (New York: Century Foundation, 1999), p. 94.
47. Thorbjorn Broddason, "The Sacred Side of Professional Journalism," *European Journal of Communication* 9 (1994).
48. Theodore L. Glasser, "The Motives for Studying Journalism," *Journalism Studies* 2, no. 4 (2001): 625.
49. Habermas, *Between Facts and Norms*.
50. Jeremy Iggers, *Good News, Bad News: Journalism Ethics and the Public Interest* (Boulder, Colorado: Westview Press, 1998), Tuchman, "Objectivity as Strategic Ritual: An Examination of Newsmen's Notions of Objectivity.".
51. Gans, *Deciding What's News*, p. 310.
52. Ibid, p. 334.

53. Media Seminar, Institute of Policy Studies, Singapore, 19 September 2002.
54. Ibid.
55. Downing, *Radical Media: Rebellious Communication and Social Movements*, 8.
56. The author was a participant in The Working Committee process. The debate is documented in Constance Singam *et al.*, eds., *Building Social Space in Singapore: The Working Committee's Initiative in Civil Society Activism* (Singapore: Select Books, 2002).
57. Premesh Chandran, Interview with author, Kuala Lumpur, Malaysia, 28 March 2002.
58. Farish A. Noor, E-mail to author, 6 April 2003.
59. Habermas, *Justification and Application: Remarks on Discourse Ethics*.
60. Singam *et al.*, eds., *Building Social Space in Singapore: The Working Committee's Initiative in Civil Society Activism*.
61. Momamed Rahmat, Interview with author, Kuala Lumpur, Malaysia, July 2002.
62. Lee Boon Yang, Lunch Talk by Minister for Information, Communications and the Arts at the Singapore Press Club Lunch, Singapore Government Press Release. September 2004. Available from <http://www.mita.gov.sg/pressroom/press_031112.html>.
63. Ibid.
64. Lee Hsien Loong, Prime Minister Lee Hsien Loong's National Day Rally 2004 Speech, Sunday 22 August 2004, at the University Cultural Centre, NUS. Singapore Government Media Release. Available at <http://app.sprinter.gov.sg/data/pr/2004083101.htm>.
65. Downing, *Radical Media: Rebellious Communication and Social Movements*, p. 34.

BIBLIOGRAPHY

Abbott, Jason P. "Democracy@Internet.Asia? The Challenges to the Emancipatory Potential of the Net: Lessons from China and Malaysia." *Third World Quarterly* 22, no. 1 (2001): 99–114.

Abrams Et Al. v. United States, 250 U.S. 616, 1919.

Adams, Paul C. "Cyberspace and Virtual Places." *Geographical Review* 87, no. 2 (1997): 155–71.

Anderson, Perry. "The Antinomies of Antonio Gramsci." *New Left Review*, no. 100 (1997): 5–80.

Anil, Samtani. "Re-Visiting the Singapore Internet Code of Practice." *Journal of Information, Law and Technology*, no. 2 (2001).

Armstrong, David. *A Trumpet to Arms: Alternative Media in America.* Boston, Mass.: South End Press, 1981.

Arquilla, John, David Ronfeldt, and Michele Zanini. "Information-Age Terrorism." *Current History* 99, no. 636 (2000): 179.

Atton, Chris. *Alternative Media.* London: Sage Publications, 2002.

Bagdikian, Ben H. *The Media Monopoly.* 5th ed. Boston: Beacon Press, 1997.

Baker, C. Edwin. *Human Liberty and Freedom of Speech.* Oxford: Oxford University Press, 1989.

Baker, C. Edwin. *Media, Markets, and Democracy.* Cambridge: Cambridge University Press, 2002.

Ballard, James David, Joseph G. Hornik, and Douglas McKenzie. "Technological Facilitation of Terrorism." *American Behavioral Scientist* 45, no. 6 (2002): 989–1016.

Barlow, John Perry. A Declaration of the Independence of Cyberspace 1996 [cited February 2003]. Available from <http://www.eff.org/~barlow/Declaration-Final.html>.

Basuki, Tedjabayu. "Indonesia: The Web as a Weapon." *Development Dialogue* 2 (1998): 96–103.

Benford, Robert D. and David A. Snow. "Framing Processes and Social Movements: An Overview and Assessment." *Annual Review of Sociology* 26 (2000): 611–39.

Bennett, W. Lance. "Cracking the News Code: Some Rules That Journalists Live By." In *Do the Media Govern?: Politicians, Voters, and Reporters in America,* ed. Shanto Iyengar and Richard Reeves, pp. 103–17. Thousand Oaks, Calif.: Sage Publications, 1997.

Berrigan, Frances J. *Access: Some Western Models of Community Media.* Paris: United Nations Educational, Scientific and Cultural Organization, 1977.

Bimber, Bruce. "The Internet and Political Transformation: Populism, Community, and Accelerated Pluralism." *Polity* 31, no. 1 (1998): 133–60.

Blumenthal, M. and D. Clark. "Rethinking the Design of the Internet: The End to End Arguments Vs. The Brave New World." In *Communications Policy in Transition: The Internet and Beyond,* ed. S. Greenstein and B. Compaine. Cambridge, Mass.: MIT Press, 2001.

Bolter, J.D. *Turing's Man: Western Culture in the Computer Age.* Chapel Hill: Univ. of North Carolina Press, 1984.

Bray, John. "Tibet, Democracy and the Internet Bazaar." *Democratization* 7, no. 1 (2000).

Broddason, Thorbjorn. "The Sacred Side of Professional Journalism." *European Journal of Communication* 9 (1994): 227–48.

Brunn, Stanley D. and Charles D. Cottle. "Small States and Cyberboosterism." *Geographical Review* 87, no. 2 (1997): 240–58.

Carey, James W. "The Press and Public Discourse." *The Center Magazine* (1987), pp. 4–16.

Carroll, Glenn. "Concentration and Specialization: Dynamics of Niche Width in Populations of Organizations." *American Journal of Sociology* 90, no. 6 (1985): 1262–83.

———. *Publish and Perish: The Organizational Ecology of Newspaper Industries.* Greenwich, Conn.: JAI Press, 1987.

Carroll, Glenn and Michael Hannan. *The Demography of Corporations and Industries.* Princeton, NJ: Princeton University Press, 2000.

Case, William. "Semi-Democracy in Malaysia: Withstanding the Pressures for Regime Change." *Pacific Affairs* 66, no. 2 (1993): 183–205.

———. *Politics in Southeast Asia: Democracy or Less.* Richmond, Surrey: Curzon, 2002.

Castells, Manuel. *The Rise of the Network Society.* 2nd ed. Vol. 1, The Information Age: Economy, Society and Culture. Oxford: Blackwell, 2000.

Chambers, Simone and Anne Costaine, eds. *Deliberation, Democracy and the Media.* Lanham, Maryland: Rowman & Littlefield Publishers, 2000.

Charity, A. *Doing Public Journalism.* New York: Guildford Press, 1995.

Choucri, Nazli. "Introduction: Cyberpolitics in International Relations." *International Political Science Review* 21, no. 3 (2000): 243–63.

Chua, Beng-Huat. *Communitarian Ideology and Democracy in Singapore.* London, New York: Routledge, 1995.

Chroust, Peter. "Neo-Nazis and Taliban on-Line: Anti-Modern Political Movements and Modern Media." *Democratization* 7, no. 1 (2000).

Cleaver, H.M., Jr. "The Zapatista Effect: The Internet and the Rise of an Alternative Political Fabric." *Journal of International Affairs* 51, no. 2 (1998): 621–40.

Curran, James. "Mass Media and Democracy: A Reappraisal." In *Mass Media and Society*, ed. James Curran and Michael Gurevitch. London: Edward Arnold, 1991.

Dahl, Robert. *Who Governs?* New Haven: Yale University Press, 1961.

Dahlberg, Lincoln. "Cyberspace and the Public Sphere: Exploring the Democratic Potential of the Net." *Convergence* 4, no. 1 (1998): 70–84.

Dahlgren, Peter. "The Public Sphere and the Net: Structure, Space and Communication." In *Mediated Politics: Communication in the Future of Democracy*, ed. W. Lance Bennett and Robert M. Entman. Cambridge: Cambridge University Press, 2001.

Dewey, John. *The Public and Its Problems*: Henry Holt, 1927.

Diamond, Larry. "Thinking About Hybrid Regimes." *Journal of Democracy* 13, no. 2 (2002): 21–35.

DiMaggio, Paul, Eszter Hargittai, W. Russell Neuman, and John Robinson. "The Internet's Impact on Society." *Annual Review of Sociology 2001* 27 (2001): 307–36.

Downing, John D.H. *Radical Media: Rebellious Communication and Social Movements*. Thousand Oaks, Calif.: Sage Publications, 2001.

Eliasoph, Nina. "Routines and the Making of Oppositional News." *Critical Studies in Mass Communication* 5, no. 4 (1988): 313–34.

Ferdinand, Peter. "The Internet, Democracy and Democratization." *Democratization* 7, no. 1 (2000).

Fisher, C.S. "Studying Technology and Social Life." In *Technology, Space and Society: Emerging Trends*, ed. M. Castells. Beverly Hills, Calif.: Sage, 1985.

Fishman, Mark. *Manufacturing the News*. Austin, Texas: University of Texas Press, 1980.

Flaherty, Lisa M., Kevin J. Pearce, and Rebecca B. Rubin. "Internet and Face-to-Face Communication: Not Functional Alternatives." *Communication Quarterly* 46, no. 3 (1998): 250–68.

Ford, Tamara Villarreal and Geneve Gil. "Radical Internet Use." In *Radical Media: Rebellious Communication and Social Movements*, ed. John D.H. Downing. Thousand Oaks, Calif.: Sage, 2001.

Fortier, François. *Virtuality Check: Power Relations and Alternative Strategies in the Information Society*. London and New York: Verso, 2001.

Froehling, O. "The Cyberspace 'War of Ink and Internet' in Chiapas, Mexico." *Geographical Review* 87, no. 2 (1997): 291–307.

Foucault, Michel. "Governmentality." In *The Foucault Effect: Studies in Governmentality*, ed. Graham Burchell, Colin Gordon and Peter Miller, pp. 87–104. Chicago: University of Chicago Press, 1991.

Fraser, Nancy. *Rethinking the Public Sphere: A Contribution to the Critique of Actually Existing Democracy*. Working Paper No. 10. Milwaukee, Wisconsin: Center for Twentieth Century Studies, 1990–1.

Gamson, W.A. and G. Wolfsfeld. "Movements and Media as Interacting Systems." *Annals of The American Academy of Political and Social Science* 528 (1993): 114–25.

Gans, Herbert J. *Deciding What's News: A Study of CBS Evening News, NBC Nightly News, Newsweek, and Time.* New York: Pantheon Books, 1979.

Geertz, Clifford. "Thick Description: Toward an Interpretive Theory of Culture." In *The Interpretation of Cultures*, pp. 3–30. New York: Basic Books, 1973.

George, S. and L.M. Martinez. "Digital advocacy and the women's movement: global success, grassroots challenge." In *Asian Cyberactivism: Freedom of Expression and Media Censorship*, ed. S. Gan, J. Gomez and U. Johannen. Bangkok, Thailand: Friedrich Naumann Stiftung, 2004.

Gershman, C. "The Internet and Democracy Building — the N.E.D. Experience." Paper presented at the The Internet and Democracy Building International Workshop organized by the U.K. Foreign and Commonwealth Office, Wilton Park, U.K., 27–28 April 2001.

Gitlin, Todd. *The Whole World Is Watching: Mass Media in the Making and Unmaking of the New Left.* Berkeley, Los Angeles, London: University of California Press, 1980.

Glasser, Theodore L. "The Idea of Public Journalism." In *The Idea of Public Journalism*, ed. Theodore L. Glasser, pp. 3–18. New York: Guilford Press, 1999.

———. "The Motives for Studying Journalism." *Journalism Studies* 2, no. 4 (2001): 623–7.

Gomez, Edmund Terence, and K.S. Jomo. *Malaysia's Political Economy: Politics, Patronage and Profits.* 2nd ed: Cambridge University Press, 1999.

Gomez, James. *Internet Politics: Surveillance & Intimidation in Singapore.* Singapore: Think Centre, 2002.

Gordon, Colin. "Government Rationality: An Introduction." In *The Foucault Effect: Studies in Governmentality*, ed. Graham Burchell, Colin Gordon and Peter Miller, pp. 1–52. Chicago: University of Chicago Press, 1991.

Gouldner, Alvin. *The Dialectic of Ideology and Technology: The Origins, Grammar, and Future of Ideology.* New York: The Seabury Press, 1976.

Gupta, Akhil. "Blurred Boundaries: The Discourse of Corruption, the Culture of Politics, and the Imagined State." *American Ethnologist* 22, no. 2 (1995): 375–402.

Habermas, Jurgen. *Justification and Application: Remarks on Discourse Ethics.* Cambridge, Mass.: MIT Press, 1993.

———. *The Structural Transformation of the Public Sphere.* Cambridge, Mass.: MIT Press, 1991.

———. *Between Facts and Norms.* Cambridge, Mass.: MIT Press, 1996.

Hachigian, Nina. "China's Cyber-Strategy." *Foreign Affairs*, March/April (2000): 118–33.

Hachten, William A. "Media Development without Press Freedom: Lee Kuan Yew's Singapore." *Journalism Quarterly* 66, no. 4 (1989): 822–7.

Hacker, Kenneth L. "Missing Links in the Evolution of Electronic Democratization." *Media, Culture and Society* 18 (1996): 213–32.

Hague, Barry N. and Brian D. Loader, eds. *Digital Democracy: Discourse and Decision Making in the Information Age.* London and New York: Routledge, 1999.

Hall, Stuart. "The Rediscovery of 'Ideology': Return of the Repressed in Media Studies." In *Culture, Society and the Media*, ed. Michael Gurevitch, Tony Bennett, James Curran, and Janet Woollacott. London and New York: Methuen, 1982.

Hallin, Daniel C. and Paolo Mancini. "Speaking of the President: Political Structure and Representational Form in U.S. And Italian Television News." *Theory and Society* 13, no. 6 (1984): 829–50.

Hallin, D.C. and P. Mancini. *Comparing Media Systems: Three Models of Media and Politics.* Cambridge, UK: Cambridge University Press, 2004.

Hanson, Ward. *Principles of Internet Marketing.* South-Western College Publishing, 2000.

Hao, Xiaoming, K. Zhang, and H. Yu. "The Internet and Information Control: The Case of China." *Electronic Journal of Communication* 6, no. 2 (1996).

Hayek, F.A. *The Constitution of Liberty.* London: Routledge & Kegan Paul, 1960.

Held, David. *Political Theory and the Modern State.* Stanford, Calif.: Stanford University Press, 1989.

Herman, Edward S. "The Propaganda Model Revisited." In *Capitalism and the Information Age: The Political Economy of the Global Communication Revolution*, ed. Robert W. McChesney, Ellen Meiksins Wood, and

John Bellamy Foster, pp. 191–205. New York: Monthly Review Press, 1998.

Hertog, James K. and Douglas M. McLeod. "Anarchists Wreak Havoc in Downtown Minneapolis: A Multi-Level Study of Media Coverage of Radical Protest." *Journalism and Mass Communication Monographs* 151 (1995).

Hill, David T. and Krishna Sen. "The Internet in Indonesia's New Democracy." *Democratization* 7, no. 1 (2000).

Hill, Kevin A. and John E. Hughes. "Computer-Mediated Political Communication: The Usenet and Political Communities." *Political Communication* 14, no. 1 (1997): 3–27.

———. "Is the Internet an Instrument of Global Democratization." *Democratization* 6, no. 2 (1999): 99–127.

Hilley, John. *Malaysia: Mahathirism, Hegemony and the New Opposition.* London; New York: Zed Books, 2001.

Ho, K.C., Zaheer Baber, and Habibul Khondker. "'Sites' of Resistance: Alternative Websites and State-Society Relations." *British Journal of Sociology* 53, no. 1 (2002): 127–48.

Howard, Philip. "Can Technology Enhance Democracy? The Doubters' Answer." *Journal of Politics* 63, no. 3 (2001): 949–55.

Hughes, Thomas P. *Rescuing Prometheus.* New York: Pantheon Books, 1998.

Iggers, Jeremy. *Good News, Bad News: Journalism Ethics and the Public Interest.* Boulder, Colorado: Westview Press, 1998.

Janowitz, Morris. "Professional Models in Journalism: The Gatekeeper and the Advocate." *Journalism Quarterly* 52 (1975): 618–26, 662.

Johnson, Thomas J. and Barbara K. Kaye. "Cruising Is Believing? Comparing Internet and Traditional Sources on Media Credibility Measures." *Journalism and Mass Communication Quarterly* 75, no. 2 (1998): 325–40.

Johnson, Thomas J., Mahmoud A.M. Braima, and Jayanthi Sothirajah. "Doing the Traditional Media Sidestep: Comparing the Effects of the Internet and Other Nontraditional Media with Traditional Media in the 1996 Presidential Campaign." *Journalism and Mass Communication Quarterly* 76, no. 1 (1999): 99–123.

Jordan, Tim. "Language and Libertarianism: The Politics of Cyberculture and the Culture of Cyberpolitics." *The Sociological Review* 49, no. 1 (2001): 1–17.

Jussawalla, M., M.H. Toh, and L. Low. "Singapore: An Intelligent City–State." *Asian Journal of Communication* 2, no. 3 (1992): 31–54.

Kalathil, S. and T.C. Boas. "The Internet and State Control in Authoritarian Regimes: China, Cuba, and the Counterrevolution." In *Carnegie Endowment Working Papers 21*. Washington, DC: Carnegie Endowment for International Peace, 2001.

Kalathil, Shanthi and Taylor C. Boas. *Open Networks Closed Regimes: The Impact of the Internet on Authoritarian Rule*. Washington, DC: Carnegie Endowment for International Peace, 2003.

Katz, Elihu. "The End of Journalism? Notes on Watching the War." *Journal of Communication* 42 (1992): 5–13.

Keohane, Robert, and Joseph S. Nye Jr. "Power and Interdependence in the Information Age." In *Governance.Com: Democracy in the Information Age*, ed. Elaine Ciulla Kamarck and Joseph S. Nye Jr., pp. 161–78. Cambridge, Mass., Washington, DC: Brookings Institution Press, 2002.

Khan, Z. "Cyber jihad: Fighting the infidels from Pakistan." In *Asian Cyberactivism: Freedom of Expression and Media Censorship*, ed. S. Gan, J. Gomez and U. Johannen, pp. 474–512. Bangkok, Thailand: Friedrich Naumann Stiftung, 2004.

Kirkman, Geoffrey S., Carlos A. Osorio, and Jeffrey D. Sachs. *The Networked Readiness Index: Measuring the Preparedness of Nations for the Networked World* 2002 [cited March 2003]. Available from <http://www.cid.harvard.edu/cr/pdf/gitrr2002_ch02.pdf>.

King, Gary, Robert Keohane, and Sidney Verba. *Designing Social Inquiry: Scientific Inference in Qualitative Research*. Princeton, New Jersey: Princeton University Press, 1994.

Knudson, Jerry W. "Rebellion in Chiapas: Insurrection by Internet and Public Relations." *Media, Culture & Society* 20, no. 3 (1998): 507–18.

Kovach, Bill and Tom Rosenstiel. *Warp Speed: America in the Age of Mixed Media*. New York: Century Foundation, 1999.

Krasner, Stephen. "Approaches to the State: Alternative Conceptions and Historical Dynamics." *Comparative Politics* (January 1984): 223–46.

Lawler, Philip F. *The Alternative Influence: The Impact of Investigative Reporting Groups on America's Media*. Lanham, Maryland: University Press of America and The Media Institute, 1984.

Lessig, Lawrence. *Code.* New York: Basic Books, 1999.

———. *The Future of Ideas.* New York: Vintage, 2002.

Levin, Brian. "Cyberhate: A Legal and Historical Analysis of Extremists' Use of Computer Networks in America." *American Behavioral Scientist* 45, no. 6 (2002): 958–88.

Linz, Juan J. and Alfred Stepan. *Problems of Democratic Transition and Consolidation.* Baltimore and London: The Johns Hopkins University Press, 1996.

Lippmann, Walter. *Public Opinion.* New York: Macmillan, 1922.

Ma, Eric Kit-Wai. "Rethinking Media Studies: The Case of China." In *De-Westernizing Media Studies,* ed. James Curran and Myung-Jin Park, pp. 21–34. London: Routledge, 2000.

Maslog, C.C., R.L. Navarro, L.N. Tabing, and L.V. Teodoro, eds. *Communication for People Power: An Introduction to Community Communication.* Philippines: UNESCO, Project Tambali, 1997.

Mauzy, Diane and Robert Milne. *Singapore Politics under the People's Action Party.* London; New York: Routledge, 2002.

McAdam, D., J.D. McCarthy, and M.N. Zald, eds. *Comparative Perspectives on Social Movements Opportunities, Mobilizing Structures, and Framing.* Cambridge: Cambridge University Press, 1996.

McAdam, Doug. "The Political Process Model." In *Political Process and the Development of Black Insurgency, 1930–1970.* Chicago and London: University of Chicago Press, 1999.

McAdam, Doug, Sidney Tarrow, and Charles Tilly. *Dynamics of Contention.* Cambridge: Cambridge University Press, 2001.

McChesney, Robert W. "The Political Economy of Global Communication." In *Capitalism and the Information Age: The Political Economy of the Global Communication Revolution,* ed. Robert W. McChesney, Ellen Meiksins Wood, and John Bellamy Foster, pp. 1–26. New York: Monthly Review Press, 1998.

McChesney, Robert W. *Rich Media, Poor Democracy: Communication Politics in Dubious Times.* Urbana and Chicago: University of Illinois Press, 1999.

McDaniel, Drew O. *Broadcasting in the Malay World.* Norwood, New Jersey: Ablex, 1994.

Merrill, John C., Peter J. Gade, and Frederick R. Blevens. *Twilight of Press Freedom: The Rise of People's Journalism.* Mahwah, New Jersey: Lawrence Erlbaum, 2001.

Meyer, David S. "Protest and Political Process." In *The Blackwell Companion to Political Sociology*, ed. Kate Nash and Alan Scott, pp. 164–72. Oxford, England: Blackwell, 2001.

Miliband, Ralph. *The State in Capitalist Society*. London: Weidenfeld and Nicolson, 1969.

Milne, Robert and Diane Mauzy. *Malaysian Politics under Mahathir*. London; New York: Routledge, 1999.

Minges, Michael and Vanessa Gray. *Multimedia Malaysia: Internet Case Study*. International Telecommunication Union, 2002 [cited March 2003]. Available from <http://www.itu.int/ITU–D/ict/cs/>.

Minges, Michael, Magda Ismail, and Larry Press. *The E-City: Singapore Internet Case Study*. International Telecommunication Union, 2001 [cited March 2003]. Available from <http://www.itu.int/ITU–D/ict/cs/>.

Morley, David. *Home Territories: Media, Mobility and Identity*. London: Routledge, 2000.

Morton, Charlotte. "The 'Arbeiter Illustrierte Zeitung' in Weimar Germany." *Media, Culture and Society* 7, no. 2 (1985): 187–203.

Nass, C. and L. Mason. "On the Study of Technology and Task: A Variable-Based Approach." In *Organization and Communication Technology*, ed. J. Fulk and C. Steinfeld. Newbury Park: Sage, 1990.

Nerone, John C., ed. *Last Rights: Revisiting 'Four Theories of the Press'*. Urbana: University of Illinois Press, 1995.

Neuman, W. Russell, Lee McKnight, and Richard Jay Solomon. *The Gordian Knot: Political Gridlock on the Information Highway*. Cambridge, Massachusetts; London, England: MIT Press, 1997.

O'Donnell, S. "Analysing the Internet and the Public Sphere: The Case of Womenslink." *Javnost – The Public* 8, no. 1 (2001): 39–57.

Olson, Mancur. *Power and Prosperity: Outgrowing Communist and Capitalist Dictatorships*. New York: Basic Books, 2000.

Pagnucco, Ron. "The Comparative Study of Social Movements and Democratization: Political Interaction and Political Process Approaches." In *Research in Social Movements, Conflict and Change*, ed. Louis Kriesberg, Michael Dobkowski, and Isidor Wallimann, pp. 145–83. Greenwich, Connecticut and London, England: JAI Press, 1995.

Papacharissi, Z. "The Virtual Sphere: The Internet as a Public Sphere." *New Media and Society* 4, no. 1 (2002): 9–27.

Pavlik, John V. and Steven S. Ross. "Journalism Online: Exploring the Impact of New Media on News and Society." In *Understanding the Web: Social, Political, and Economic Dimensions of the Internet*, ed. Alan B. Albarran and David H. Goff, pp. 117–34. Ames, Iowa: Iowa State University Press, 2000.

Picard, Robert G. "Media Concentration, Economics, and Regulation." In *The Politics of News, the News of Politics*, ed. Doris Graber, Denis McQuail, and Pippa Norris. Washington, DC: C.Q. Press, 1998.

Przeworski, Adam. *Democracy and the Market: Political and Economic Reforms in Eastern Europe and Latin America.* Cambridge: Cambridge University Press, 1991.

Putnam, Robert. "Bowling Alone: America's Declining Social Capital." *Journal of Democracy*, January 1995.

Rahmah Hashim and Arfah Yusof. "Malaysia." In *Internet in Asia*, ed. Sankaran Ramanathan and Jorg Becker. Singapore: Asian Media Information and Communication Centre, 2001.

Reno, Attorney General of the United States Et Al. v. American Civil Liberties Union Et Al., 000 U.S. 96–511, 1997.

Rheingold, Howard. "A Slice of My Life in My Virtual Community." In *High Noon on the Electronic Frontier: Conceptual Issues in Cyberspace*, ed. Peter Ludlow, pp. 413–44. Cambridge, Mass.: MIT Press, 1996.

Richards, David L. "Making the National International: Information Technology and Government Respect for Human Rights." In *Technology, Development, and Democracy: International Conflict and Cooperation in the Information Age*, ed. Juliann Emmons Allison, pp. 161–86. Albany, New York: State University of New York Press, 2002.

Rodan, Garry. "The Internet and Political Control in Singapore." *Political Science Quarterly* 113, no. 1 (1998): 63–89.

———. "Asian Crisis, Transparency and the International Media in Singapore." *The Pacific Review* 13, no. 2 (2000): 217–42.

———. "Singapore: Information Lockdown." In *Losing Control: Freedom of the Press in Asia*, ed. Louise Williams and Roland Rich, pp. 169–89. Asia Pacific Press at the Australian National University, 2000.

Rosen, Jay. *What Are Journalists For?* Yale University Press, 1999.

Rozumilowicz, Beata. "Democratic Change: A Theoretical Perspective." In *Media Reform: Democratizing the Media, Democratizing the State*, ed. Monroe E. Price, Beata Rozumilowicz, and Stefaan G. Verhulst, pp. 27–46. London: Routledge, 2002.

Russell, A. "Chiapas and the New News: Internet and Newspaper Coverage of a Broken Cease-Fire." *Journalism* 2, no. 2 (2001): 197–220.

Sabri Zain. *Face Off: A Malaysian Reformasi Diary (1998–99)*. Singapore: BigO Books, 2002.

Saltzer, J.H., D.P. Reed, and D.D. Clark. *End-to-End Arguments in System Design* 1981 [cited February 2003]. Available from <http://web.mit.edu/Saltzer/www/publications>.

Scammell, Margaret and Holli Semetko, eds. *The Media, Journalism and Democracy*. Aldershot: Ashgate, 2000.

Schedler, Andreas. "The Menu of Manipulation." *Journal of Democracy* 13, no. 2 (2002): 36–50.

Schmitter, Philippe C. "More Liberal, Preliberal, or Postliberal?" In *The Global Resurgence of Democracy*, ed. Larry Diamond and Marc F. Plattner, pp. 328–35. Baltimore and London: The Johns Hopkins University Press, 1996.

Schudson, Michael. *Discovering the News: A Social History of American Newspapers*. Basic Books, 1978.

———. *The News Media and the Democratic Process*. New York: Aspen Institute, 1983.

Schumpeter, Joseph A. *Capitalism, Socialism and Democracy*. 3rd ed. New York: Harper & Row, 1950.

Scott, James. *Seeing Like a State: How Certain Schemes to Improve the Human Condition Have Failed*. New Haven: Yale University Press, 1998.

Scott, James C. *Domination and the Arts of Resistance: Hidden Transcripts*. New Haven: Yale University Press, 1990.

Seow, Francis T. *The Media Enthralled: Singapore Revisited*. Boulder, Colorado: Lynne Rienner Publishers, 1998.

Shoemaker, Pamela J. "Media Treatment of Deviant Groups." *Journalism Quarterly* 61, no. 1 (1984): 66–82.

———. "The Communication of Deviance." In *Progress in Communication Sciences*, ed. Brenda Dervin and Melvin J. Voigt, pp. 151–75. Norwood, New Jersey: Ablex, 1987.

Shore, Elliott. "Selling Socialism: The 'Appeal to Reason' and the Radical Press in Turn-of-the-Century America." *Media, Culture and Society* 7, no. 2 (1985): 147–68.

Siebert, Fred S., Theodore Peterson, and Wilbur Schramm. *Four Theories of the Press: The Authoritarian, Libertarian, Social Responsibility and Soviet Communist Concepts of What the Press Should Be and Do.* Urbana: University of Illinois Press, 1956.

Sigal, Leon V. "Who? Sources Make the News." In *Reading the News*, ed. Robert Karl Manoff and Michael Schudson, pp. 9–37. New York: Pantheon Books, 1986.

Singam, Constance, Chong Kee Tan, Tisa Ng, and Leon Perera, eds. *Building Social Space in Singapore: The Working Committee's Initiative in Civil Society Activism.* Singapore: Select Books, 2002.

Skocpol, Theda. "Bringing the State Back In: Strategies of Analysis in Current Research." In *Bringing the State Back In*, ed. Peter Evans, Dietrich Rueschemeyer, and Theda Skocpol: Cambridge University Press, 1985.

Sparks, Colin. "The Working-Class Press: Radical and Revolutionary Alternatives." *Media, Culture and Society* 7, no. 2 (1985): 133–46.

———. "From Dead Trees to Live Wires: The Internet's Challenge to the Traditional Newspaper." In *Mass Media and Society*, ed. James Curran and Michael Gurevitch. New York: Oxford University Press, 2000.

———. "Media Theory after the Fall of European Communism: Why the Old Models from East and West Won't Do Anymore." In *De-Westernizing Media Studies*, ed. James Curran and Myung-Jin Park. London: Routledge, 2000.

Spinelli, Martin. "Democratic Rhetoric and Emergent Media: The Marketing of Participatory Community on Radio and the Internet." *International Journal of Cultural Studies* 3, no. 2 (2000): 268–78.

Stanton, John J. "Terror in Cyberspace." *American Behavioral Scientist* 45, no. 6 (2002): 1017–32.

Stephens, Mitchell. *A History of News.* New York: Viking, 1988.

Steuer, J.S. "Defining Virtual Reality: Dimensions Determining Telepresence." *Journal of Communication* 42, no. 4 (1992): 73–93.

Swidler, Ann. "Culture in Action: Symbols and Strategies." *American Sociological Review* 51, no. 2 (1986): 273–86.

Syed Ahmad Hussein. "Muslim Politics and the Discourse on Democracy." In *Democracy in Malaysia: Discourses and Practices*, ed. Francis Loh and Khoo Boo Teik. Richmond, Surrey: Curzon, 2002

Tarrow, Sidney. *Power in Movement: Social Movements and Contentious Politics.* 2nd ed: Cambridge University Press, 1998.

Taubman, Geoffry. "A Not-So World Wide Web: The Internet, China, and the Challenges to Nondemocratic Rule." *Political Communication* 15 (1998): 255–72.

Terranova, Tiziana. "Free Labor: Producing Culture for the Digital Economy." *Social Text* 18, no. 2 (2000): 33–57.

Thomas, Julian. "Liberal Machines." *American Behavioral Scientist* 43, no. 9 (2000): 1548–60.

Tuchman, Gaye. "Objectivity as Strategic Ritual: An Examination of Newsmen's Notions of Objectivity." *American Journal of Sociology* 77 (1972): 660–79.

Ubayasiri, K. "A virtual Eelam: Democracy, Internet and Sri Lanka's Tamil Struggle." In *Asian Cyberactivism: Freedom of Expression and Media Censorship*, ed. S. Gan, J. Gomez, and U. Johannen, pp. 474–512. Bangkok, Thailand: Friedrich Naumann Stiftung, 2004.

Wahl-Jorgensen, Karin. "The Construction of the Public in Letters to the Editor: Deliberative Democracy and the Idiom of Insanity." *Journalism* 3, no. 2 (2002): 183–204.

Wang, Georgette. "Regulating Network Communication in Asia: A Different Balancing Act?" *Telecommunications Policy* 23, no. 3/4 (1999): 277–87.

Wang, Lay Kim. "Media and Democracy in Malaysia." *Javnost – The Public* 8, no. 2 (2001): 67–87.

Warkentin, Craig and Karen Mingst. "International Institutions, the State, and Global Civil Society in the Age of the World Wide Web." *Global Governance* 6, no. 2 (2000): 237–57.

Weber, Max. *Economy and Society: An Outline of Interpretive Sociology.* Ed. Guenther Roth and Claus Wittich. 2 vols. Vol. 1. Berkeley: University of California Press, 1978.

Weingast, Barry. "The Political Foundations of Democracy and the Rule of Law." *American Political Science Review* 91, no. 2 (1997): 245–63.

Whine, Michael. "Cyberspace — a New Medium for Communication, Command, and Control by Extremists." *Studies in Conflict and Terrorism* 22, no. 3 (1999): 231–45.

Williams, Raymond. *Marxism and Literature*. Oxford, New York: Oxford University Press, 1977.

———. "Means of Communication as Means of Production." In *Problems in Materialism and Culture: Selected Essays*, pp. 50–63. London: Verso, 1980.

Wintrobe, Ronald. *The Political Economy of Dictatorship*: Cambridge University Press, 1998.

Wong, Kean. "Malaysia: In the Grip of the Goverment." In *Losing Control: Freedom of the Press in Asia*, ed. Louise Williams and Roland Rich, pp. 115–37. Asia Pacific Press at the Australian National University, 2000.

Zaharom Nain. "Globalized Theories and National Control: The State, the Market, and the Malaysian Media." In *De-Westernizing Media Studies*, ed. James Curran and Myung-Jin Park, pp. 139–53. London: Routledge, 2000.

———. "The Media and Malaysia's Reformasi Movement." In *Media Fortunes, Changing Times: Asean States in Transition*, ed. Russell Hiang-Khng Heng. Singapore: Institute of Southeast Asian Studies, 2002.

———. "Rhetoric and Realities in Malaysian Television Policy in an Era of Globalization." *Asian Journal of Communication* 6, no. 1 (1996): 43–64.

Zittrain, Jonathan and Benjamin Edelman. *Empirical Analysis of Internet Filtering in China*. Berkman Center for Internet & Society, Harvard Law School, 2003 [cited May 2003]. Available from <http://cyber.law.harvard.edu/filtering/china>.

Zulfikar Mohamad Shariff. "Fateha.com: challenging control over Malay/ Muslim voices in Singapore." In *Asian Cyberactivism: Freedom of Expression and Media Censorship*, ed. S. Gan, J. Gomez, and U. Johannen, pp. 318–68. Bangkok, Thailand: Friedrich Naumann Foundation, 2004.

INDEX